Cut Your Cholesterol

Cut Your Cholesterol

Featuring the Exclusive

Live It Down Plan

David L. Katz, M.D.
and Debra L. Gordon

Reader's Digest

The Reader's Digest Association
Pleasantville, New York/ Montreal

Design by Susan Welt, Andrew Ploski

Address any comments about *Cut Your Cholesterol* to:
Reader's Digest
Editor-in-Chief, Reader's Digest Health Publishing
Reader's Digest Road, Pleasantville, NY 10570-7000

Credits | **Photography** | **38** Susan Goldman/Arlene Vallon, Reader's Digest Association, GID (RDA/GID), **42** Image Source/elektra Vision/PictureQuest, **57** Lisa Koenig, RDA/GID, **60** PhotoDisc, **74** Martin Brigdale, RDA/GID, **77** Jean-Blaise Hall/PhotoAlto/PictureQuest, **81** Gus Filgate, RDA/GID, **82**, **85** Martin Brigdale, RDA/GID, **88-90** William Lingwood, RDA/GID **91** Image Source/elektra Vision/PictureQuest, **93** Alan Richardson, RDA/GID, **95** William Lingwood, RDA/GID, **97** Martin Brigdale, RDA/GID, **98** Gus Filgate, RDA/GID, **100** William Lingwood, RDA/GID **102** David Murry & Jules Selmes, RDA/GID, **103** William Lingwood, RDA/GID, **105** Elizabeth Watt **107** William Lingwood, RDA/GID, **109** Martin Brigdale, RDA/GID, **110** Alan Richardson, RDA/GID, **111** Martin Brigdale, RDA/GID, **112** Alan Richardson, RDA/GID, **113** Mark Thomas, RDA/GID, **115** PhotoDisc **119** William Lingwood, RDA/GID, **125-134** Lisa Koenig, RDA/GID, **141** Beth Bischoff, **143** Christine Bronico, **144-159** Beth Bischoff, **167** BananaStock, Life, **170** BOTH Beth Bischoff, **173** Stockbyte/PictureQuest, **174** imagesource, **186** PhotoDisc, **231-235**, **241** William Lingwood, RDA/GID, **243** Martin Brigdale, RDA/GID, **246** William Lingwood, RDA/GID, **247** Martin Brigdale, RDA/GID
Illustrations | **13** World Health Report | Medical Illustrations, **17, 23, 28-29** Keith Kasnot | All heart illustrations, Annemarie Gilligan

Library of Congress Cataloging-in-Publication Data

Katz, David L.
    Cut your cholesterol : featuring the exclusive live it down plan /
David L. Katz and Debra L. Gordon.
        p. cm.
    Includes index.
ISBN 10: 0-7621-0475-9 (hardcover)
ISBN 10: 0-7621-0499-6 (paperback)
ISBN 13: 978-0-7621-0499-4 (paperback)
    1. Hypercholesteremia—Prevention—Popular works.
2. Cholesterol—Health aspects—Popular works. I. Gordon, Debra L., 1962- II. Title.
    RC632.H83 K38 2003
    616.3'99705—dc21

                                    2003003926

Printed in China

3 5 7 9 10 8 6 4 2 (hardcover)

5 7 9 10 8 6 4 (paperback)

For more Reader's Digest products and information, visit our online store at:
www.rd.com (in the United States)
www.readersdigest.ca (in Canada)

Note to our readers | The information in this book should not be substituted for, or used to alter, medical therapy without your doctor's advice. For a specific health problem, consult your physician for guidance.

Working with my coauthor, Debra Gordon, has been a very great pleasure. Deb put me in the enviable position of being able to "think out loud" while she wrestled with the need to make such thoughts sort themselves out on the page. For her efficiency, professionalism, sense of humor, and constant good cheer, I offer my most heartfelt thanks. I have much the same to say of our editor at Reader's Digest, Marianne Wait. A great editor makes authors feel the love they want, even while imposing the discipline they need to assure that a book actually results from their efforts, and does so more or less on time. Marianne—I feel the love! The book itself is testimony to the discipline. You are, indeed, a great editor, and I thank you.

I acknowledge an unpayable debt to the many pioneers of heart disease prevention—from Ancel Keys to Dean Ornish, William Castelli to Walter Willet—who have blazed the trails of knowledge the rest of us are privileged to follow. Closer to home, I am thankful to my father, Dr. Donald Katz, a cardiologist whose devotion to his profession, and his patients, inspired me long ago, and still does.

Finally, and foremost, I thank my wife, Catherine, and our children, Rebecca, Corinda, Valerie, Natalia, and Gabriel. They love me enough to forgive me the time I spend at the keypad, instead of with them. I love them enough to have some difficulty forgiving myself.

David L. Katz, M.D.

This book is the result of a wonderful partnership between myself, my coauthor, David Katz, M.D., and my editor, Marianne Wait. It's one of the best teams I've ever worked on. David wins the award as the coolest physician I've encountered in my long career. Not only does he know just how to translate the most complex medical jargon into plain English, always with a twist of humor and a dollop of advice, but he is one of the few people I know who spends as much, if not more, time on e-mail as I do. Given the messages I've received time-stamped 2 or 3 A.M., I'm convinced he rarely, if ever, sleeps.

Marianne was tireless in her insistence that we keep the reader forefront in our minds and relentless in her quest for advice that went beyond the stale and mundane. She pushed me to go the extra mile   always with her wonderful sense of humor   and *Cut Your Cholesterol* is a much better book for it.

I would be remiss if I didn't also thank our eagle-eyed copy editor, Sean Nolan. He reminded me once again of how thankful I have always been for the fact that there are copy editors on this earth.

Finally, I have to thank my husband, Keith, and my three sons, Jonathan, Callum, and Iain, for eating—and eventually learning to enjoy—the whole wheat pasta, bean-filled everything, extra servings of vegetables, and other changes this book engendered.

Debra L. Gordon

David L. Katz, M.D., MPH, FACPM, is associate clinical professor of public health and medicine at the Yale University School of Medicine and a board-certified specialist in both internal medicine and preventive medicine/public health with 15 years of clinical practice experience. Dr. Katz founded and directs the Yale Prevention Research Center, where he serves as principal investigator for numerous studies related to obesity prevention and control, nutrition, behavior change, and chronic disease prevention. He also founded and directs the Integrative Medicine Center at Griffin Hospital in Derby, Connecticut. A nationally recognized authority on nutrition, Dr. Katz conducts nutrition courses at Yale for both medical and nursing students, and lectures frequently throughout the United States and abroad. His other books include *Nutrition in Clinical Practice* and *The Way to Eat*. Dr. Katz lives in Connecticut with his wife and five children.

Debra L. Gordon is an award-winning journalist who has been writing about health and medicine for more than 15 years. She cut her teeth covering the medical beat for the *Virginian-Pilot* in Norfolk, Virginia, and later was medical reporter for the *Orange County Register* in southern California. She is the coauthor of *Maximum Food Power for Women* and author of *Seven Days to a Perfect Night's Sleep*. She currently lives in northeastern Pennsylvania, where she is a full-time freelance writer.

Contents

Why "*Live It Down*"?

There is an adage I once heard at a conference that I find deeply compelling: "The single best way to predict the future is to create it!" With the help of the *Live It Down Plan,* you can indeed create a future filled with better health for you and your family.

Taking hold of the power to create your medical destiny begins with a reconsideration of cause and effect. You may know that heart disease is the leading cause of death in the United States among both men and women. (Women often incorrectly identify breast cancer as their biggest health threat, while heart disease actually accounts for 10 times as many deaths.) But heart disease is not truly a cause. It's a consequence. The real culprit in the United States is a combination of poor diet, physical inactivity, tobacco use, and so on down a list of personal lifestyle choices that contribute to heart disease.

By the end of this list, fully half of the deaths from heart disease in this country are accounted for by behaviors that can be modified. Modified by whom? Not by doctors. By you. In fact, the best available data suggest that by making the right lifestyle choices, most people could reduce their risk of death from heart disease by 80 percent or more—without drugs. That's why we've created the *Live It Down Plan*: to help you make those choices. If everyone in the United States were to adopt this Plan, I think heart disease could be essentially eradicated.

> By making the right lifestyle choices, most people could reduce their risk of death from heart disease by 80 percent or more—without drugs.

Despite the title, this book isn't just about cholesterol, because it's not just high cholesterol that causes heart attacks. The list of usual suspects—high cholesterol, high blood pressure, diabetes—is being continuously extended to a litany of newcomers: C-reactive protein, homocysteine, Lp(a), small and dense LDL, endothelial dysfunction. The *Live It Down Plan* attacks them all. It also helps lower high blood pressure, defend against diabetes, improve the health of your arteries so they'll be less prone to plaque buildup, and more.

Perhaps you are tempted to think that changing your lifestyle is not worth the effort. After all, there are plenty of medications that lower cholesterol. Why not simply rely on this ever-proliferating arsenal? The truth is that some of you may need medication—because of risk factors that represent an acute danger and/or because of a genetic predisposition that diet and exercise can't correct. But no medical technology, no combination of pills, can fully measure up to the health-promoting power of a well-chosen lifestyle. By following the *Live It Down Plan*, most of you could theoretically reduce your personal risk of heart attack to something very close to zero.

The steps you'll take on the Plan, such as starting a walking program, adding more fiber to your diet, eating fish three times a week, and taking fish-oil capsules every day, don't require heroic efforts. But they can yield dramatic results. For instance, one study showed that people who took fish-oil supplements dropped their total cholesterol 12 percent.

The Plan's eating strategy is based on modern science as well as everything we know about the diet our ancestors adapted over the ages—in essence, the way we were meant to eat. As a result, you'll get an ideal array of micronutrients, optimal sources of protein, and the perfect balance of omega-6 and omega-3 fatty acids. (Most Americans today consume far too many omega-6 fatty acids.) And because stress has a host of negative effects on your heart, we've included a chapter on that topic, with plenty of tips on how to mitigate the health effects of a hectic life. Just learning a simple breathing technique, for instance, can help.

On the *Live It Down Plan* most people will lower their cholesterol by 30 points or more in just 12 weeks. But even that significant benefit is just a small part of what you can expect to gain. By blending nutrition, physical activity, supplements, and mind-body medicine, the *Live It Down Plan* offers you the power to completely reshape your health. The very same strategies that will protect your heart will lower your cancer risk, help you control your weight, reduce your risk of stroke, help prevent or control diabetes, and even slow the aging process.

Tests may predict your future health, but only you can create it! Here, and nowhere else, is all the detailed information you need to devise your best medical destiny. If you Live It Down, we predict you'll be living it up for many years to come!

David L. Katz, M.D., MPH, FACPM

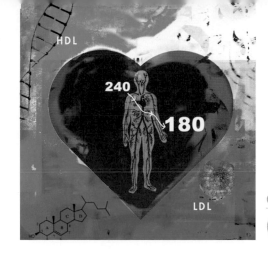

The Ups and Downs of Cholesterol

As the old saying goes, "What goes up must come down." In the case of high cholesterol, you must bring your level down if you want to reduce your risk of heart attack and stroke. But the question is how to get it down. Unfortunately, gravity isn't going to help.

If you're facing this problem (and you probably are if you're reading this book), you're anything but alone. About half of all adults in America have cholesterol levels that are too high. Even if you don't know your cholesterol numbers, if you're overweight (as three in five adults are) or sedentary (as two in five adults are), it's quite likely your levels of cholesterol and other blood fats are out of whack.

So what's to be done? If you've already been diagnosed with high cholesterol, your doctor has probably told you to watch what you eat, get more exercise, and maybe fill a prescription. But chances are that's the only help you got. You probably didn't get specific advice about which foods you should eat more of or which to avoid. (Did you know that nuts are good for your arteries, or that eggs are back on the menu?) You probably weren't told that relieving stress can help your body clear cholesterol from the bloodstream, or that certain supplements can help stave off a heart attack. It's even possible that you got outdated or even wrong information. For example, the very low-fat diets some doctors recommend could actually make your problem worse by raising your triglyceride level (which you'll read more about later) and lowering your level of "good" cholesterol—the kind that protects you from heart attacks.

Whatever information your doctor gave you, it likely didn't include a step-by-step 12-week plan to help you make the exact lifestyle changes that have been proven to lower cholesterol. But now you have one in this book: the *Live It Down Plan*.

Cutting your cholesterol doesn't require heroic measures, just small changes to some of the everyday habits you've acquired over the years—the same ones that likely contributed to your cholesterol problem in the first place. These small changes are what the *Live It Down Plan* is all about. Just by dipping your bread in olive oil instead of smearing it with butter, and skipping the greasy pork sausages for breakfast (at least most of the time), you could lower your cholesterol 5 to 10 percent in just a few weeks. That translates to a 10 to 20 percent reduction in your heart disease risk. Add less than a cup of beans a day to your diet or switch to a high-fiber cereal, and your levels could plummet another 20 points, which could effectively cut your heart disease risk in half.

By following the *Live It Down Plan* for 12 weeks, most people will drop their cholesterol 30 points or more. Best of all, the same actions you'll take on the Plan—like eating more fruits, vegetables, and fiber, fitting more physical activity into your everyday life, and learning to relax—will also boost your protection against everything from high blood pressure to diabetes to cancer. No cholesterol-lowering pill can promise these benefits. But before you embark on the Plan, you'll definitely want to know more about the main problem at hand: cholesterol. So read on.

A Numbers Game

We all walk around with lots of numbers in our head, and for many of us, in the last 10 years or so our "cholesterol number" became one of them. Because as almost everyone knows, too much cholesterol gums up the arteries, setting the stage for a heart attack. Yet if you turn back the clock 100 years, no one was talking about cholesterol. In fact, clogged arteries remained an uncommon condition well into the 20th century. In 1910 William Osler, M.D., often called the father of modern medicine, described angina pectoris—painful chest spasms caused when narrowed arteries impede the flow of blood to the heart—as a rare disease, claiming he hadn't even seen a case until late in his practice. Today more than 7 million Americans have angina, and it's a rare general practitioner, let alone cardiologist, who isn't all too familiar with this condition. Angina is considered a definitive sign of coronary heart disease, or CHD, the No. 1 killer of both men and women in the United States.

Much of our knowledge about this silent killer comes from the residents of the small Massachusetts town of Framingham. It was 1948, at the height of postwar prosperity, when indoor malls were just coming into their own, cars were replacing feet as the primary mode of transportation, smoking was cool, and a steak dinner was the ultimate dining experience. That's the year scientists from the U.S. Public Health Service chose the town

Geography as Destiny

Not surprisingly, high cholesterol poses a bigger problem in more developed nations. The impact on public health is measured in disability-adjusted life years, or DALYs. One DALY equals one year of healthy life lost.

KEY: Proportion of disability-adjusted life years attributable to cholesterol problems.
☐ <0.5%   ☐ 0.5–0.9%   ☐ 1–1.9%   ☐ 2–3.9%   ☐ 4–7.9%   ■ 8–15.9%

Source: The World Health Report 2002

to help them learn more about the growing epidemic of heart disease.

Back then no one used the phrase "risk factor," knew that high blood pressure or high cholesterol could lead to heart disease, or understood that you could modify those risk factors and thus lower your chances of developing CHD.

Since the Framingham Heart Study began, more than 10,000 citizens—including the offspring of the first 5,209 healthy residents who signed on—have participated in what became one of the most important health studies in history. In addition to the ones listed above, the study is responsible for other landmark findings, including:

- The link between diabetes and CHD.
- The identification of diet and obesity as CHD risk factors.
- The discovery that a high level of HDL ("good" cholesterol) is associated with reduced risk of death.
- The identification of homocysteine, apolipoprotein E, and lipoprotein (a) as possible risk factors for heart disease.

You'll read more about all of these later in the book.

Cholesterol: Myth vs. Reality

Myth: Cholesterol is inherently bad.
Reality: All mammals need cholesterol to survive.

Myth: High cholesterol is dangerous.
Reality: High cholesterol is not a problem by itself. But an unfavorable ratio of "good" to "bad" cholesterol, along with factors such as your weight, the amount of exercise you get, and your family health history could be trouble.

Myth: People who have heart attacks have high cholesterol.
Reality: Although high cholesterol is a significant risk factor in heart disease, some people develop heart disease and have heart attacks even though their cholesterol levels are normal or even low.

Myth: You must cut out cholesterol-containing foods if you are to lower your blood cholesterol levels.
Reality: Cholesterol in the blood comes from your diet but also from the cholesterol your liver makes. In fact, your liver makes far more cholesterol than you eat. So cutting back on dietary cholesterol may have little effect.

Myth: I should avoid eggs to maintain a healthy cholesterol level.
Reality: Several published studies show that an egg or two a day has little effect on people with normal cholesterol levels.

Myth: If I follow a low-fat diet and exercise a lot, my cholesterol levels will go down.
Reality: Some people's genetic makeups mean that lifestyle changes alone—no matter how rigorously they're followed—won't be enough to bring cholesterol levels into the safe zone. These people will require medication in addition to lifestyle changes.

Myth: Young people don't have high cholesterol.
Reality: Everyone from age 20 up should have their cholesterol measured. Studies have shown that plaque can build up in the arteries that supply blood to the heart as early as the late teens.

What Exactly Is Cholesterol?

Although cholesterol has gotten a bad rap over the years, it's not, by itself, a bad thing. Cholesterol is a soft, faintly yellow, naturally occurring waxy substance found in cell walls and membranes throughout your body, including your brain, nerves, muscles, skin, liver, intestines, and heart. It's one of several fats, or lipids, your body produces. Without enough cholesterol, you simply couldn't live.

You use cholesterol to produce sex hormones (including estrogen, progesterone, and testosterone), vitamin D, and bile acids that help you digest fat. However, you need only a relatively small amount to take care of all of these things. And your body (your liver, intestines, and even skin) manufactures plenty of it—about three or four times more cholesterol than most Americans eat. That means you could go the rest of your life without ever consuming another bite of cholesterol and you'd be just fine. (Although there's no need to do so; you'll read later on that eating too many foods that contain cholesterol is not the main cause of high blood cholesterol.)

The Good, the Bad, and the Worse

Like so many things, cholesterol isn't bad for you unless there's too much of it, at which point it begins to cause trouble. The story isn't quite that simple, however. As you probably already know, there are different kinds of cholesterol—some bad, some good. And how much you have of each type makes a tremendous difference in your likelihood of developing CHD.

It's actually not cholesterol per se that's good or bad for you, but the "vehicle" through which it travels your bloodstream. Because cholesterol is waxy, it can't mix with blood, which is watery. Like oil in a salad dressing, it remains separate. To enter the cells and

> Your body manufactures three or four times more cholesterol than most Americans eat.

tissues where it's needed, then, it hooks up with proteins, creating special transporters called lipoproteins. Think of these as submarine-like bubbles that carry cholesterol around the body. Some of these "submarines" are friends, but most are foes.

LDLs: Low-Density Lipoproteins

Low-density lipoproteins, or LDLs, are the primary foes—the archenemies, in fact. LDLs carry most of the cholesterol (75 to 80 percent) in the blood, depositing it into the cells, including the arteries. There these particles contribute to the formation of plaque, which narrows the arteries. That reduces the amount of blood that can get through, diminishing the amount of oxygen that reaches the heart.

Some LDL types are more dangerous than others. Smaller, denser LDL particles are more damaging to blood vessels because it's easier for them to cross the lining of the vessel and burrow into the vessel wall.

Most people won't know what type of LDL they have because the tests to determine it are too expensive and complicated for the typical doctor's office. If you already have CHD, or have a strong family history of CHD, and your doctor has sent you to a cardiac specialist, that doctor may run more detailed tests to better understand your risk. But it doesn't matter much, as the focus remains the same regardless: Lower the amount of LDL in your body.

So what's the ideal LDL level? As you'll read in Chapter 3, that depends on your personal history and other risk factors for CHD. But if you're a man 45 or older or a woman 55 or older and don't have CHD, diabetes, hypertension, or a family history of premature CHD, and don't smoke, here's what you should aim for (levels are measured in milligrams per deciliter, or mg/dl—a deciliter is about 3 ounces):

LDL level	Category
Less than 100 mg/dl	Optimal
100–129 mg/dl	Near optimal
130–159 mg/dl	Borderline high
160–189 mg/dl	High
190 mg/dl and above	Very high

Everything from your weight to whether or not you smoke to your family health history—even the amount of stress you're under—affects your LDL level. Of course, your diet makes a difference, too, particularly the types of fats you eat. You'll read much more about these fats in Chapter 4.

HDLs: High-Density Lipoproteins

High-density lipoproteins, or HDLs, are the good guys—the "garbage trucks" of the bloodstream, as described by C. Noel Bairey Merz, M.D., director of the Preventive and Rehabilitative Cardiac Center at Cedars-Sinai Medical Center in Los Angeles. HDLs typically transport about 20 to 25 percent of the cholesterol in your blood, carrying it away from tissues to your liver, which disposes of it. The more HDL in your bloodstream, the more artery-clogging cholesterol is being removed.

Research finds that for every 1 percent increase in your HDL level, your risk of a heart attack drops 3 to 4 percent. By comparison, a 1 percent drop in your LDL level reduces your risk of a heart attack just 2 percent. HDL is so beneficial that a high level may offer enough protection to cancel out a heart disease risk factor like having diabetes or being overweight.

Having low HDL, on the other hand, often signifies other problems. For instance, many people with low HDL also have high levels of other dangerous blood fats, such as triglycerides and remnant lipoproteins (more on this later). That makes sense, since low HDL means fewer "garbage trucks" disposing of the "trashy" cholesterol. Low HDL can also be a sign of insulin resistance and metabolic syndrome, or Syndrome X, risks you'll learn about in Chapter 2.

HDL level	Category
Less than 40 mg/dl	Low (risky)
40–59 mg/dl	Average (neutral)
60 mg/dl and above	High (protective)

Smoking, being overweight, being sedentary, and consuming a high-carbohydrate diet (more than 60 percent of your calories) contribute to low HDL. So does a family history of low HDL. In fact, about half of HDL imbalances are due to genetics. Women are lucky in that they generally have a higher HDL level than men. But some doctors think women need these higher levels to remain healthy, and they suggest an HDL level even higher than 60 (the usual target) is most desirable for women.

Good Guys and Bad Guys

Inside your arteries there's a battle going on. LDLs are the enemy force, and HDLs the defenders. If your ratio of "enemies" to "defenders" is favorable, you win—plaque will not form. Here's how it plays out. VLDLs, produced in the liver, travel through the bloodstream, where they shed triglycerides for use by cells. In the process they give rise to LDLs. HDLs, manufactured in the liver, travel through the circulation, seeking LDLs. An HDL particle fuses to an LDL and "opens" it with a "lock-and-key" mechanism to take some of its cholesterol. The HDL then carries the cholesterol back to the liver and out of circulation.

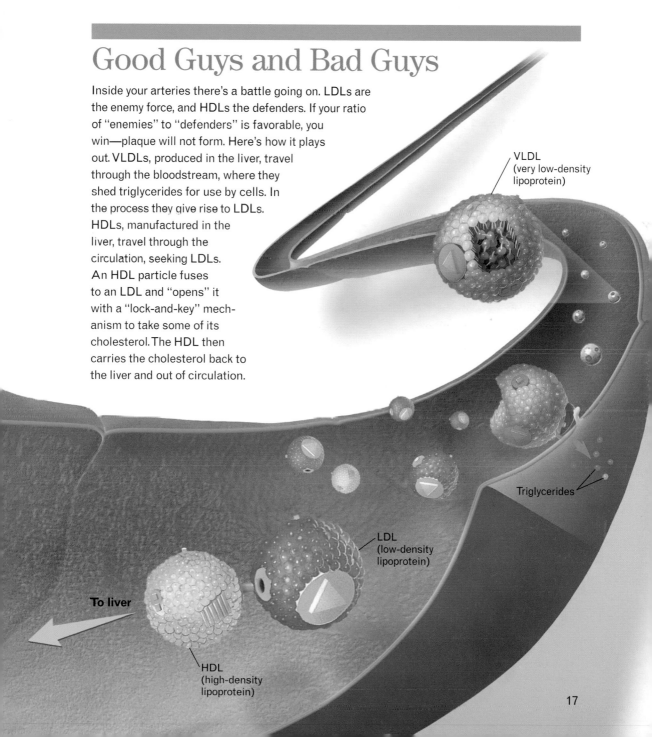

VLDL
(very low-density
lipoprotein)

Triglycerides

LDL
(low-density
lipoprotein)

To liver

HDL
(high-density
lipoprotein)

Total Cholesterol

The basic cholesterol test measures LDL and HDL, along with two other components you'll read about shortly: very low-density lipoproteins (VLDL) and triglycerides. Together these make up your total cholesterol count.

So what should your total cholesterol be? The goal has changed twice since it was first devised in 1988. It's not an arbitrary number, however. It's set by the National Institutes of Health's Expert Panel on Detection, Evaluation, and Treatment of High Blood Cholesterol in Adults, a true mouthful that you don't have to remember. The panel periodically releases a report—the third one came out in 2001—called the Adult Treatment Panel Report.

Based on the latest research, experts believe a safe total cholesterol level is about 150 mg/dl. (By contrast, the average total cholesterol level in the United States is between 200 and 210.) As you'll find out later in the book, this total cholesterol target isn't a one-size-fits-all measure. The goal you set depends not only on where your cholesterol levels are today, but also on other risk factors, including your weight, physical activity, diet, and family health history.

The Ratio's the Key

What's even more important than your total cholesterol, LDL, or HDL alone is the proportion of good to bad cholesterol in your blood. As long as you strike the right balance, you're probably in the clear.

Here's one reason that HDL and LDL numbers on their own don't tell the whole story: People who eat diets low in animal fat tend to have low HDL, even though their heart disease risk is small. "If you simply looked at populations in the world," notes John Larosa, M.D., president and professor of medicine at the University of New York Health Science Center at Brooklyn, "those with the lowest HDLs—that is, populations with the lowest amount of animal fat in their diet—have the lowest risk of coronary disease. So HDL is a good predictor of risk in populations only as long as LDL levels are fairly high."

There are several ways doctors measure the proportion of different types of cholesterol in the blood. One is by calculating your ratio of total cholesterol to HDL. You can figure out this number by dividing your total cholesterol by your HDL. If your total cholesterol is 240 and your HDL is 60, your ratio is 4:1. An acceptable ratio is less than 5:1, although an even better ratio is less than 4.5:1 for men and 4:1 for pre-menopausal women. A truly ideal ratio is 3.5:1.

Non-HDL Cholesterol

Another up-and-coming indicator of your overall risk of heart disease is your non-HDL cholesterol count. You see, not all "bad" cholesterol is equally bad. While LDL has long been the focus of cholesterol reduction efforts, researchers have recently identified several other lipoproteins, including VLDL and IDL (intermediate-density lipoproteins) that also affect your cardiovascular health. To take these into account, they've come up with a new measurement and focus of treatment: non-HDL cholesterol. Your non-HDL cholesterol count is simply your total cholesterol minus HDL, or put another way, the sum of your LDL, VLDL, and IDL.

In late 2002 researchers published an article in *Circulation*, the journal of the American Heart Association, confirming that if you have heart disease, your non-HDL level can help predict your risk of a heart attack or angina (chest pain) and determine treatments. "LDL cholesterol, even though it is a 'bad' cholesterol, tells only part of the story," said lead author Vera Bittner, M.D., MSPH, professor of medicine in the division of cardiovascular diseases at the University of Alabama at Birmingham. "We found that while LDL cholesterol is important, the non-HDL cholesterol is the more important predictor—at least in this group of people with heart disease."

Many people won't know their levels of VLDL and IDL, and that's okay. Current recommendations call for obtaining at least a total cholesterol and HDL level to determine CHD risk. If these levels don't raise any red flags, there's no reason to investigate further (unless you have CHD or a strong family history of heart disease). But if the levels are elevated, you'll probably need more detailed tests, possibly including VLDL and IDL counts.

If your LDL goal is:	Your non-HDL goal should be:
Less than 160 mg/dl	Less than 190 mg/dl
Less than 130 mg/dl	Less than 160 mg/dl
Less than 100 mg/dl	Less than 130 mg/dl

Other Lipoproteins Being Studied

As if HDL, LDL, and VLDL weren't enough to track, researchers are discovering other types of lipoproteins that play a role in your CHD risk. Again, the standard cholesterol test doesn't measure them, but most are included in a complete lipid profile.

Chylomicrons

You probably haven't heard of this class of lipoproteins, as researchers are just beginning to understand their role as a risk factor in CHD. But chylomicrons (ki-LO-mi-krons) give rise to all other forms of lipoproteins. When you eat, the fat in your meal passes through your digestive system into your intestine. There the cells lining the small intestine transform the fat into small droplets of fat and protein that contain

The Boy with Orange Tonsils

Lovely Tangier Island off the coast of Virginia offers a glimpse of a simpler life, where golf carts are the preferred mode of travel, residents speak with a unique Old English dialect, three-quarters of the population share one of four last names, and the teeming waters of the Chesapeake Bay provide the economic sustenance for a majority of its residents. But about 40 years ago doctors learned that Tangier Island offered something else: a genetic disorder of cholesterol transport. They dubbed the disorder Tangier disease.

The medical mystery began with a 5-year-old boy with orange tonsils, a very low HDL level, and an enlarged liver and spleen. Because his HDL level was so low, he was unable to eliminate enough cholesterol from his body, resulting in the orange tonsils (cholesterol is faintly yellowish). Only about 40 cases worldwide have been reported.

In 1999 scientists discovered the gene responsible for this disease and for a less serious condition that also results in low HDL. The gene encodes a protein that helps rid cells of excess cholesterol. The gene is defective in people with Tangier disease.

The discovery of this gene may lead to a better understanding of the relationship between HDL and heart disease, possibly resulting in new drugs that regulate HDL levels.

cholesterol and triglycerides. These droplets are the chylomicrons.

They head out of your gut and into your bloodstream, eventually encountering enzymes that break them down into chylomicron remnants. The remnants continue on to your liver, where they're repackaged as other forms of cholesterol and triglycerides. The reason that statins, the major class of cholesterol-lowering drugs (Zocor, Lipitor, Pravachol, etc.), don't work very well to lower triglyceride levels is that they don't seem to affect chylomicrons, the major transporter of triglycerides. (We'll talk more about statins in Chapter 8.)

Researchers don't know why, but the higher the level of chylomicron remnants in your blood, the greater your risk of CHD. Certain cholesterol-lowering drugs, such as Lopid (gemfibrozil) and other fibrates, help lower your chylomicron level, as do supplements of fish oil (more on this in Chapter 5).

There are no established targets for chylomicrons. Because they are transient, they don't sustain a stable blood level.

Lipoprotein (a)

Lipoprotein (a), also known as Lp(a)—doctors call it "el-pee little-a"—is found only in the blood of hedgehogs, certain monkeys, and humans. It's made up of a small portion of LDL, with an adhesive protein (apoprotein A) surrounding it. This gives Lp(a) a Velcro-like stickiness that makes it more likely to cause blood clots and lead to the formation of artery-narrowing plaques. It also seems to prevent clots from dissolving, increasing the danger that a clot will block the flow of blood to your heart or brain. Although Lp(a) carries only a small amount of cholesterol, an elevated level is three to four times more powerful as a marker of CHD than other measures, such as LDL.

If you have high Lp(a), your risk of developing CHD over the next 10 years is 70 percent higher than someone with normal levels. The risk is particularly significant in women. The landmark Heart and Estrogen/Progestin Replacement Study (HERS) found that women with the highest Lp(a) levels had a 54 percent greater risk of recurrent heart problems than those with the lowest levels. And the Framingham Heart Study found that levels above 30 mg/dl doubled the risk of heart attack in 3,000 women.

> Although Lp(a) carries only a small amount of cholesterol, an elevated level is three to four times more powerful as a marker of heart disease than other measures, such as LDL.

While there is no official target level for Lp(a), studies suggest that for many people, levels starting at 30 mg/dl may raise your risk of heart disease. African-Americans are the exception; their levels are typically two to three times higher than those of Caucasians.

If you have a family history of heart disease, especially if you're a woman nearing menopause or postmenopause, ask your doctor about having your Lp(a) level tested.

With all of that said, there's not much you can do to modify your Lp(a) level. Unlike other kinds of cholesterol, Lp(a) in the blood is mainly determined by genes, so drugs and dietary changes have little effect on it. But that doesn't mean there's no point in finding out your level. If, for instance, you have high Lp(a) with another CHD risk factor, like smoking or being overweight, that could justify setting an even lower goal for your LDL or being more aggressive in your efforts to change your lifestyle.

Apolipoproteins

As noted earlier, cholesterol can't get around the body without hooking up with proteins that act as transporters. Different types of cholesterol tend to hook up with different types of proteins. HDL pairs with apolipoprotein A—or apo(a) for short— and LDL bonds with apolipoprotein B—apo(b). So it's no big surprise that a low level of apo(a) and a high level of apo(b) may indicate trouble.

One large study of people who had had heart attacks found that low apo(a) and high apo(b) levels quadrupled the odds of a second heart attack. The combination may also pose dangers for those who haven't had a heart attack. In fact, research suggests that your apolipoprotein levels may predict your likelihood of having a heart attack even better than your LDL or HDL levels.

At some point doctors may start relying more on these protein levels as a sign of CHD risk. But right now the test is still relatively new, expensive, and not standardized for the basic doctor's office, so don't expect to have one; it isn't part of the typical complete lipid profile, either. The exception is if you have a high triglyceride level. That can make it more difficult to get an accurate reading of non-HDL cholesterol. Thus, a high apo(b) level may be the tiebreaker to help your doctor decide whether to start you on cholesterol-lowering drugs. There's also some thought that apo(b) may actually turn out to be a very accurate indicator of heart disease risk in women, whose triglyceride levels tend to run high to begin with.

Normal ranges for apo(a) are 101–199 mg/dl for women and 94–178 mg/dl for men. For apo(b) normal ranges are 49–103 mg/dl for women and 52–109 mg/dl for men.

Cholesterol and Strokes

For years doctors questioned the role high cholesterol played in strokes. But a large study published in summer 2002 may have answered that question. Researchers at Tel Aviv University in Israel followed 11,177 patients with CHD for six to eight years. As levels of total cholesterol and LDL increased, so did the likelihood that the patients would have an ischemic stroke—the most common form, in which a blood clot blocks the flow of blood to the brain. Another study, in *Circulation*, the journal of the American Heart Association, found a strong connection between high triglyceride levels and stroke in heart disease patients. Triglycerides can make blood cells stickier, increasing the risk of clots.

Remnant-Like Particle Cholesterol

One other form of cholesterol that researchers are studying is remnant-like particle cholesterol, referred to as RLP-C. These are lipoproteins that contain the greatest proportion of triglycerides, chylomicrons, chylomicron remnants, VLDL, VLDL remnants, and IDL. They're veritable stuffed balloons of risk factors for heart disease.

In one major Japanese study, researchers measured levels of total cholesterol, LDL, HDL, triglycerides, Lp(a), and RLP-C in the blood of 208 patients, of whom 57 had high cholesterol and 151 had normal cholesterol. They found that an unfavorable ratio of RLP-C to HDL (a normal ratio is less than 1:4) in patients with overall normal cholesterol levels was highly associated with narrowing of the coronary arteries. In

Anatomy of a Lipoprotein

Cholesterol travels around the bloodstream in bubbles called lipoproteins. Different types of lipoproteins contain different amounts of cholesterol and triglycerides. And they vary greatly in size. HDL is much smaller than LDL, which is much smaller than VLDL.

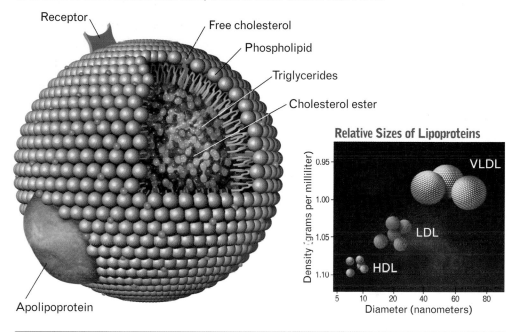

other words, here's a clear example of why having a normal total cholesterol level may not be good enough to prevent heart disease.

Currently, there is no readily available test for RLP-C levels, although as more research emerges on its role in cardiac disease, that will change.

Another Blood Fat: Triglycerides

Eat too much and you gain weight. It's one of the simplest facts in medicine. But the repercussions of gluttony go beyond weight gain. When you eat more calories than you need, your body converts them into a form of fat called triglycerides and sends them to your fat cells for storage. Although triglycerides aren't technically a form of cholesterol, they are a blood fat, or lipid, just like cholesterol. They're also sharing space in those same lipoprotein bubbles that carry cholesterol around, so it's nearly impossible to consider one without considering the other.

Normally, you should have only small amounts of triglycerides in your bloodstream. If your level is high (above 200 mg/dl 8 to 10 hours after your last meal), there's a problem. The higher your level, the more triglycerides are delivered to your liver, where they are transformed into LDL and VLDL—which, as you saw earlier, significantly contribute to CHD.

Doctors used to think that an elevated blood triglyceride level alone didn't cause atherosclerosis or CHD, but now they're not so sure. In one major German study in which 4,849 middle-aged men were followed for eight years, their triglyceride levels alone—regardless of HDL or LDL levels—turned up as a risk factor for CHD. Of course, the risk of suffering a heart attack or other incident related to CHD went up even more when the men had high triglycerides, high LDL, and low HDL. At the very least, think of triglycerides as the canary in the coal mine: If your level is high—even if everything else seems normal—take warning.

Triglycerides can be dangerous for several reasons. For one, lipoproteins rich in triglycerides also contain cholesterol. So high triglycerides may be a sign of a current or forthcoming problem with your LDL level. High triglycerides also make it more likely that your LDL will cause lesions in your coronary artery walls, setting in motion the cascade of events that can lead to CHD. If you're a woman you need to worry about this blood fat even more than men because studies find that high triglyceride levels represent a much greater risk for heart disease in women than in men.

Triglycerides tend to be high if you smoke, drink a lot of alcohol, are obese, are sedentary, are going through menopause, or eat too many simple carbohydrates (like sugar and white flour). Certain diseases, such as type 2 diabetes, kidney or liver disease, and hypothyroidism—as well as genetic predisposition—can also increase your risk of high triglycerides.

If you don't have any of these factors, your triglyceride level is usually less than 100 mg/dl. But if you do, your level will likely rise into the 150–199 mg/dl range. If it's above 200 mg/dl, it's likely there's some genetic influence as well.

Triglyceride level (mg/dl)	Risk of CHD
500 mg/dl and above	Very high
200–499 mg/dl	High
150–199 mg/dl	Borderline high
Less than 150 mg/dl (under 100 is ideal)	Normal

Getting Tested

Generally, your doctor will order a cholesterol test as part of your routine health exam. You should fast for 9 to 12 hours before the test. If you've recently had a

Continued on page 26

Which Tests to Get?

How much do you need to know about your levels of cholesterol and other blood components to understand your risk of heart disease and how to lower it? That depends on several factors. For some people, a basic cholesterol screening will suffice. Others will want to investigate further. Use this chart as a general guide to help you determine which blood tests you may need.

Test	Who Should Have It	Are More Tests Needed?
Routine Cholesterol Screening This test includes total cholesterol and HDL counts.	Every healthy adult age 20 and older, at least once every five years.	**No** If there's no obvious reason to suspect an increased risk of heart disease (such as a family history of heart disease) and the results are normal, no further testing should be required. **Yes** If the results are abnormal, or if they are normal but there are other reasons to suspect an increased risk, you should have a complete lipid profile.
Complete Lipid Profile This test includes counts for HDL, LDL, VLDL, and triglycerides.	People with abnormalities on routine cholesterol screening; those at increased risk of heart disease for other reasons; and those being treated for any lipid disorder.	**No** If the results explain your apparent heart disease risk and are adequate to guide any treatment decisions, no further testing should be required. **Yes** If you are at above-average risk for heart disease (for instance, due to a strong family history of CHD) and your results are either normal or insufficiently abnormal to explain your personal risk, you should have additional testing to rule out other, more subtle risk factors.
Additional Tests Other tests measure the following: • Apolipoprotein A • Apolipoprotein B • Apolipoprotein E • Lipoprotein (a) • Homocysteine* • LDL subtypes (e.g., small, dense LDL) • C-reactive protein* • Oxidative burden and antioxidant capacity* • Fibrinogen* • Uric acid*	Specialized testing is warranted when heart disease, or apparent risk for heart disease, is not fully explained by a complete lipid profile (for instance, if you have a strong family history of heart disease and yet your lipid levels are relatively normal) or whenever more guidance for treatment is required.	Under fairly unusual circumstances, such as when heart disease or heart disease risk factors don't respond as expected to therapy, more elaborate testing may be suggested by a specialist.

* You'll read about these risk factors in Chapter 2.

Continued from page 24

stroke, surgery, infection, weight loss, pregnancy, or a change in your usual diet, the results may be skewed, so try to wait until you're back to normal before taking the test. The basic cholesterol test reveals total cholesterol and HDL levels. In some cases, your doctor may order a more detailed test, known as a complete lipid profile, for more information. (See "Which Tests to Get?" on page 25.) Medicare and most other health insurance plans cover these tests.

Other tests to know about include:

Skin cholesterol test. Approved by the FDA in June 2002, Cholesterol 1,2,3, is the world's first noninvasive (read: no needle stick) cholesterol test. The three-minute test, performed at a doctor's office, measures the amount of cholesterol in the skin on the palm of your hand. Clinical studies found that using the test, in addition to identifying other risk factors, accurately assessed heart disease risk. The best part? You don't have to fast, and you get your results in just three minutes. The test involves placing two drops of liquid in the palm of your hand. The chemicals bind to the cholesterol on your skin, changing color, the color is then read by a special handheld reader.

Home cholesterol tests. The official recommendation stipulates that you have your blood cholesterol tested every five years if your first test results are normal, and more often if they're abnormal or you're being treated for high cholesterol or CHD. But sometimes you want to know how you're doing without the hassle of a doctor's appointment. A home cholesterol test is a handy solution.

There are several to choose from. Generally, a small device analyzes a drop of your blood in a matter of minutes. But buyer beware: Most of these tests measure only your total cholesterol. While this information may be helpful, it doesn't tell you everything you need to know. Recently, tests that measure HDL, LDL, and triglycerides have come on the market. To use them you send a blood sample to an accredited laboratory for analysis, then receive the results in the mail. Read the package carefully to make sure you're getting one of these tests.

Beware the Quick Screening

So you had one of those health-fair cholesterol tests, and your readings came back high. Before you panic, be sure to follow up with your doctor. While these tests are a good first step, any abnormal or high results should be checked again. The most accurate lipid profile is one taken after fasting for at least eight hours. Even a single cup of coffee with sugar or milk can skew the results. Also, check that the blood is sent to an accredited laboratory, preferably one approved by the College of American Pathologists' Commission on Laboratory Accreditation. Most large hospitals and interstate laboratories have this certification.

Heart Disease 1, 2, 3

You don't really need to remember all of the nitty-gritty details on the various types of cholesterol, just the bottom line: If your cholesterol levels are out of whack, you're heart disease risk is increased. Exactly how cholesterol wreaks havoc is fairly complicated.

All cells have receptors, or "doors," that suck LDL into them. If you have too much cholesterol in your blood, the cells make fewer receptors so they can avoid, quite literally, drowning in cholesterol. This, in turn, leads to more cholesterol floating in your bloodstream. While some of it gets returned to your liver for disposal via the garbage-bearing HDL, some of it stays in the bloodstream. If it hangs around long enough, it may become oxidized. And some of it burrows into your artery walls, where it's even more likely to become oxidized.

To understand oxidation, think about what happens to a metal chair when it's left out in the backyard: It rusts. That's what happens to cells in the body when they're attacked by free radicals—unstable molecules that damage cells. Free radicals are a by-product of just about any bodily process that involves oxygen.

Why doesn't cholesterol in the bloodstream always become oxidized? Because of wonderful compounds called antioxidants, which do just what their name implies; more on antioxidants in later chapters.

Your body has a system to deal with this oxidized cholesterol, dispatching special-

Continued on page 30

How Heart Disease Happens

When you think of heart disease, you probably picture a simple process whereby cholesterol sticks to artery walls and gums them up, eventually closing them off. What actually happens is somewhat different—and considerably more complicated.

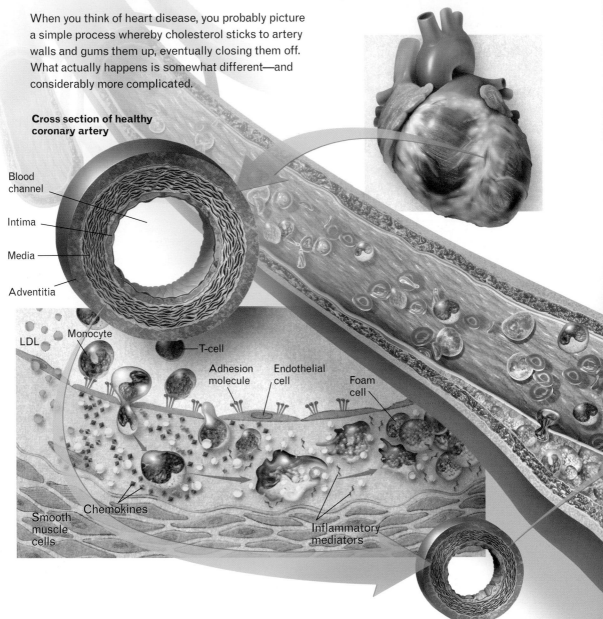

Cross section of healthy coronary artery

Blood channel

Intima

Media

Adventitia

LDL

Monocyte

T-cell

Adhesion molecule

Endothelial cell

Foam cell

Chemokines

Smooth muscle cells

Inflammatory mediators

Stage I Heart Disease: The Scene Is Set

Excess LDL particles in the blood burrow into the artery wall. In response, white blood cells called monocytes rush to the site of the injury. They latch onto adhesion molecules and are lured inside the artery wall by chemical messengers called chemokines. Once inside, monocytes engulf the LDL to dispose of it. But if there is too much LDL, the monocytes become stuffed and turn foamy. These "foam cells" collect in the blood vessel wall, eventually forming a fatty streak. This is stage I in the development of plaque.

Stage II: A Narrowed Artery

As plaque accumulates, it creates a bulge inside the artery wall, narrowing the artery at this site. Think of the bulge as a wound. The body tries to protect the wound by forming a hard cap over it, much like a scab. If the plaque stops growing, the cap may stabilize it, making it less likely to rupture. But if the plaque continues to grow, the cap becomes thin, weak, and more likely to burst.

Stage III: Plaque Burst!

The cap may be further weakened by inflammatory chemicals, produced by foam cells, that eat away at it. Stress at the site of the plaque (for instance, from an increase in heart rate or blood pressure due to emotional stress or exertion) may cause it to rupture. As the contents spew into the artery, the body sends a distress signal that triggers a clotting response. If a clot blocks the artery, a heart attack results.

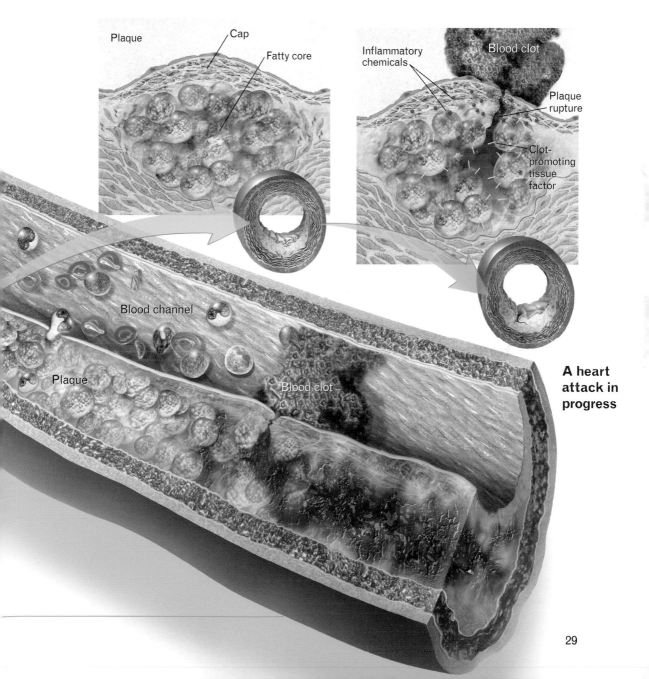

Plaque

Cap

Fatty core

Inflammatory chemicals

Blood clot

Plaque rupture

Clot-promoting tissue factor

Blood channel

Plaque

Blood clot

A heart attack in progress

Continued from page 27

Warning Signs of Heart Disease

The following signs of heart disease should not be ignored:

Angina. A feeling of tightness, pressure, or pain that appears with exertion or stress and disappears with rest. Usually felt in the chest, throat, upper abdomen, or arms.

Shortness of breath. Difficulty breathing, whether you're exerting yourself, at rest, or asleep.

Edema. Swelling of your ankles, usually at the end of the day.

Palpitations. Forceful, rapid, or irregular heartbeat.

Fatigue. Decreased ability to exercise, tiring easily.

Fainting. Sudden loss of consciousness or light-headedness.

ized white blood cells called monocytes to gobble it up. If there's too much oxidized cholesterol, however, the monocytes get stuffed. They take on a foamy appearance, hence their new name, "foam cells." These foam cells collect in the blood vessel wall, where they turn dangerous and begin producing free radicals, which further oxidize the cholesterol. Eventually a fatty streak forms—the dreaded plaque. This is stage I of atherosclerosis, or hardening of the arteries.

Nearly everyone, regardless of their diet or lifestyle, will have at least a low level of damage in their blood vessels by the time they die. And thanks to growing rates of obesity and physical inactivity, even children under 10 are now susceptible.

Stage II Heart Disease

Eventually this mess of cholesterol, foam cells, and other debris builds up, pushing outward from the artery wall. This cholesterol-rich "bump" looks like the pus that develops in an open wound. As with such wounds, white blood cells rush to the site to repair the damage, forming a hard coating, or cap, over it. Meanwhile, the bump continues to grow, eventually becoming so big it narrows the artery, decreasing blood flow and the supply of oxygen and nutrients to the heart. If your heart doesn't get enough oxygen-rich blood, you may feel a squeezing sensation in your chest. This is called angina. It often happens when you exercise, because that's when your heart needs additional oxygen.

Stage III Heart Disease

To understand what may happen next, visualize a rushing mountain stream. As it flows, it knocks aside rocks, plants, and other debris in its way, sending that debris downstream. The same thing can happen in your blood vessels. As the blood flows, it can "rip" the cap off the plaque, letting the pus out just as if you ripped the scab off a wound. The larger the plaque, the more likely it is to rupture. Also, the type of LDL that makes up the plaque could play a role in how easily it bursts; recent research shows that very small, dense LDL particles make these plaques more fragile.

Once a plaque bursts, blood platelets begin sticking to the exposed surface of the ruptured plaque, eventually blocking flow through the vessel altogether and triggering a heart attack or stroke (or, if these blockages occur in the arteries leading to your legs, peripheral artery disease).

Unfortunately, there may not be any warning signs of heart disease before a heart attack occurs, especially in women. Some people experience angina, but others only learn they have a problem when they find themselves in the hospital, hooked up to machines, and a nurse leaning over them telling them about the heart attack they just suffered. That's why it's so important to identify your risk factors, such as high cholesterol, and do what you can to tilt the odds in your favor.

Should You Have an EBCT?

What if an X-ray could help diagnose heart disease or predict risk? Some researchers think it can. Using electron beam computed tomography (EBCT), a type of CT scan, doctors can examine artery walls for calcium deposits; a lot of calcium indicates a lot of plaque. In people with CHD symptoms, the degree of arterial calcification is a stronger predictor of heart attack risk than high cholesterol, age, family history, diabetes, high blood pressure, or smoking. Even in people without symptoms, studies find that calcification indicates CHD, prompting preventive measures.

However, whether EBCT adds much value to other, less expensive screening tests is debatable. If, for example, someone has high cholesterol, high blood pressure, and diabetes, do they need EBCT to know they're at high risk? And if they have no cardiovascular risk factors to modify (in other words, their cholesterol and blood pressure are fine, they don't have diabetes, and they don't smoke),

do they need EBCT to give them a clean bill of health?

If someone has a strong family history of CHD but no clear risk factors, it might be worth an EBCT to tease out any hidden problem. And there's another potential benefit of EBCT: A picture may be worth a thousand words in terms of motivation. Someone seeing their abnormal arteries with their own eyes may be more inspired to make lifestyle changes than someone who is simply told their cholesterol is high. But that can work both ways; in one study of post-menopausal women, normal calcium scores were less likely to change the subjects' unhealthy behaviors.

The bottom line is the test has predictive value and may help clarify risk of CHD. But it's not clear yet who should have it or whether it's cost effective. There's no reason to go on your own to one of the many screening centers offering EBCT; only have the test if your doctor recommends it.

Examining Your Arteries

Is there any way to tell how much plaque you have before a heart attack occurs? If you're having angina or have several risk factors for heart disease, your doctor may order a series of tests to determine if you have coronary artery blockages. These include:

Electrocardiograms. In this test, known as an ECG or EKG, electrodes are attached to your chest to detect any irregular heart rhythm or damage from a heart attack and determine whether your heart is getting enough blood and oxygen.

Imaging techniques. These can determine if you have any artery blockages and if so, how severe they are. The most common ones are:

Radioisotope scan. A radioactive dye is injected into the bloodstream, and a special machine takes pictures of your heart and arteries as the dye passes through.

Echocardiogram. This test uses sound waves instead of dye or X-rays to trace a picture of your heart, revealing any damage to the muscle or abnormal blood flow.

CT scan. A more advanced form of X-ray, the CT machine takes detailed pictures of your heart from various angles, providing a cross-sectional view.

MRI. Using a magnetic field and radio waves, MRI records energy signals emitted by the atoms that make up the cells of the body. MRI can measure blood flow through arteries, providing information about blockages.

Cardiac catheterization, or angiography. In this procedure—an invasive test—a pencil-sized plastic tube is threaded through an artery in your groin. A catheter is then passed through the tube toward the heart and into a coronary artery. Iodine-based dye is then injected, and a special camera takes pictures to show any blockages.

EBCT. This sophisticated test measures calcification of the arteries, a possible indication of CHD. (See "Should You Have an EBCT?" on page 31.)

Once your doctor determines you have plaques, the goal is to stabilize them and prevent a heart attack. But it's far better to prevent the plaques in the first place. Bringing down your cholesterol is a key strategy for both. For instance, having 60 percent of the surface area of a coronary artery covered in plaque is considered significant atherosclerosis. If your cholesterol is 150 you'll be 80 years old before you get that much plaque. But if your cholesterol is 300 you'll reach that level before you hit 40.

Of course, cholesterol isn't the only factor that plays a role in the development of heart disease. In Chapter 2 we'll explore some of the other factors—inflammation, high blood pressure, even germs—that can significantly affect your risk.

Beyond Cholesterol

Imagine taking your car in for servicing and only having the oil checked. It wouldn't make sense, would it? Yet that's essentially what you're doing if you focus only on your cholesterol counts to gauge the health of your arteries. True, those numbers are a strong indication of your risk of heart disease. But they don't tell the whole story. In fact, as many as half of all people with heart disease have normal cholesterol levels.

What else is going on here? Researchers are beginning to uncover the answers to that question, and those answers include myriad factors, ranging from blood components like C-reactive protein and interleukin-18 to your state of mind and even the length of your legs.

Sometimes it seems as if the risk factors and markers for heart disease grow as fast as grass during a rainy July. There are so many, in fact, that one study found just 18 percent of American adults had no risk factors for heart attack. If you have only one risk factor, the odds of trouble are probably relatively low (depending on the factor, of course). Chalk up more than one, however, and the danger becomes compounded. In this phenomenon, called synergism, the total risk is greater—and much more dangerous—than the sum of its parts.

Think of the formation of plaque as a process that is controlled by various "on" switches. High cholesterol is only one of them. Starting on the next page you'll read about 11 other switches—and discover what you can do to turn them "off."

1. Nitric Oxide

The same chemical responsible for men's erections (and, indirectly, for the success of Viagra) also plays a vital role in the health of your arteries, and thus your heart. The chemical is nitric oxide (NO), which is primarily produced in the blood vessels' endothelium, or lining. There it increases blood flow, prevents fatty deposits from sticking to blood vessel walls, keeps walls from getting too thick and stiff, and prevents the arteries from narrowing.

"The lining of the vessel is very important for cardiac health," says John P. Cooke, M.D., Ph.D., head of Stanford University's vascular unit and one of the first researchers to pinpoint the role of NO in cardiovascular health. "When the endothelium is healthy it's like Teflon, and things don't stick." When it's unhealthy, it becomes more like Velcro, attracting blood-borne gunk like flies to flypaper.

If your artery walls don't make enough nitric oxide, they become like Velcro, attracting blood-borne gunk like flies to flypaper.

All of the major culprits in heart disease—overweight, lack of exercise, smoking, high cholesterol, high blood pressure, high levels of homocysteine and lipoprotein (a)—damage the endothelium. And a damaged endothelium doesn't make enough NO, which results in more damage in an increasingly dangerous spiral. "But we can restore endothelial health and the lining of the vessel through exercise and nutrition," Dr. Cooke says. Certain nutritional supplements (like arginine) and drugs used to treat heart disease (like aspirin and statins) can also help.

By the Numbers

If doctors could measure endothelial function—how blood vessels behave—they would have a good indication of your nitric oxide production, and in fact, your overall risk for coronary heart disease (CHD). Measuring endothelial function is like asking your arteries, "How's it going?" If the answer is "well," your arteries are happy with the composition of the blood and are probably relatively free of plaque.

Doctors can measure endothelial function in various ways, most of which involve using ultrasound to measure changes in the diameter of certain arteries. This testing is usually used for research purposes only. But soon there may be a way to test endothelial function right in the doctor's office. In late 2000 the FDA approved a new, noninvasive instrument called CVProfilor DO-2020 that can measure the elasticity of your arteries, an indication of NO production. Normal ranges vary depending on your age and sex. The test isn't in routine use yet, but that day may be coming.

☑ How the *Live It Down Plan* Can Help

The *Live It Down Plan* is designed to promote the overall health of your heart and blood vessels, not just lower your cholesterol. There are several ways it contributes to better endothelial function. First, it calls for plenty of foods that contain the amino acid arginine, from which NO is produced. These foods include beans, soy, almonds, walnuts, oats, and such cold-water fish as salmon, tuna, and mackerel.

Also, endothelial function is highly sensitive to saturated fat. Just one meal high in saturated fat can temporarily cut endothelial function almost in half. And of course you'll cut your intake of saturated fat on the Plan.

Finally, exercise plays a tremendous role in the production of NO and the health of the endothelium, Dr. Cooke says, because the increased blood flow that occurs during exercise encourages the endothelium to make more NO. Over the long term, if you exercise every day, your endothelial cells not only release more NO but also make more of the enzyme that converts arginine into NO. It's like expanding the size of the NO factory. "That's why the coronary arteries of long-distance runners have twice the capacity to relax and expand as those of same-aged couch potatoes," Dr. Cooke says.

---

2. Inflammation and C-Reactive Protein

Remember the last time you scraped your knee? As it healed, it grew red and warm, sometimes leaking pus. That was inflammation at work. Whenever there's an injury to any part of your body, the flow of blood increases as white blood cells rush to the area like rescue workers responding to a train wreck. Ironically, this very process can also damage tissue.

What does inflammation have to do with heart disease? As it turns out, plenty. When the lining of the artery is damaged—say, when LDL particles burrow into the artery wall—white blood cells flock to the site, resulting in inflammation. Thus, more LDL equals more inflammation. Inflammation not only further damages the artery walls, leaving them stiffer and more prone to plaque buildup, but it also makes any plaque that's already there more fragile and more likely to burst. Other factors that damage the artery wall and trigger inflammation include smoking, high blood pressure, and even germs (more on those in a minute).

How do you know if your arteries are inflamed? By testing your level of C-reactive protein (CRP), which is produced in the liver whenever inflammation occurs. If your arteries are under attack, your CRP level rises. An estimated 25 million to 35 million healthy middle-aged Americans with normal cholesterol have CRP levels that put them at higher risk of heart attack and stroke.

In a landmark study on CRP and heart disease, researchers at Boston's Brigham and Women's Hospital measured CRP levels in 1,086 apparently healthy men. They followed the men over the next eight years, tracking heart attacks, strokes, and blood clots. The result: The risk of a first heart attack rose fivefold when both cholesterol and CRP were high.

Researchers involved in the Harvard Women's Health Study reported similar results, noting that women with the highest levels of CRP had a sevenfold increase in risk of heart attack or stroke. Even if they didn't smoke, had normal cholesterol levels, and had no family history of heart disease, the women with high CRP were still more likely to have a heart attack or stroke. And a study published in late 2002 found that women with high CRP were twice as likely to die from a heart attack or stroke as those with high cholesterol.

Doctors now suspect that inflammation plays such a powerful role in heart disease that it trumps even cholesterol as a risk factor.

It's important to note that these studies involved healthy people. For those with a known cause of inflammation—such as rheumatoid arthritis or an active infection—CRP may not be a reliable indication of heart disease risk.

CRP may function as a marker of inflammation in the blood vessels, but it also can play a direct role in damaging the arteries by interfering with an enzyme involved in nitric oxide production. As you learned earlier, less nitric oxide means artery walls that attract more plaque-forming gunk. CRP also seems to be a marker for metabolic syndrome, a risk factor you'll read more about later in this chapter.

Another marker of inflammation is a molecule called interleukin-18 (IL-18). A four-year German study on patients with CHD found that those with high levels of this molecule were three times as likely to die from heart disease as those with low levels. Earlier studies had linked high levels of IL-18 to quicker buildup of plaque and more unstable plaque. The results are still preliminary, researchers warn, and the test for IL-18 is too complex for the typical doctor's office.

Still, given the evidence on CRP and IL-18, doctors now suspect that inflammation plays such a powerful role in heart disease that it trumps even high cholesterol as a risk factor—although you can't treat one and ignore the other, because they are linked. LDL increases inflammation, and inflammation generates free radicals, which oxidize the LDL particles and accelerate the formation of plaque. Many of the same factors that increase inflammation—such as obesity, diabetes, and metabolic syndrome—also increase cholesterol.

By the Numbers

CRP testing is becoming increasingly common as doctors are finding that people with elevated CRP—even if their LDL is below 150—may benefit from lifestyle changes and statin drugs. If you have high levels of CRP *and* high cholesterol, your risk of heart attack and stroke is nine times that of someone with normal levels of both.

The risks of heart attack and stroke begin to rise with a CRP level as low as 0.55 milligram to 0.99 milligram per liter. Above 2.5 milligrams your risk is twofold or even fourfold. Ask for the high-sensitivity CRP test (hs-CRP) at your next checkup. It costs about $20 and is widely available. The standard CRP test, used for diagnosing conditions such as arthritis and inflammatory bowel disease, simply isn't sensitive enough.

Despite CRP's value in predicting heart disease risk, it will never be used by itself, doctors say, because it may be elevated in people with other forms of inflammation (such as arthritis) whose CHD risk is normal.

☑ How the *Live It Down Plan* Can Help

The good news is that CRP levels seem to predict a heart attack six or eight years in the future. That's plenty of time to modify your lifestyle (and, if necessary, take medication). One imperative is quitting smoking. Smoking inflames the arteries and is associated with higher levels of CRP. If you smoke, we strongly suggest you quit. Ask your doctor for advice on how to do it.

The *Live It Down Plan* will help reduce your CRP level through:

Supplements. Fish-oil supplements help reduce inflammation throughout the body. This action may be one reason studies find that people taking fish-oil supplements are less likely to die from a heart attack than those who don't take the supplements.

Aspirin. The Plan recommends a daily aspirin for people at increased risk for heart disease. In a seminal 1998 study on CRP and heart disease risk, researcher Paul M. Ridker, M.D., and his colleagues found that men with the highest levels of CRP reaped the greatest benefits from taking aspirin.

Weight loss. When Dr. Ridker evaluated the connection between weight and CRP, he found that the more overweight you are, the higher your CRP level. That's not surprising, since fat cells are a major source of interleukin-6, a protein that plays a key role in inflammation. More interleukin-6 means a higher CRP level. The Plan will help you lose weight through healthful eating and exercise.

Exercise. A study published in August 2002 found that the more active people were, the lower their CRP levels. The study, which evaluated data from a national health and nutrition survey of nearly 14,000 people, reported that just 8 percent of vigorous exercisers had elevated CRP levels, compared with 13 percent of moderately active and 21 percent of sedentary adults. The *Live It Down Plan* recommends moderate physical activity four or more days a week.

3. Germs

Since bacteria, viruses, and other germs are a common cause of inflammation in general (think about the white blood cells the body dispatches to fight an infection), researchers have begun investigating a possible link between germs and heart disease.

Some of the bugs that have been implicated are the culprits behind chronic, low-grade infections. They include *helicobacter pylori*, the bacterium that causes most ulcers; *chlamydia pneumoniae*, a bacterial organism that causes mild pneumonia in young adults; and even *streptococcus mutans*, the bacteria that cause cavities in your teeth (see "One More Reason to Brush," below.) Also on this list is herpes simplex virus type 1 (HSV-1), the virus that causes cold sores.

A study published in the journal *Circulation* in 2000 found that older people who had been infected with HSV-1 had twice the risk of having a heart attack or dying from heart disease as those never infected by the virus. Another study looked at 572 heart disease patients who had been admitted to the hospital for tests. The researchers followed the subjects for an average of 3.2 years and found that the death rate was 3.1 percent in those who tested positive for exposure to as many as three infectious agents, 9.8 percent for those exposed to four to five, and 15 percent

One More Reason to Brush

Think about this the next time you rush through brushing your teeth or decide to skip flossing: You're more likely to have elevated C-reactive protein (CRP) levels—and a higher risk of heart disease—if you have gum disease.

Gum diseases are bacterial infections that destroy the gum and bone that hold your teeth in your mouth. When this happens your gums separate from the teeth, forming pockets that fill with plaque and even more bacteria. About 15 percent of adults between ages 21 and 50, and 30 percent over 50, have gum disease. And overall, studies find that people with gum disease are almost  twice as likely to suffer from CHD as those who don't have it. Researchers speculate that gum disease may allow oral bacteria to enter the blood-stream, triggering the liver to make inflammatory pro-teins like CRP. The bacte-ria may also play a direct role in injuring the arteries.

for those exposed to six to eight. The greatest risk came from exposure to the bacteria *chlamydia pneumoniae*, *mycoplasma pneumoniae* (which also causes pneumonia), and *helicobacter pylori*.

Bacteria and viruses trigger an overall immune response in the body, which may damage arteries. But some may wreak further havoc. *Cytomegalovirus*, a germ implicated in CHD, causes endothelial cells to generate large amounts of a molecule that interferes with nitric oxide production. Another study suggests some *chlamydia pneumoniae* bacteria may hitch a ride to the heart inside certain immune system cells.

> **Bacteria and viruses trigger an overall immune response that may damage arteries. And some germs may wreak further havoc.**

The whole germ theory got a big boost when British doctors gave antibiotics to CHD patients who tested positive for prior infection with *chlamydia pneumoniae*. Blood flow in a major artery in the patients' arms improved with the antibiotics, and blood levels of two markers for endothelial problems dropped, suggesting that the condition of the delicate lining of the arteries and other blood vessels improved. Another study found a three-month course of antibiotics resulted in longer life and reduced the risk of future heart attacks in people hospitalized for heart attack or unstable angina.

Researchers aren't sure exactly why antibiotics might help. They may kill residual bacteria left over from an acute infection. (Autopsies have revealed *chlamydia pneumoniae* living in coronary artery walls.) Another possibility: Certain antibiotics appear to have anti-inflammatory actions. Researchers are actively investigating this mystery.

Meanwhile, don't look for cardiologists to start handing out antibiotics any time soon. The world, and the United States in particular, is facing a serious public health threat from the growing incidence of antibiotic resistance, in which even the most powerful antibiotics are no longer effective against an increasing number of bacteria. The medical community will need many more studies proving conclusively that antibiotics can help with CHD—and which antibiotics work best. And despite the above data supporting a germ-heart disease connection, two large studies have found no association between the number of infections a person suffers and subsequent heart attacks and strokes.

❤ How the *Live It Down Plan* Can Help

The diet recommended in the Plan is associated with optimal immune function, which reduces inflammation and increases the body's defense against common infections.

Also, quitting smoking can reduce your risk of infection. Studies find that smoking turns your entire body into a breeding ground for germs. Smokers are particularly prone to respiratory infections. In a study published in the journal *Stroke*, researchers

Case 19,471: A Mystery Solved

The discovery of the link between homocysteine and heart disease owes much to an obscure case published in the November 23, 1933, *New England Journal of Medicine.* It described an 8-year-old boy admitted to Massachusetts General Hospital after four days of headache, drowsiness, and vomiting. He died three days later. An autopsy revealed the cause of death: hardening of the arteries resulting in stroke. It was hardly a disease doctors expected to find in a child.

Thirty-two years later, a 9-year-old girl admitted to the same hospital had signs of homocystinuria, a genetic defect identified just a few years previously in which the liver can't dispose of homocysteine, resulting in abnormally high levels of the amino acid. It turned out the little boy who had died in 1933 was her uncle.

The cases intrigued Kilmer S. McCully, M.D., then a pathologist at Massachusetts General Hospital. He began investigating the disease and found that in these children (and a 2-month-old baby) the arteries were thickened and damaged, even though there was no buildup of cholesterol.

In 1969 McCully published a paper outlining his discovery and proposing a link between B vitamins, methionine, and heart disease. (Homocysteine is converted into methionine, a harmless substance, with the help of B vitamins. When the body is deficient in B vitamins, the conversion is slowed and homocysteine levels rise.)

Although it took another 30 years before McCully's theories became widely accepted, today doctors often screen high-risk patients for homocysteine levels.

found that current and former smokers who had common chronic infections—such as bronchitis, ulcers, urinary tract infections, and even gum disease—were more than three times as likely to develop early CHD as people without such infections. Secondhand smoke can be just as devastating, the researchers found, so encourage your loved-ones to quit, for their sake and yours.

4. Homocysteine

When Kilmer S. McCully, M.D., first proposed a link between levels of an amino acid called homocysteine and heart disease in 1969, the medical community largely ignored him. But four decades and hundreds of studies later, that community is finally in agreement—or as close to agreement as it ever comes—in linking high levels of homocysteine to an increased risk of heart disease, stroke, and peripheral vascular disease (reduced blood flow to the hands and feet).

Homocysteine is formed when the body breaks down dietary protein, especially protein from animal sources. Then B vitamins, particularly folate, B_6, and B_{12}, break down homocysteine so your cells can use it for energy.

But if this breakdown phase fails to occur—say, if you don't get enough B vitamins—homocysteine builds up to an unhealthy level. It then damages endothelial cells, preventing the production of nitric oxide. It may also make blood cells stickier, encouraging clotting, which can eventually trigger a stroke or heart attack. In a study of 386 women at the University of Washington in Seattle, those with the most homocysteine in their blood had double the heart attack risk of those with the least. They also had the lowest levels of folate. Further, a 2002 study published in the journal *Stroke* found that high levels of homocysteine increased the risk of stroke fivefold.

> **In one study people with the most homocysteine in their blood had double the heart attack risk of those with the least.**

Other research links high levels of homocysteine to the development of dementia or Alzheimer's disease. In one study people with the highest levels of homocysteine at the start of the study were nearly twice as likely to develop dementia.

Thankfully, the homocysteine problem is one of the easiest ones to solve. It's generally as simple as getting more B vitamins. When researchers gave people who underwent angioplasty (a catheter procedure to open blocked blood vessels with a balloon) a combination of the three B vitamins, they found that not only were homocysteine levels lower, but the incidence of repeat blockages dropped, cutting the number of repeat angioplasties in half. And in a Harvard study of 80,000 nurses, those with the highest intake of folate (about 696 micrograms a day) cut their risk of developing heart disease nearly in half.

The older you are, the more you smoke, and the less you move all seem to be tied to higher homocysteine levels. High cholesterol and blood pressure also tend to go hand in hand with high levels of homocysteine. And too much protein in your diet—think Atkins and the Zone—can also increase homocysteine levels.

By the Numbers

Check with your doctor to find out whether a homocysteine test is appropriate for you; it may be worth taking if you have other known risk factors for heart disease. (See page 25 for more information on blood tests.)

Homocysteine level	Heart disease risk
5–15 micromoles per liter	Normal
> 9 micromoles per liter	Risk begins to rise

☑ How the *Live It Down Plan* Can Help

The Plan has all of the elements—including a focus on nonanimal protein, plenty of B-vitamin-rich grains, beans, and vegetables, a daily multivitamin, and exercise—that studies show reduce homocysteine levels. The moderate levels of alcohol included in the Plan for most participants may also help. An Australian study of 350 obese men and women found that those who drank six 8.5-ounce glasses of red wine per week had blood homocysteine concentrations 17 percent lower than those who didn't consume any alcohol, and 13 percent lower than those who reported primarily drinking beer or spirits.

A Coffee Connection?

For most people coffee contributes little to overall heart disease risk. But if you're a java junkie, keep reading. A 2001 study published in the *Journal of Clinical Nutrition* found that drinking four or more cups of coffee a day affects cholesterol and homocysteine levels. Researchers broke 191 healthy, nonsmoking, coffee-drinking volunteers aged 24 to 69 into three groups: no coffee, one to three cups a day, or more than four cups a day. Those who cut out the brew altogether saw their homocysteine and cholesterol levels drop.

Another study, published in the same journal, found that in adults who drank strong filtered coffee, homocysteine levels rose 18 percent. Researchers concluded that if you're used to drinking four or more cups of coffee a day, abstaining might reduce by 10 percent the risk of heart disease attributed to high homocysteine levels.

5. Metabolic Syndrome and Diabetes

Few conditions sound as mysterious as the one often called Syndrome X. What is it, and why should you care?

During the groundbreaking Framingham Heart Study, when the link between high cholesterol and heart attack risk became clear, researchers noticed a certain group of people with low LDL levels who nevertheless had a high risk of heart disease. Why? Further study revealed a cluster of heart disease risk factors dubbed Syndrome X: high levels of insulin and glucose (blood sugar), a high triglyceride level, low HDL, small and dense LDL particles (the kind more likely to burrow into artery walls and cause plaque), high blood pressure, and being overweight.

The hallmark of the syndrome, now called metabolic syndrome, is insulin resistance. This means the body can't effectively use insulin, the hormone that helps glucose enter cells. The body tries to compensate by churning out more insulin, to little avail; too much glucose still remains in the bloodstream. Insulin resistance generally stems from a combination of genetic susceptibility and weight gain—very few thin people have this condition.

Gerald Reaven, M.D., believes that metabolic syndrome may be responsible for at least half of all heart attacks.

Gerald Reaven, M.D., professor emeritus of medicine at the Stanford University School of Medicine and co-author of *Syndrome X: Overcoming the Silent Killer That Can Give You a Heart Attack,* estimates that between 60 million and 75 million Americans have metabolic syndrome. He believes it may be responsible for at least half of all heart attacks. The growing obesity epidemic in the United States is contributing to the rising incidence of metabolic syndrome, which is threatening to reverse the overall reduction of CHD risk in the country, undoing decades of hard work. Factors that contribute to weight gain—physical inactivity, a high-fat diet, and junk food (often in the form of highly processed carbohydrates)—also contribute to metabolic syndrome.

Other signs of the syndrome include high levels of fibrinogen, a protein that increases the risk of blood clots, and increased PAI-1, a protein that slows the breakdown of those clots. In other words, if you have metabolic syndrome, it's more likely that a clot will form where plaque has ruptured. A high level of lipoprotein (a) is another common characteristic. And some people with metabolic syndrome, though certainly not all, also have high LDL levels, compounding the problem.

The seriousness of metabolic syndrome as a CHD risk factor is clear. In a study of 4,483 people, those with metabolic syndrome were three times more likely to have CHD, a stroke, or a heart attack as those without the syndrome. Another study found that for every 30 percent increase in insulin there is a 70 percent increase in the risk of heart disease over a five-year period.

Diabetes and Heart Disease

About 5 to 10 percent of people with metabolic syndrome will go on to develop type 2 diabetes, and that percentage is probably rising, given the current obesity epidemic. Diabetes significantly increases heart disease risk. In fact, some 80 percent of people with diabetes eventually die of CHD. Diabetes can contribute to an imbalance between HDL and LDL. And like people with metabolic syndrome, diabetics tend to have smaller, denser LDL particles, which lead to more plaque. To make matters worse, glucose (blood sugar) latches onto lipoproteins, and sugar-coated LDL stays in the bloodstream longer than normal LDL, presenting more opportunity for oxidation.

Glucose also binds to proteins on the surface of endothelial cells, damaging the artery wall. This blood vessel assault is one of the factors that leads to blindness and kidney damage in people with diabetes, and researchers suspect the same forces are at work with CHD. But since the blood vessels leading to the eyes and kidneys are smaller and more delicate than those leading to the heart, that damage turns up sooner.

By the Numbers

There is no single test for metabolic syndrome, but if you have three or more of the following factors, you probably have it:

Risk factor	Measure	
Large waist circumference	Men:	> 40 inches
	Women:	> 35 inches
High fasting triglyceride level		≥ 150 mg/dl
Low HDL	Men:	≤ 40 mg/dl
	Women:	≤ 50 mg/dl
High blood pressure		≥ 130/85 mm/Hg
High fasting glucose levels		110–125 mg/dl

You have diabetes if your fasting blood glucose levels are 126 mg/dl or higher. Normal fasting blood glucose levels are between 80 and 120 mg/dl.

▼ How the *Live It Down Plan* Can Help

The key to reversing metabolic syndrome is to bring the body's insulin needs back in line. One of the best ways to do this is by losing weight. Shedding excess pounds makes cells more sensitive to insulin, so less is required. The Finnish Diabetes

Program and the Diabetes Prevention Program found that a 7 percent loss of body weight cut the risk of developing type 2 diabetes by more than half.

If you're overweight, you'll likely drop pounds on the *Live It Down Plan* because you'll be eating more healthfully and exercising more. The Plan also includes a fairly generous amount of protein, which helps you feel full with less food. The eating strategy you'll follow also helps combat insulin resistance directly by focusing on complex, high-fiber carbohydrates, which help reduce the amount of insulin your body needs. This is because soluble fiber, abundant in many grains, beans, lentils, and some fruits and vegetables, slows the absorption of glucose into the bloodstream after a meal, which reduces both blood sugar levels and insulin requirements.

6. High Blood Pressure

Blood pressure is the force of blood against the walls of your arteries. The more forceful it is—the higher it is—the more likely it is that the walls of your arteries will be damaged. An estimated one in four American adults has high blood pressure. Typically, there are no symptoms, which is why regular blood pressure checks are just as important as regular teeth cleanings.

Uncontrolled high blood pressure results in stiff, inflexible artery walls that are a veritable magnet for white blood cells, cholesterol, and other blood components that accumulate and form plaque. It's easy to envision the damage high-pressure blood flow can wreak if you already have plaque buildup: That blood rushing past at high force is just what it takes to nick the "cap" off the plaque, setting the stage for a heart attack. (See page 29.)

High blood pressure damages arteries, and damaged arteries are more susceptible to plaque buildup.

By the Numbers

Blood pressure fluctuates throughout the day; it tends to be higher when you wake up in the morning and lower in the evening. And many factors can influence it—like what you eat that day and whether or not you're feeling stressed. So doctors don't like to diagnose high blood pressure until you've been tested on at least three separate occasions.

Blood pressure (mm/Hg)	Classification
≤120/80	Optimal
<130/85	Normal
>140/90	High

☑ How the *Live It Down Plan* Can Help

The *Live It Down Plan* will significantly improve your blood pressure readings through various means. First, the eating strategy: Studies show that a diet rich in grains, fruits, vegetables, and nonfat dairy products—like the *Live It Down Plan* diet—can reduce blood pressure by about 10 percent, and more than 15 percent when combined with sodium restriction. Exercise, weight loss, and stress relief also help lower blood pressure. In fact, studies find that meditation can be as effective as medication in lowering blood pressure.

We also encourage you to quit smoking, which on its own should be enough to substantially lower your blood pressure. The nicotine in a single cigarette is potent enough to raise blood pressure levels above normal, and it can take 30 minutes to an hour for the effects of a cigarette to wear off and for blood pressure to return to baseline. Weight loss, another benefit of the Plan, can reduce blood pressure as well.

---

7. Depression

In one of the strongest indications of the power of the mind to influence the body, a growing collection of evidence finds that people who are depressed have a significantly higher risk of developing heart disease. In a study of almost 3,000 men and 5,000 women, depressed men were 70 percent more likely to develop CHD than those who weren't depressed. While depressed women were just 12 percent more likely to develop heart disease overall, those who were severely depressed were 78 percent more likely. In fact, a 1998 study found that women who are depressed have a risk of dying from heart disease equal to that of women who smoke or who have high blood pressure.

One study found that depression was as dangerous to the heart as smoking or high blood pressure.

The link works the other way around, too: While about 1 in 20 American adults experiences major depression in a given year, that number jumps to about one in three among those who have survived a heart attack.

The more severe the depression, the more dangerous it is to your health. But some studies suggest that even mild depression, including feelings of hopelessness experienced over many years, may damage the heart. Other studies suggest depression may affect how well heart disease medications work.

Researchers aren't sure what the connection between depression and heart disease is, but theories abound. One is that people who are depressed tend not to take very good care of themselves. They're more likely to eat high-fat, high-calorie "comfort" foods, less likely to exercise, and more likely to smoke. But beyond lifestyle, there is probably also a physiological link between depression and heart disease. Recent studies found that people with severe depression tended to have a deficiency of heart-healthy omega-3 fatty acids. People who are depressed also often have chronically elevated levels of stress hormones, such as cortisol. These keep the body primed for fight or flight, raising blood pressure and prompting the heart to beat faster, all of which put additional stress on coronary arteries and interfere with the body's natural healing mechanisms.

A whole branch of medicine is devoted to the complex links between mental health, the nervous system, the hormone system, and the immune system. Called psychoneuroimmunology, this science is gradually sorting out how the mind-body connection affects our vulnerability to, or defense against, heart disease.

Overall, an estimated 10 percent of American adults experience some form of depression every year. Although available therapies can alleviate symptoms in more than 80 percent of people treated, less than half of those with depression get the help they need.

◪ How the *Live It Down Plan* Can Help

A major component of the Plan is regular, moderate exercise. A 1999 study conducted at the Duke University School of Medicine found that exercising 30 minutes a day, three days a week, was just as beneficial in treating depression as medication alone, and nearly as beneficial as medication combined with exercise. Of course, regular exercise is also a great way to reduce your risk of heart disease and lower your cholesterol. On the Plan you'll also get plenty of omega-3 fatty acids (from food and fish-oil supplements) and B vitamins, both beneficial in preventing depression.

Diagnosing Depression

The following are signs of depression. If you're experiencing one or more of them, see your doctor or a mental health care provider.

Despair: persistent feelings of sadness, emptiness, worthlessness; excessive crying; inappropriate guilt; recurring thoughts of suicide or death.

Apathy: loss of interest in activities, including sex.

Trouble concentrating: difficulty making decisions, restlessness.

Fatigue: loss of energy, constantly feeling tired.

Low self-esteem: poor self-image, misdirected guilt.

Sleep or eating problems: changes in weight or appetite, changes in sleep patterns or early-morning waking.

Poor hygiene: often manifested in sloppy appearance.

Persistent physical ailments: headaches or digestive problems, for example.

The *Live It Down Plan* diet can also help defend against a form of depression called seasonal affective disorder (SAD), which often strikes in the winter. Increased production of serotonin, a brain chemical that is associated with mood, relieves SAD. The complex carbohydrates favored by the Plan will help increase serotonin levels by increasing the amount of tryptophan that reaches the brain. Tryptophan, an amino acid, is a precursor of serotonin.

8. Uric Acid

You've probably heard of gout. It's caused by the buildup of uric acid, a by-product of the breakdown of purines (components in many foods we eat). Over time an elevated uric acid level leads to the formation of needle-like crystals in joints. These crystals trigger gout attacks. Researchers now suspect a high level of uric acid may also be a sign of heart disease. The key word is "may," since two large studies yielded entirely different results.

In a 1999 study researchers evaluated data on 6,700 people and concluded that uric acid didn't play a role in the development of CHD or in death from CHD. They suggested that any link noted in the past was probably due to the connection between high uric acid and other risk factors, namely, being overweight. But a year later a study of 6,000 people found just the opposite: Women with high levels of uric acid (more than 8.61 mg/dl) were three times more likely to die from heart disease than women with low levels (less than 6.15), and men with high levels (more than 10.75) were 1.7 times more likely to die from heart disease than those with low levels (less than 8.30).

Researchers suspect that a high level of uric acid, which causes gout, may also be a sign of heart disease.

Researchers aren't sure what the connection may be, but they do know that insulin resistance, another CHD risk factor, often results in high levels of uric acid. Both are connected with being overweight.

By the Numbers

Normal levels vary slightly based on the lab and method of measurement used. What follows are general guidelines.

Gender	Normal uric acid level
Men	Up to 7.0 mg/dl
Women	Up to 6.0 mg/dl

☑ How the *Live It Down Plan* Can Help

Elevated levels of uric acid are linked to a high intake of meat, sugar, and starches, all of which are limited on the *Live It Down Plan* diet. Also, if you're overweight, the Plan will help you make the kind of lifestyle changes necessary to reach a healthier weight for your body type. And studies find that a daily low-dose aspirin (another *Live It Down Plan* component for most people at increased CHD risk) reduces the production of uric acid.

---

9. Hypothyroidism

High cholesterol is usually tied to lifestyle, genetic factors, or a combination of the two. But there are other causes. One explanation for high cholesterol that isn't attributable to lifestyle is hypothyroidism, or an underactive thyroid gland. Now comes research that even a slightly underactive thyroid, not bad enough for the problem to be called hypothyroidism, also poses a major heart disease risk. This condition is known as subclinical hypothyroidism.

Between 1990 and 1993, Dutch researchers evaluated women to see if they had blockages in their aortas (the large blood vessel leading from the heart to the rest of the body) or any evidence of a past heart attack. At the same time they collected blood tests of thyroid function. The study found that almost 11 percent of the women had subclinical hypothyroidism when they began the study, and those women were almost twice as likely as the women with no thyroid problems to have blockages in their aortas. They were also twice as likely to have had heart attacks.

The connection is probably related to the role the thyroid plays in controlling metabolism. If the gland doesn't produce enough thyroid hormone, metabolism can slow, reducing the body's ability to clear cholesterol from the bloodstream. (If your metabolism goes into slow motion, cholesterol hangs around longer, so it's more likely to oxidize and cause damage to your arteries.) There may also be a connection between hypothyroidism and homocysteine levels; recent studies have found elevated levels of homocysteine in people with hypothyroidism.

New research finds that even a slightly under-active thyroid poses a major heart disease risk.

While hypothyroidism has a fairly recognizable constellation of symptoms—weight gain, fatigue, depression, hair loss, muscle and joint pain—subclinical hypothyroidism is more insidious. Symptoms are rarely obvious, and doctors often don't pick up on it because you may have normal test results.

By the Numbers

The gold-standard test for thyroid conditions measures a hormone made in the pituitary gland called thyrotropin-stimulating hormone (TSH). TSH regulates the amount of thyroid hormone made and released by the thyroid gland. The pituitary is in charge of this system, so when the TSH level is normal, the pituitary is satisfied with the thyroid's function. Other tests, called free T4 and T3, measure levels of the hormone itself. Typically, an elevated TSH level would lead your doctor to test your free T4 and T3 levels. Although there is controversy as to what is "normal" TSH and what is subclinical hypothyroidism, "it's generally accepted that subclinical hypothyroidism is a TSH greater than 5, with normal free T4 tests and T3," says Hossein Gharib, M.D., president of the American Association of Clinical Endocrinologists. Some researchers believe that a TSH greater than 3, Dr. Gharib says, is already on the high side. A TSH greater than 5 plus a low free T4 is hypothyroidism.

Subclinical hypothyroidism occurs in about 15 percent of women over the age of 60 and in about 8 percent of elderly men (although since the condition is less studied in men, this latter figure may actually be higher).

What You Can Do

Before your doctor starts you on any cholesterol-lowering drug, ask about being tested for hypothyroidism. Once the condition is treated and TSH levels return to normal, the majority of patients show an estimated 20 to 30 percent reduction in cholesterol levels. The recommended treatment, even for subclinical hypothyroidism, is the synthetic thyroid hormone levothyroxine, sold under various brand names, including Synthroid.

---

10. Iron Overload

An increasing body of evidence suggests that high levels of iron may explain several heart disease anomalies. For instance, men who regularly donate blood (and thus rid themselves of iron) have a lower risk of heart disease, as do premenopausal women, who regularly lose blood (and thus iron) through menstruation.

Iron overload depletes an antioxidant that helps prevent LDL from "rusting," or oxidizing.

A genetic condition called hemochromatosis is associated with high levels of iron. About 1 out of 10 people carries the gene for it, and 1 out of 250 to 300 people exhibits the condition. A comparable state can also result from taking iron pills for more than 10 years or receiving numerous blood transfusions. Certain people with liver disease may also experience iron overload. Generally there are few, if any, symptoms. And therein lies the danger, for hemochromatosis causes severe depletion of glutathione, an important antioxidant. Antioxidants like glutathione help prevent the LDL from "rusting," or oxidizing, which makes it stickier and starts the process of plaque formation. Several studies found that iron overload is most damaging to the heart if you also have a high LDL level. It makes sense, since the higher your LDL count is, the more LDL is available to be oxidized. One study found that every 1 percent rise in blood iron increased the risk of heart disease 4 percent.

Researchers suspect high iron levels may also affect cardiovascular risk in other ways. In a 1999 study Japanese researchers found that iron overload raised levels of a chemical that is a marker of oxidation and impaired endothelial function. Iron probably affects endothelial function by interfering with nitric oxide production. When researchers lowered the subjects' iron levels, their endothelial function improved.

The Luck of the Draw

The *Live It Down Plan* will help you attack most of the risk factors discussed in this chapter. But some, like the ones listed below, you're stuck with. Even so, keep in mind that your power to reduce your overall CHD risk is still monumental.

Leg length. A British study of 2,512 men ages 45 to 59 found those with the shortest legs had more heart attacks and new incidents of angina than men with longer legs. Researchers in Wales monitored the men for 15 years to gauge their risks of developing heart disease and found men with shorter legs—even those who weren't short overall—had higher levels of fibrinogen and cholesterol and were more likely to be insulin resistant. Researchers suspect that nutritional and environmental circumstances during childhood, which affected growth rates and leg length, also play a role in cardiac health.

Baldness. When researchers at Harvard Medical School compared patterns of baldness with incidence of CHD in 22,071 male physicians, they found that the balder a man was (particularly if he had baldness on top of the head), the higher his CHD risk.

Earlobe creases. More than 30 studies over the past 30 years have suggested an increase in heart disease risk among certain people (not Asians or Native Americans) whose earlobes have a crease. In one study in which 264 patients from a coronary care unit or catheterization lab were followed for 10 years, researchers found those with creased earlobes were indeed more likely to have had a coronary event, and those with two creased earlobes were more likely still.

In the cases of baldness and earlobe creases, the connection with heart disease is likely genetic. That is, the gene for baldness and earlobe creases may also play a role in the development of CHD.

The jury is still out on the significance of the iron-heart disease link. A population-based study published in 2000 found no association between iron levels above the normal range and deaths from CHD.

What You Can Do

If there is a history of hemochromatosis in your family, you should have regular blood tests for iron overload. A genetic test for hemochromatosis is now available. If you have a high iron condition, don't take any iron supplements, including multivitamins that contain iron. (Look for a brand that doesn't contain iron.) Limit the amount of red meat you eat, and avoid drinking alcohol. Too much iron plus alcohol can result in liver disease or make existing liver disease worse.

11. Fibrinogen

Fibrinogen is a protein that helps your blood clot (picture the fibers in a cloth soaking up liquid). That's a good thing unless, as too often happens, you wind up with too much of a good thing. Then fibrinogen plays a role in the development of CHD by making blood thick and sticky—just what your arteries don't need. Studies published in the American Heart Association's journal *Circulation* in 2000 found that people with high levels of fibrinogen were more than twice as likely to die of a heart attack as those with low levels.

This protein makes blood thick and sticky—just what your arteries don't need.

As with most cardiac risk factors, the effects of fibrinogen are influenced by the company it keeps. This marker may not mean all that much if you don't have any other major cardiac risk factors that make you more prone to plaque formation. But if you do, your fibrinogen level becomes more important.

By the numbers

The normal range for fibrinogen is 170–450mg/dl.

☑ How the *Live It Down Plan* Can Help

High cholesterol, smoking, inactivity, and a poor diet all seem to induce the body to produce more fibrinogen. The Plan will help with all of these. It will also protect you in another important way by teaching you to relax.

For some reason, fibrinogen levels are related to stress. People with stressful occupations and lower socioeconomic standing tend to have higher levels. In fact, a 2002 Dutch study published in the journal *Psychosomatic Medicine* found that a mental state known as "vital exhaustion" (which is just what its name implies—a state of excessive fatigue, irritability, and hopelessness) correlates with high levels of fibrinogen. The study also linked it to less early-morning fibrinolysis, the process by which blood clots break down.

Omega-3 fatty acids have been shown to reduce fibrinogen levels, and you'll get plenty of those on the Plan through fish and fish-oil supplements. And moderate alcohol consumption, also a part of the *Live It Down Plan* for most participants, can reduce fibrinogen levels up to 20 percent. In addition, the *Live It Down Plan's* daily low-dose aspirin for most people at increased risk for CHD can reduce blood clots through its anti-inflammatory and anticlotting activity.

Other Risk Factors

Other factors—or, more precisely, markers—may be related to CHD, although there isn't as much evidence yet to support their role as independent risks as there is for the ones discussed so far. They include:

Low magnesium. When researchers at the Centers for Disease Control and Prevention analyzed nutritional data and causes of death for nearly 13,000 men and women, they found that those with the highest levels of magnesium were 31 percent less likely to die from heart disease. No surprise, since the mineral plays a major role in keeping your heart beating regularly.

The recommended daily allowance of magnesium is 350 milligrams for men and 280 milligrams for women. A national survey conducted between 1988 and 1991 found that men averaged only 321 milligrams and women only 238 milligrams. Further, while many of us are focused on getting enough calcium, most don't know that it's just as important to maintain a favorable ratio of calcium to magnesium, ideally 2:1. A 4:1 dietary calcium-magnesium ratio is blamed, in part, for the high rate of heart disease among middle-aged men in Finland. In contrast, the calcium-magnesium ratio of healthy centenarians in Italy suggests that high magnesium consumption might even prolong life.

High oxidative burden. There are now ways of measuring the relative abundance of "oxidants," such as free radicals, in the blood. These compounds can injure the lining of blood vessels, interfere with nitric oxide production, and make LDL more likely to stick to artery walls. This relative abundance is known as the oxidative burden. Smokers tend to have an especially high oxidative burden, while people living a healthy lifestyle and eating plenty of antioxidant-rich fruits and vegetables tend to have a low one.

Carotid artery thickness. According to an article in the *British Medical Journal*, the thickness of the walls in your carotid arteries (the arteries on either side of your neck) may indicate the amount of atherosclerosis you have and your risk of heart attack and stroke. This is an easily accessible spot to use ultrasound to measure atherosclerosis. Finding it in one place generally means it exists elsewhere in the body.

Get With the Program

Congratulations! After plodding tirelessly through all of the weighty information in this chapter, you are now fully armed against your enemies. You know that inflammation is a formidable threat—and that aspirin and fish-oil supplements can help you combat it. You know that eating plenty of walnuts, oats, and cold-water fish will boost your body's production of nitric oxide, which keeps artery walls slick so nothing can stick to them. You know that simply taking a daily multivitamin can lower your homocysteine level and potentially slash your risk of heart attack. Too much to remember? Don't worry—you'll be doing all of these things on the *Live It Down Plan*. With so much more to offer you than cholesterol-lowering drugs (or drugs alone), the *Live It Down Plan* is a potent, overall defense of your total heart health. Read on to find out how to put the Plan into action.

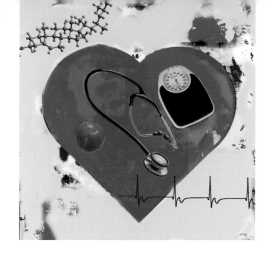

What You and Your Doctor Can Do

When you find out your cholesterol levels have been red-flagged, your reactions may run the gamut from nonchalance to fear to fatalism. For some people, knowing they have a cholesterol problem is what finally makes the obscure risk of heart disease seem real—and moves them to action.

Perhaps you're a 52-year-old woman going through menopause, and the normal blood test results you've always received have suddenly gone haywire. Or you're a 40-year-old man who had his cholesterol checked for the first time—and found out some uncomfortable news. Maybe you're surprised or even resentful. But remember: Cholesterol numbers don't come out of nowhere. Quite likely you are overweight, don't get enough exercise, smoke, or live life as if you're perpetually running for a train that's just pulling out of the station. Focusing solely on your cholesterol generally won't be enough to lower your risk of coronary heart disease (CHD); to avoid a heart attack or stroke you'll want to launch an attack on all of these fronts. And the *Live It Down Plan* will show you how.

The Plan is not just for people with high cholesterol. It's how we *all* should live to reduce our risk of serious health problems, including cancer and diabetes. So if you're embarking upon the Plan because you have high LDL, low HDL, or metabolic syndrome, don't go it alone: Engage your family and friends—they'll benefit, too. And if you've picked up this book because your wife or father or friend has high cholesterol, and you're whispering secret thanks that *your* cholesterol is normal, remember that cholesterol levels are not stationary. They change as we age—generally going up. Following the *Live It Down Plan* will help you keep them in line.

Before you embark it's important to get a good picture of where you stand now, so you know what cholesterol target to aim for on the Plan and whether you'll need extra help from medication along the way.

Risk Factors You're Stuck With

Okay, so some things you really *are* born with. For instance, researchers have found several genetic abnormalities that can lead to high cholesterol and make lowering your cholesterol through lifestyle changes alone difficult, if not impossible. If this is true for you, you'll probably need cholesterol-lowering medication. That doesn't mean you can skip the lifestyle changes, however; the two together work best. The following risk factors fall into the category of things you can't change.

Genes

About 1 in 100 people can chalk up high cholesterol to a genetic basis called familial combined hyperlipidemia (FCHL). Although FCHL has been under study for nearly 30 years, many aspects of it remain a mystery. The disease results from defects in the way the body metabolizes lipoproteins; this leads to high total cholesterol, high triglycerides, or both. People with FCHL also have higher levels of small LDL particles—the ones most likely to accumulate in the arteries and cause plaque. If you have FCHL, you're also more likely to have insulin resistance, which itself is a risk factor for heart attacks.

If you've followed the *Live It Down Plan* for 12 weeks and don't see any improvement in your cholesterol, talk to you doctor about genetic testing and the possibility of medication. Lifestyle changes may not be enough for you.

Other genetic risks include:

HPA-2 Met. This gene variation makes blood stickier and more likely to clot. It may also predispose men to a blood clot in the heart. If you have it, there's nothing you can do about it—all the more reason to attack the risk factors you *can* modify by following the *Live It Down Plan*.

Apo-E4. This gene is linked with a higher risk of CHD. If you have it and you eat a heart-healthy diet, your risk of heart disease isn't increased (unless you drink too much or smoke). But if you have the gene and you eat the typical high-fat American diet, your cholesterol levels skyrocket. Alcohol tends to increase cholesterol levels in people with this gene, and people with the gene who smoke have a sharply increased risk of CHD.

Apo-E2 or apo-E3. Like apo-E4, these genes predispose you to heart disease. And cholesterol levels in people with these genes don't respond as well to lifestyle

Hormones and Heart Disease

We know that estrogen plays a role in helping women maintain healthy levels of cholesterol before menopause. After menopause, as estrogen levels plummet, LDL tends to rise, HDL drops, and triglycerides increase. In theory, hormone replacement therapy (HRT) should solve those problems. And when researchers looked back on large populations of women who chose to take HRT, the numbers seemed to support this theory. But the story isn't so simple after all.

In 2002 the government halted part of a major trial, the Women's Health Initiative, after realizing that Prempro, a brand of pill that combines estrogen and another hormone, progestin, not only failed to protect women from heart disease, it actually increased the incidence slightly. The drug also slightly raised the incidence of breast cancer, stroke, and blood clots in postmenopausal women.

Researchers don't know if it was the form of the estrogen used, the form of progestin, or the combination that caused the problems. Many suspect that another form of HRT would yield different results. Meanwhile, doctors no longer prescribe HRT just for heart protection.

So what's a menopausal woman to do? The *Live It Down Plan* will help bring HDL and LDL levels back in line. Additionally, some studies suggest a high intake of foods (such as soy) that contain estrogen-like compounds called phytoestrogens can lower cholesterol. The *Live It Down Plan* recommends soy as one alternative to animal protein. Whether phytoestrogens directly protect against heart disease is still under study, but soy offers valuable nutrients without the saturated fat of meat, and thus is a good addition to a heart-healthy diet.

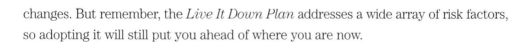

changes. But remember, the *Live It Down Plan* addresses a wide array of risk factors, so adopting it will still put you ahead of where you are now.

Family History

Even if you have no genetic abnormalities (or don't know whether you do), you may be at increased risk for CHD if your grandfather, father, or brother developed heart disease before the age of 55, or your grandmother, mother, or sister developed it before the age of 65. Perhaps genetics is to blame for your family history—or simply bad habits like smoking and poor eating. Either way you can lower your own risk by following the *Live It Down Plan*.

Age and Sex

More men than women develop CHD. And on average, men develop it 10 years before women do. But once women hit menopause, their risk of dying from heart disease equals that of men. In the end, 47 percent of all heart attacks occur in women.

Before menopause women usually have total cholesterol levels lower than those of men the same age. After menopause, however, women often have an increase in LDL and a decrease in HDL. After age 50 they often have higher total cholesterol levels than men of the same age. Even what would typically be considered a protective

> In the end, 47 percent of all heart attacks occur in women.

HDL level—in excess of 60 mg/dl—often isn't enough to guard women from heart disease after menopause. Thus, some experts suspect there may be no such thing as a "safe" HDL level for women; the higher, the better.

Ethnicity

Race plays a role in your risk of CHD. For instance, some African Americans with CHD appear to have a genetic trait that increases the danger of high triglycerides, particularly in women. One study found that African Americans produce less nitric oxide in response to stress; this substance is critical for opening blood vessels and increasing blood flow. Native Americans, particularly those in North and South Dakota, also face a much higher risk of CHD than Caucasians, while Hispanics have a lower risk than all of these groups. Whether race-related risks are mostly attributable to genetics or lifestyle habits is uncertain.

Risk Factors You Can Change

More than anything else, how you live your life determines your likelihood of developing CHD. Even if you have risk factors you can't do a thing about, making changes to your lifestyle can go a long way toward ensuring you don't ever suffer a heart attack or other so-called "coronary event."

Smoking

Smoking accounts for about one in five deaths from cardiovascular disease. Women who smoke are two to six times more likely to suffer a heart attack than those who don't. The risk increases with the number of cigarettes smoked each day. But if you quit, within one year your CHD risk plummets 50 percent; within 15 years your relative risk of dying from CHD approaches that of a lifetime nonsmoker.

About 70 percent of smokers say they want to quit. If you're one of them, talk to

Stuff the Stogies

If you think cigar smoking is a safe alternative to cigarette smoking because you don't inhale the smoke from a cigar, think again.

A large study published in 1999 in the *New England Journal of Medicine* found cigar smokers were more likely to develop cardiovascular disease than nonsmokers, and twice as likely as nonsmokers to suffer from cancer of the mouth, throat, esophagus, or lungs.

Cigar smoking causes almost twice as many heart attacks and strokes as it does lung cancer, because nicotine causes arteries to narrow and increases heart rate, whether it's inhaled or absorbed through the mouth; cigars have 10 to 400 times more nicotine than the average cigarette. Too bad Ulysses S. Grant, Sigmund Freud, and Babe Ruth didn't know this: All three died from cigar-related diseases.

your doctor about stop-smoking strategies. In addition to providing the kind moral and medical support you'll need, your doctor can prescribe medications shown to help smokers break the habit.

How does smoking affect your heart disease risk? It lowers HDL and damages the blood vessels, making them less elastic (thereby reducing blood flow and causing high blood pressure) and turning them into virtual Velcro, so that gunk (like fatty deposits) is more likely to stick to them. Smoking also reduces oxygen levels in the blood, which further irritates vessel walls.

Smoking may also contribute to insulin resistance and the cascade of events that leads to metabolic syndrome (described on page 43). When researchers at Stanford University had 20 smokers and 20 nonsmokers drink a sweet solution, they found that while glucose levels of both remained about the same, the smokers had much higher levels of insulin, a sign of insulin resistance. Also, while total cholesterol levels were the same in both groups, VLDL was higher and HDL lower in smokers.

Unless your cholesterol is off the charts, quitting smoking may be even more important than fixing the cholesterol problem. Research has shown that male smokers with low cholesterol have a substantially higher risk of death than nonsmokers with high cholesterol. Of course, doing both is best.

Lack of Exercise

Could our lives be any easier? We have clickers to change the channel, increase the stereo volume, even turn lights on and off. We can drive through for hamburgers, dry cleaning, and doughnuts. We can hire someone to clean the house, cut the grass, and walk the dog. Is it any wonder that one in four Americans is not physically active at all?

Or that more than 6 in 10 don't get enough exercise to do any good for their health?

While lack of exercise is bad for the whole body (and the mind), it's particularly bad for the heart. If you're sedentary, you're almost twice as likely to suffer a heart attack as someone who exercises regularly. Exercise increases HDL, reduces LDL, improves insulin sensitivity, and lowers blood pressure. It also helps to control your weight and keep your heart in shape. If you do have high cholesterol or other CHD risk factors, exercise can help nullify some of those risks by creating healthier, stronger blood vessels— in some instances, even new blood vessels for blood to flow through.

> **If you're sedentary, you're almost twice as likely to suffer a heart attack as someone who exercises regularly.**

If you're living the couch potato life, your body is storing calories as fat instead of burning them, which leads to high triglycerides and LDL. In fact, lack of exercise is so dangerous for your heart that some experts think a history of no regular physical activity should count as a risk factor for heart disease— one just as dangerous as high LDL.

You don't have to do much to make a difference; just 20 minutes of brisk walking per day will help your body burn calories instead of storing them as fat.

Your Diet

There's simply no way around it: You are what you eat. And if you eat a diet high in saturated fat and trans fatty acids (the stuff McDonald's cut back on in late 2002), you're more likely to have high cholesterol.

The fewer fruits, vegetables, whole grains, and fiber you get, the more likely you are to have high cholesterol as well as an overall increased risk of heart disease, even without the high cholesterol. Chapter 4 outlines the eating strategies of the *Live It Down Plan*. They are designed not only to lower your cholesterol and your risk of heart disease but to help unclog your arteries as well.

No Time to Waist

A trim waistline cuts more than a dashing figure—it may cut your risk of heart disease, too, since weight carried around the midsection increases the risk. Use a tape measure to measure the smallest part of your natural waist, usually just above the belly button. A circumference of more than 40 inches in men or 35 inches in women can indicate an increased risk of CHD.

Your Weight

America has a weight problem. Just consider the seat situation. To accommodate our girth, seats in auditoriums, stadiums, even subway cars have been widened. And some airlines are beginning to enforce policies whereby people who spill out of the seat they purchase must buy a second. According to the latest figures, nearly 65 percent of American adults are either overweight or obese.

Are You Overweight?

Knowing your weight isn't enough to determine if you're overweight or obese. For that you need to know your Body Mass Index (BMI), a measure that takes into account both height and weight.*

BMI	19	20	21	22	23	24	25	26	27	28	29	30	31	32	33	34	35	36
HEIGHT	WEIGHT IN POUNDS																	
4'10"	91	96	100	105	110	115	119	124	129	134	138	143	148	153	158	162	167	172
4'11"	94	99	104	109	114	119	124	128	133	138	143	148	153	158	163	168	173	178
5'0"	97	102	107	112	118	123	128	133	138	143	148	153	158	163	168	174	179	184
5'1"	100	106	111	116	122	127	132	137	143	148	153	158	164	169	174	180	185	190
5'2"	104	109	115	120	126	131	136	142	147	153	158	164	169	175	180	186	191	196
5'3"	107	113	118	124	130	135	141	146	152	158	163	169	175	180	186	191	197	203
5'4"	110	116	122	128	134	140	145	151	157	163	169	174	180	186	192	197	204	209
5'5"	114	120	126	132	138	144	150	156	162	168	174	180	186	192	198	204	210	216
5'6"	118	124	130	136	142	148	155	161	167	173	179	186	192	198	204	210	216	223
5'7"	121	127	134	140	146	153	159	166	172	178	185	191	198	204	211	217	223	230
5'8"	125	131	138	144	151	158	164	171	177	184	190	197	203	210	216	223	230	236
5'9"	128	135	142	149	155	162	169	176	182	189	196	203	209	216	223	230	236	243
5'10"	132	139	146	153	160	167	174	181	188	195	202	209	216	222	229	236	243	250
5'11"	136	143	150	157	165	172	179	186	193	200	208	215	222	229	236	243	250	257
6'0"	140	147	154	162	169	177	184	191	199	206	213	221	228	235	242	250	258	265
6'1"	144	151	159	166	174	182	189	197	204	212	219	227	235	242	250	257	265	272
6'2"	148	155	163	171	179	186	194	202	210	218	225	233	241	249	256	264	272	280
6'3"	152	160	168	176	184	192	200	208	216	224	232	240	248	256	264	272	279	287
6'4"	156	164	172	180	189	197	205	213	221	230	238	246	254	263	271	279	287	295

Key: Underweight   Healthy   Overweight   Obese   Severely Obese

*Note that these are general ranges. People with very muscular builds may have a high BMI without being overweight. And the BMI tends to underestimate body fat in older people, who have usually lost muscle mass.

Source: Centers for Disease Control and Prevention

Being overweight has repercussions far beyond where you buy your clothes. It's associated with increased LDL and decreased HDL. Where you gain weight also matters. Pounds packed around the waist (the old spare tire or beer belly) increase your risk of CHD as well as your risk of metabolic syndrome, described in Chapter 2. Extra padding around the hips (more typical for women) is less dangerous.

Wherever you carry your extra weight, if you're a woman it may be even more important for you to lose the pounds. One long-term study of 116,000 women found that almost 40 percent of their CHD risk was related to weight.

Stress and Hostility

The phrase "stress" has become so ubiquitous in our culture that it can at times seem meaningless. But to your heart and blood vessels, it's anything but. Stress—especially the chronic type you suffer with financial, health, or marital problems—plays a critical role in your risk for CHD. For instance, one study found that levels of LDL rose about 5 percent in a group of middle-aged male airline pilots when they experienced episodes of high occupational stress. Stress also affects your endothelial function (which indicates the all-important health of your artery walls) and how quickly you're able to clear triglycerides from your blood after eating. (Remember, the higher your triglyceride level, the more triglycerides are delivered to your liver, where they are transformed into LDL and VLDL—the "bad" and "very bad" kinds of cholesterol.) Stress can also raise your blood pressure and make your blood more likely to clot.

So What's The Plan?

We'll go into more detail on every aspect of the *Live it Down Plan* in the following four chapters. You'll walk through the Plan week by week starting on page 206. But here are the basics in a nutshell.

As you might expect, the cornerstone of the Plan focuses on how you eat. If you're anticipating a draconian diet that limits you to lettuce and tofu, relax; you'll still get plenty of enjoyment from food. In fact, the *Live It Down Plan* enables you to get roughly one-fourth of all of your calories from fat, as long as it's the heart-healthy kind of fat. And it doesn't restrict your intake of dietary cholesterol. (Yes, that's right, eggs and shrimp are back on the menu).

What's more, there's no focus on limiting calories unless you're overweight, defined as a Body Mass Index (BMI) of 26 or higher (see page 61). That's because the best way to control your weight is to eat right and get more exercise, not count calories—even if you are overweight. In the end, exercise and a healthy diet are more important than what the scale shows. Studies find that even people considered overweight can still have healthy cholesterol levels and other measures that indicate

Fringe Benefits

Controlling your cholesterol can do much more than simply protect you from heart disease and stroke. A growing body of evidence suggests that what's good for the heart may also be good for the mind, and that low levels of cholesterol may help prevent Alzheimer's disease.

In one of the strongest studies linking the two, Finnish researchers tracked nearly 1,500 people for an average of 21 years. They found that high cholesterol and blood pressure appeared to increase Alzheimer's risk even more than the so-called Alzheimer's gene (apo E-4), often cited as the most important genetic risk factor for the disease.

And when researchers at Case Western Reserve University compared the diets of 96 Alzheimer's patients to those of healthy patients, they found that those who tended to eat a diet low in fat and high in fish, vegetables, whole grains, and antioxidants like vitamins C and E (in other words, the *Live It Down* eating plan) reduced their risk of Alzheimer's disease. Other studies found that people taking cholesterol-lowering statin drugs also lowered their risk of developing Alzheimer's up to 79 percent.

Researchers suspect that high levels of cholesterol may lead to brain plaques, clumps of protein that accumulate on nerve cells.

a low risk for CHD if they're following a lifestyle like the one in the *Live It Down Plan*.

The rest of the eating strategy breaks down like this: 20 percent protein—that includes meat, poultry, eggs, soy, fish, and beans, with the greatest emphasis on the latter two—and 55 percent carbohydrates, primarily coming from complex carbohydrates like vegetables, fruits, and whole grains. We'll help you follow this strategy whether you're eating in or dining out.

Next, we want you to move. The type of exercise—walking, swimming, martial arts, digging in your garden—doesn't matter, as long as you get your heart beating faster, stretch your muscles, and burn some calories so they don't get stored as cholesterol-raising fat. The Plan includes a walking program that gives you just about all of the exercise you need in an easy, safe, and convenient form. You'll also find a series of simple morning stretches along with two easy strength-training routines (a 10-minute routine and a 30-minute routine) that will keep you toned and also pump up your metabolism to help you burn more calories.

A few key dietary supplements can help slash your risk of heart disease, and you'll be taking them on the Plan. The recommendations vary depending on your situation. Everyone will take daily fish-oil supplements (for valuable omega-3 fatty acids) and a multivitamin/multimineral. Most people will take a daily baby aspirin. Some people may add a natural cholesterol-lowering supplement like gugulipid, policosanol, or red yeast rice extract; the trace mineral chromium to enhance insulin sensitivity; or the antioxidant coenzyme Q10 if they are taking a statin drug to treat their cholesterol.

Finally, we're going to teach you how to do something that's more difficult for most Americans than bypassing a super-size meal: relax. From a new way to breathe to a new way of viewing the world, we'll explain how you can bring a small island of peace and calm into each and every day.

Never Too Late

Even if you already have heart disease, it's not too late to help your heart. If you have CHD, your risk of heart attack or some other "coronary event" is much higher than that of someone who doesn't— so your need for the *Live It Down Plan* is that much more urgent, and its potential benefit that much greater.

Why *Live It Down*?

Why try to lower your cholesterol through lifestyle when a pill can do the trick? Several reasons. First, while cholesterol-lowering drugs are a boon to people who really need them (you'll discover after you take the quizzes later in this chapter whether you're one of them), even the best drugs have side effects. And despite their effectiveness, no cholesterol-lowering medications will work as well as they should if you continue to eat a diet high in saturated fat, if channel surfing is your only form of exercise, or if you're sinking your retirement funds into cigarettes.

Another major benefit of the *Live It Down Plan*: It helps disarm or defend against other CHD risk factors that cholesterol-lowering drugs don't affect. We're talking about everything from high blood pressure to diabetes, insulin resistance, and metabolic syndrome. The Plan also attacks inflammation (remember, elevated C-reactive protein—a marker of inflammation—may be more dangerous than high cholesterol), and blood components like triglycerides and homocysteine.

Setting Your Cholesterol Goals

The *Live It Down Plan* will help you reduce your cholesterol. How much you need to bring it down depends on your CHD risk factors. In a nutshell, the greater your risk for a heart attack or stroke—in other words, the more risk factors you have—the lower your ideal cholesterol level.

If you have high cholesterol, the main goal is to lower your LDL. Why, you might ask, is this true when your ratios of HDL and LDL to total cholesterol are what count the most? First, because it's much easier to lower LDL than raise HDL. Few drugs or supplements reliably raise HDL (niacin is probably the best). Intense physical activity is effective, but few people are willing to work that hard. Alcohol also moves the needle, but of course the "dose" is limited by alcohol's inherent dangers. Lowering LDL is also the most direct way to slow plaque buildup, since LDL plays the most direct role in forming the stuff.

Perhaps the best way to think about your cholesterol goal is in terms of improving your HDL/LDL ratio. This can be done by raising HDL, lowering LDL, or both. And since it's easier to reduce LDL, that's where the focus falls.

To figure out how low your LDL target should be, take the following quiz. It will help you assess your current risk for CHD or heart attack. Remember, the greater your risk, the lower your cholesterol target should be.

What's Your Heart Disease Risk?

Take this quiz to determine your risk for CHD or heart attack. The answers will help you set LDL goals and let you know if you may need to start on a cholesterol-lowering drug.

Step 1

Count Your Risk Factors

If you don't have known heart disease or diabetes, answer the following questions. If you do, go directly to step 2 on the next page. (Not sure whether or not you have heart disease? If you've had a heart attack, a bypass operation, angioplasty, or an angiogram that showed a blockage in a coronary artery, or if you suffer from angina, you probably do.)

Check all that apply:

- ☐ I smoke cigarettes.
- ☐ I have high blood pressure (140/90 mm/Hg or higher, or you're on blood pressure medication).
- ☐ I have low HDL cholesterol (less than 40 mg/dl).
- ☐ I have a family history of early heart disease (heart disease in your father or brother before age 55, or in your mother or sister before age 65).
- ☐ I'm a man 45 or older, or a woman 55 or older.

If you checked one risk factor or none: Congratulations! You are in treatment category III—the lowest risk category (turn to page 67 to see what this means). You can skip steps 2 and 3. If you checked two or more: Go to step 2 on page 66.

What's Your Heart Disease Risk? (continued)

Step 2

Calculate Your Heart Attack Risk

Take the appropriate quiz below (one each for men and women) and add up the points (the numbers in blue) to determine your risk of having a heart attack in the next 10 years.

Men

1. Age

Years	20–34	35–39	40–44	45–49	50–54	55–59	60–64	65–69	70–74	75–79
Points	-9	-4	0	3	6	8	10	11	12	13

2. Total Cholesterol

mg/dl	Age 20–39	40–49	50–59	60–69	70–79
<160	0	0	0	0	0
160–199	4	3	2	1	0
200–239	7	5	3	1	0
240–279	9	6	4	2	1
>280	11	8	5	3	1

4. Blood Pressure

Systolic BP	If untreated	If treated
<120	0	0
120–129	0	1
130–139	1	2
140–159	1	2
>160	2	3

3. Smoking Status

Age	20–39	40–49	50–59	60–69	70–79
Nonsmoker	0	0	0	0	0
Smoker	8	5	3	1	1

5. HDL level

mg/dl	Points
>60	-1
50–59	0
40–49	1
<40	2

Score

Point Total	10-Year Risk (%)
<0	<1%
0–4	1
5–6	2
7	3
8	4
9	5
10	6
11	8
12	10
13	12
14	16
15	20
16	25
>17	>30

Your 10-Year Risk = ____ %

Women

1. Age

Years	20–34	35–39	40–44	45–49	50–54	55–59	60–64	65–69	70–74	75–79
Points	-7	-3	0	3	6	8	10	12	14	16

2. Total Cholesterol

mg/dl	Age 20–39	40–49	50–59	60–69	70–79
<160	0	0	0	0	0
160–199	4	3	2	1	1
200–239	8	6	4	2	2
240–279	11	8	5	3	2
>280	13	10	7	4	2

4. Blood Pressure

Systolic BP	If untreated	If treated
<120	0	0
120–129	1	3
130–139	2	4
140–159	3	5
>160	4	6

3. Smoking Status

Age	20–39	40–49	50–59	60–69	70–79
Nonsmoker	0	0	0	0	0
Smoker	9	7	4	2	1

5. HDL level

mg/dl	Points
>60	-1
50–59	0
40–49	1
<40	2

Score

Point Total	10-Year Risk (%)
<9	<1%
9–12	1
13–14	2
15	3
16	4
17	5
18	6
19	8
20	11
21	14
22	17
23	22
24	27
>25	>30

Your 10-Year Risk = ____ %

Step **3**

Identify Your Risk Category

Now, using the chart below, identify the category you fit. Your category helps determine your treatment approach (whether you will need cholesterol-lowering medication and how religiously you will need to follow the *Live It Down Plan*). Generally, if you haven't reached your cholesterol goal after three months of making lifestyle changes, your doctor will likely start you on medication. In some instances, depending on your risk factors and how high your LDL level is, you may need to start on medication even as you start the *Live It Down Plan*.

Your Risk Category

10-Year Risk	Category	Your LDL Goal	Medication?
More than 20%	I Highest risk	Less than 100 mg/dl	If your LDL is currently 100 to 129, you may need to start drug treatment even as you begin the *Live It Down Plan*, with the goal of getting off the medication later. If your LDL is 130 or higher, you almost certainly will need medication.
10% to 20%	II Moderate risk	Less than 130 mg/dl	If your LDL is 130 or more after three months on the Plan, you may also need drug treatment.
Less than 10%	III Lowest risk	Less than 160 mg/dl	If your LDL is 160 or more after three months on the Plan, you may also need drug treatment.

Personalizing the Plan

The *Live It Down Plan* is ideal for anyone, regardless of your cholesterol level. But some aspects of the Plan will differ slightly if you have metabolic syndrome or high triglycerides. For instance, you may need to exercise more, limit calories, and take certain supplements.

If You Have Metabolic Syndrome

You read about metabolic syndrome in chapter 2 (see page 43). People who have metabolic syndrome tend to be overweight, with much of their fat settled around their abdomens. They also tend to have insulin resistance (in other words, are on their way to developing diabetes) and are relatively inactive.

If you have metabolic syndrome, you'll need to lose weight. There's simply no way around this recommendation. In Chapter 4 we'll help you determine a daily caloric target based on your sex, age, physical activity level, and current weight.

You'll also need to follow the Plan closely if you have metabolic syndrome. No cheating, no halfway there for you. Certain elements, particularly fish-oil supplements, soluble fiber (from beans, whole grains, etc.), and exercise will be particularly important to help you increase your HDL and reduce your triglycerides. And your doctor may start you on a medication such as metformin, which has been shown to improve insulin resistance and even help prevent the development of diabetes. We'd also like you to:

Consider chromium supplements. Some research suggests chromium supplements may improve insulin sensitivity. (More on chromium in Chapter 5.)

Are You a Nonresponder?

Sometimes no amount of dietary and lifestyle change is enough to get your cholesterol down to a safe level. While some people can make just a few changes—substituting olive oil for butter, or eating fish instead of steak twice a week—and see their cholesterol drop 15 points in two weeks, others may follow the Plan to the nth degree and still find their numbers have barely budged.

These people are called "nonresponders." About 20 percent of adults fall into this category, usually due to their genetic makeup. On the other hand, those people who saw their levels plummet quickly are "hyper-responders," and, again, about 20 percent of adults fall in this category. If you're a nonresponder, it's likely you will need medication as well as lifestyle changes to bring your cholesterol down. Generally, if you've followed the *Live It Down Plan* closely for three months (no cheating!) and your levels haven't budged or have only dropped a little, talk to your doctor about medication that will help.

Control your alcohol intake. While alcohol will increase your HDL, too much can also increase triglycerides. Our advice to you is the same we'd give anyone else—if you drink, drink moderately. That means no more than one drink a day for women and anyone over 65, and no more than two drinks a day for men under 65.

What's Your Diabetes Risk?

As we noted above, if you have diabetes, it's likely you have or will have CHD unless you dramatically change your lifestyle. However, one-third of all people with diabetes don't even know they have it.

To find out if you are at risk for diabetes, see how many of the following statements apply to you:

1. I am a woman who has delivered a baby weighing more than 9 pounds at birth.
If yes, add 1 point.

2. I have a parent with diabetes.
If yes, add 1 point.

3. I have a brother or sister with diabetes.
If yes, add 1 point.

4. My weight is equal to or above that listed in the "At-Risk Weight Chart" (right).
If yes, add 5 points.

5. I am under 65 years of age and I get little or no exercise.
If yes, add 5 points.

6. I am between 45 and 64 years of age.
If yes, add 5 points.

7. I am 65 years of age or older.
If yes, add 9 points.

At-Risk Weight Chart	
Height	**At-Risk Weight**
4'10"	129
4'11"	133
5'0"	138
5'1"	143
5'2"	147
5'3"	152
5'4"	157
5'5"	162
5'6"	167
5'7"	172
5'8"	177
5'9"	182
5'10"	188
5'11"	193
6'0"	199
6'1"	204
6'2"	210
6'3"	216
6'4"	221

Source: American Diabetes Association

If you scored 10 or more points:
You are at high risk for having diabetes. Only your health care provider can check to see if you have diabetes. See your doctor for tests.

If you scored 9 points or fewer:
You are probably at low risk for having diabetes now. Keep your risk low by losing weight if you are overweight, being active most days, and eating low-fat meals that are high in fruits, vegetables, and whole grain foods.

Control your blood pressure. The *Live It Down Plan* should help lower your blood pressure, but your doctor may also decide to start you on blood pressure medication, such as a calcium channel blocker or ACE inhibitor. Beta-blockers, another type of blood pressure medication, may increase triglycerides and reduce HDL. While they may be the best choice for some patients, they're generally not the first choice for most.

If You Have High Triglycerides

If your triglyceride level is high, you usually also have an increase in VLDL remnants (see page 22), and thus a high VLDL count. Treatment depends on just how high your triglyceride level is.

Borderline High Triglycerides (150–199)

Follow the *Live It Down Plan*. If your BMI is 26 or higher, you need to lose weight—one of the best ways to lower your triglycerides. The Plan also calls for fish-oil supplements, which can reduce triglycerides.

Add two days of physical activity. Although the Plan calls for at least four days of moderate to intense physical activity, if you have a high triglyceride level, increase that activity to six days. Of course, if you aren't used to exercising, get the green light from your doctor first, and start slowly.

Talk to your doctor about medication. If you have CHD or other risk factors (such as diabetes), your doctor may consider treating you with the cholesterol-lowering drugs nicotinic acid or fibrates. (For more on these medications, see chapter 8.)

High Triglycerides (200–499)

The recommendations above apply to you also. Plus, it's more likely your doctor will start you on medication. You should also try to avoid alcohol, excess calories, and simple starches/processed carbohydrates.

Very High Triglycerides (more than 500)

It's very important that you get your triglycerides into a safer level as quickly as possible to prevent acute pancreatitis, an inflammation or infection of the pancreas. So it's quite likely your doctor will start you on medication (most likely fibrates and nicotinic acid), particularly if your triglyceride level is more than 1,000.

Ready, Set, Go

Are you ready? No, are you really ready? Changing your health habits is a challenging task, even though it's presented as absurdly simple in magazine cover lines that promise you can "Lose 10 Pounds in Two Weeks." It takes commitment to make the kind of changes called for on the *Live It Down Plan*, along with the support of family and friends. One thing that will help is understanding your own risks, as you've done in this chapter, for studies show that people are more likely to make a healthy change if they believe it's relevant to their situation.

Other ways to get on track and stay there:

Shout the news. Tell everyone in your life that you've made a new commitment to your health, from eating well to exercising to reducing your stress. Their questions and support will help you remain strong.

Track your progress. There's no better way to succeed than to see your success. The weekly logs that are part of the 12-week Plan starting on page 206 will help.

Make a list. Write down all of the reasons you think this won't work, then prove yourself wrong. For instance, if you think you can't exercise because you don't have time, list five ways you can find 30 minutes a day. Try skipping a TV show (or else exercise in front of the tube), dropping a commitment you can do without, or walking during lunch and eating your sandwich at your desk.

Take small steps. As you'll see in the week-by-week Plan, we don't expect you to go from 0 to 60 immediately. By making just a few changes at a time, you're less likely to be overwhelmed—and more likely to succeed.

Set realistic goals. Your goal shouldn't start as: "Cut out all red meat." Instead, set a more reasonable goal such as: "Eat no more than one hamburger per week for the first three weeks, then switch to chicken or veggie burgers." Make your goals very specific, and make a list of steps you need to take to reach them. In the hamburger goal, for instance, your step-by-step to prevent fast-food lunches might look like this:

1. Make a list of three different lunches I can pack.
2. Buy ingredients for lunches at the store.
3. Buy an insulated lunch bag.
4. Pack lunch the night before.

Plan for roadblocks. The holidays, a vacation, or a deadline crunch at work can all stall your progress, so plan ahead. To cope with a work crunch, for instance, bring along a bag of healthy snacks to the office and get your exercise by taking the stairs instead of the elevator.

Be flexible. Don't take an all-or-nothing approach. If you miss your daily walk one day, it doesn't mean you've failed or that there's no point in walking the next day. If you couldn't resist the french fries, vow to return to the Plan when you finish licking the grease off your fingers. Remember, this is a permanent lifestyle change, not a short-term solution.

Build in rewards. Every time your cholesterol drops treat yourself to something special, like a new golf club or a manicure.

Be patient. Studies show it takes at least three weeks of daily repetition before a change begins to feel natural, and longer before it's automatic.

Also understand that just as people move through various stages when they grieve, they move through stages when they're trying to change habits. The fact that you're reading this book means you're past stage one (precontemplation) and have reached stage two (contemplation). Stage three, preparation, means you're getting ready to put the advice in this book into action, such as by purchasing a bottle of olive oil, cholesterol-lowering margarine, or a new pair of walking shoes (you'll read about "Getting Ready" on page 205). In stage four, action, you'll begin following the 12-week Plan starting on page 206.

It won't always be a smooth road. You may backslide (maybe the sausages on the breakfast buffet were just too tempting to pass up) or become frustrated if you don't see quick results. That's okay. Just don't give up. As we've said before, this Plan is for life.

Which brings us to stage five: maintenance. You'll know you've reached this stage when you automatically order a salad at Wendy's instead of the Big Bacon classic (or stop going to Wendy's altogether and pack your own lunch instead), or walk to the post office instead of driving. You've found renewed energy, watched your cardiac risk factors—including your cholesterol—drop substantially, and perhaps even wrangled a muttered "good job" out of your overworked doctor.

Live It Down | Eating

Every aspect of the *Live It Down Plan* is important. Some psychologists would argue that good mental health and a nurturing network of friends matter most. And if you happen to be training for a triathlon, good for you— enough exercise can erase a lot of other lifestyle sins. But for most people the "heart" of the *Live It Down Plan* will be the diet. After all, eating is something all of us do every day, often with some degree of abandon, so it stands to reason that therein lies the biggest opportunity for improvement.

When researchers look for a cause-and-effect relationship between our lives and our cholesterol levels, diet always comes out on top. Various studies show drops of 25 percent or more in total cholesterol from many of the simple dietary changes that make up the *Live It Down* eating plan.

For instance, by cutting back your consumption of saturated fat (the kind in hamburgers and ice cream) to less than 7 percent of your total calories, increasing your fiber intake by 5 to 10 grams (about one serving of a raisin bran cereal) a day, and adding a couple of tablespoons of a special margarine designed to help lower cholesterol to your diet regularly, you could lower your LDL level between 17 and 30 percent. And that's before you add more bran, apples, oats, nuts, and other foods that on their own can lower your LDL several percentage points or increase your HDL.

The right foods can also reduce inflammation (think fatty fish such as salmon), regulate blood clotting (think garlic or black or green tea), lower blood pressure, and more. While healthy cholesterol levels are vital when it comes to avoiding heart disease, there is no way to overstate the countless benefits of eating well.

The Origins of the *Live It Down* Eating Strategy

There are plenty of ways to go about lowering your cholesterol through diet. For instance, there's the Mediterranean diet (high in fat, but mainly the heart-healthy kind), the Ornish diet (extremely low in all types of fat), the Dietary Approaches to Stop Hypertension diet, known as DASH (rich in grains, fruits, vegetables, and nonfat dairy), and the American Heart Association's Step I and Step II diets (relatively low in fat and protein). In many ways the success of these diets and the expert findings and opinions behind them help map out a common ground of healthful eating habits. While many experts in the field may defend their particular view or territory, we believe the greatest benefits lie where the territories overlap—a moderately low total fat intake, a healthy balance of "good" and "bad" fats, plenty of fruits and vegetables, and a moderate amount of protein. This overlap area also happens to correspond almost perfectly with what we know about how our early ancestors ate, which you'll read more about in a minute.

The *Live it Down* eating strategy is not a special "diet" you follow for a couple of months until your cholesterol levels improve. Any diet you need to get "on" implies that eventually you will get back "off" of it—and then what? Rather, this is the way

Venison and Chestnut Casserole

Game meats—like the meats our early ancestors ate—are very low in fat. This mouthwatering venison dish contains just 2 grams of saturated fat per serving. **Recipe on page 240**.

to eat for life, one we think you'll find enjoyable enough to embrace permanently once you give it a chance.

Blending Evidence and Evolution

If you capture a wild animal for a zoo, what kind of diet do you feed it? Something like what it ate in the wild, of course. The *Live It Down* eating strategy is unique because it's based on the way humans were meant to eat, the way we *did* eat back before there were drive-throughs, pig farms, or frozen food. When grabbing dinner meant chasing dinner, whether it was a deer, a mammoth, or a squirrel. When the bulk of the diet came from plant foods, and processed or refined foods were as foreign as computers. When grains were eaten largely intact, not stripped of their nutrients and fiber to become pale shadows of their former selves. Ironically, it has taken us just a few decades to change the human food supply more than it had changed over all the millennia before.

The diet the hunter-gatherers ate is the diet we're genetically programmed to consume, the one humans ate for 99.6 percent of their time on earth. While it varied depending on geographic area, the basic breakdown looked like this:

- Up to 30 percent of calories from protein.
- Between 45 and 60 percent of calories from carbohydrates (all complex carbohydrates high in fiber).
- Between 20 and 30 percent of calories from fat (primarily unsaturated).

The Live It Down Plan

♥ Eating

- A moderate amount of fat (about 25 percent of calories), mostly in the form of healthy fats from fish, nuts, and olive and canola oils.
- A moderate amount of lean protein (up to 20 percent of calories), from fish, beans, lean meats, soy, and eggs. (Yes, eggs are okay!)
- A shift to complex carbohydrates like whole grains in place of white rice, white flour, and white bread.
- Nine servings a day of fruits and vegetables.
- Yummy foods like peanut butter, chocolate, and shrimp.
- Up to one alcoholic drink a day for women and up to two drinks a day for men.

Our ancestors certainly ate meat, when they could get it, suggesting that meat by itself is not a bad thing. But the meat they ate came from wild game, not cows penned into small spaces, chickens raised in miniscule pens, or pigs crowded into corrals. Because that game grazed in the wild or on grasslands, its meat had more of the beneficial unsaturated fatty acids, called omega-3 fatty acids (which you'll read more about later). Today, because most animals raised for meat are fed diets high in processed feed—instead of grazing on grass or being fed the grains, nuts, seeds, and algae critical for the formation of omega-3 fatty acids—they contain very few of these essential nutrients. Also, wild animals have a low total fat content: around 5 percent of calories, compared to the 30 percent found in today's corn-fed domestic cattle.

Because they ate every bit of the animals they killed, including the bone marrow, liver, and other organ meats, our ancestors got quite a bit of cholesterol—even more than is found in the typical American diet. They ate lots of eggs (sometimes raiding the nests of birds), and those who lived by the sea consumed a great deal of shellfish, all high in cholesterol. But you can bet they didn't have cholesterol levels off the chart. (How do we know? For one thing, modern hunter-gatherers and indigenous peoples of preindustrial societies don't have high cholesterol.) That's why the *Live It Down Plan* doesn't focus on limiting your intake of cholesterol. While the evidence is still mixed on whether or not we can simply ignore dietary cholesterol altogether, particularly in people at high risk for heart disease, there is increasing evidence that when your overall diet is good, the cholesterol in your food has little impact on the cholesterol in your blood.

Live It Down Eating: The Big Picture

Here, then, are the essentials of the *Live It Down* eating plan.

Calories. Calories matter because if you eat too much—of any kind of food—you gain weight. And being overweight is associated with increased LDL and decreased HDL. You won't be counting calories on the *Live It Down Plan*. Rather, you'll be eating more fruits and vegetables (which are naturally low in calories) and cutting back on many of the high-fat, high-calorie, nutritionally empty foods you've probably been eating—so it's likely that you'll lose weight in the process.

If your Body Mass Index is 26 or higher (see page 61 in Chapter 3), you'll need to make a special effort to lose weight, particularly if you have metabolic syndrome, diabetes, or a high triglyceride level. One study found that losing 10 percent of your overall weight resulted in a

Continued on page 81

When Low-Fat is Too Low

You'll be eating less fat on the *Live It Down Plan*, but there's no need to cut all of it—in fact, doing so may be counterproductive. In a study from the University of Washington, researchers put 444 men with high LDL on various diets involving different levels of fat. The result: Reducing total fat to 30 percent of calories from 35 percent and keeping saturated fats at 7 to 8 percent was as effective at lowering cholesterol as diets with less total fat. In fact, when fat intake dropped to about 20 percent of calories (as some very low-fat proponents recommend), HDL fell and triglyceride levels rose.

The Truth About High-Protein Diets

Perhaps no other diet has generated as much discussion and controversy as the one created by Robert C. Atkins, M.D., more than 30 years ago. It strictly limits carbohydrates (including fruits and vegetables) and empha sizes protein and fats, including such high-fat, high-calorie foods as bacon, hamburgers, and sausage. (Phase 1 of the diet calls for 64 percent of calories from fat—and 42 grams of saturated fat.) It's based on the notion that by restricting carbohydrates, you induce the body to enter a state called ketosis, which forces it to burn fat as fuel.

But the Atkins diet, which hasn't been rigorously studied, ignores one basic nutritional fact nearly every researcher in the field agrees on: Eating saturated fat increases your risk of coronary heart disease (CHD) and generally increases cholesterol. At least 14 different studies support this finding, while an analysis of six clinical trials involving 6,356 participants found that decreasing saturated fat cut blood cholesterol levels and reduced CHD 24 percent.

Most of the studies that have been done on the Atkins diet showed some disturbing results. In one study 100 people were assigned to either a moderate fat (30 percent of calories) eating plan with no calorie restriction, a reduced-calorie diet with either 15 percent or 30 percent of calories from fat, or the Atkins diet. Only those on the Atkins diet had an increase in LDL cholesterol (6 percent), an increase in triglycerides (5.5 percent), a slight decrease in HDL, and increases in homocysteine (which damages artery walls) and fibrinogen (which contributes to blood clotting).

Not all the news on the Atkins diet has been negative, however. A short-term (six month) study reported at the American Heart Association meeting in 2002 found those on the diet lost weight, reduced their LDL, and increased their HDL. What gives? The LDL reduction was likely the result of weight loss due to calorie restriction, and the HDL increase may have been due to fish-oil supplementation.

Most important, as noted throughout this book, no single measure sums up health. Cancer, cholera, and AIDS can lower weight and cholesterol, too; it doesn't mean they're good for you. The *Live It Down* eating strategy, on the other hand, *is* good for you, providing a pattern of eating associated with lifelong health, weight control, reduced cancer risk, reduced CHD risk, and a host of other benefits.

Winning Weight-Loss Strategies

The weight-loss formula is one of the simplest in mathematics: Consume fewer calories than you burn, or burn more than you consume. It's really all a numbers game. If you need 2,000 calories a day to maintain your current weight but you take in 2,100 instead, every day your body will store that extra 100 calories. Over the course of a year you'll gain more than 10 pounds. By contrast, consume 1,900 calories a day and you'll lose more than 10 pounds in a year.

What's Your Number?

If you want to shed pounds, it helps to have an idea of how many calories you need to maintain your current weight so that you can figure out what calorie limit you'll need to live within every day to lose weight. According to the nonprofit Calorie Control Council, most people leading moderately active lives (exercising regularly—at least three times per week for 30 to 60 minutes each time) need about 15 calories per pound per day to maintain their weight. For a 130-pound woman that's 1,950 calories (130 x 15). If you're inactive, you need fewer calories. According to the Centers for Disease Control and Prevention, most inactive women need about 1,600 calories a day, and most inactive men need about 2,200.

To lose a pound a week you'll need to cut 500 calories a day from your diet. Or better yet, cut 300 calories and burn an extra 200 through exercise.

Calorie-Cutting Tactics

Eliminating those calories (as well as burning more through exercise) doesn't have to be painful. Starvation and deprivation diets simply don't work. Instead, the little things are what matter. Here are seven ideas to get you started:

1. Eat breakfast.
A study published in the February 2002 journal *Obesity Research* found that eating breakfast was a key behavior among people who averaged a 60-pound weight loss and kept it off an average of six years. Participants told researchers that skipping breakfast made them so hungry that they overate during other meals and snacked on unhealthy, high-calorie foods.

2. Measure that cereal.
The average serving of cereal is 1 cup. Yet most adults pour out at least twice that.

3. Scoop and save.
Every now and then someone comes up with such a cool kitchen utensil that you just have to rush right out and buy it. That's the Lê Scoop. Its function: to scoop out the inside dough from a bagel, leaving you with the outer crust (and, of course, less fat

and fewer calories). Fill the inside with nonfat cottage cheese sprinkled with ground flaxseeds for an easy, low-fat, low-calorie breakfast.

4. Buy the smaller size.
The larger the portion in front of you, the more you'll eat. It's a proven fact. When researchers sent 79 parents home with a video and either 1- or 2-pound bags of M&Ms along with either a medium or jumbo size tub of popcorn for each family member, they ate more M&M's from the 2-pound bag than the 1-pound bag, and about half a tub of popcorn, regardless of the tub size.

5. Make smart switches.
See how much you can save by switching from high-fat, high-calorie indulgences to lower-fat, lower-calorie options. Just by making the following substitutions, you could lose 25 pounds a year:

Instead of eating this once a week	Try this once a week	Calorie savings
Large fries	1-ounce snack-size bag of potato chips	383 calories a week, or 5.7 pounds a year
Fried chicken breast and wing	Roasted chicken breast and thigh without skin	243 calories a week, or 3.6 pounds a year
Burger	Veggie burger	216 calories a week, or 3.2 pounds a year
Three slices bacon and two eggs	Two slices deli-style ham and egg substitute	199 calories a week, or 3 pounds a year
Chocolate ice cream (1 cup)	Nonfat fudgsicle bar	240 calories a week, or 3.6 pounds a year
Pasta carbonara (1 cup)	Pasta with tomato sauce	246 calories a week, or 3.7 pounds a year
One slice cheesecake	One slice angel food cake with strawberry topping	130 calories a week, or 1.9 pounds a year

6. Skip the soda.
If you drink nondiet soda, you can cut 160 calories (per 16 ounces) out of your day just by switching to diet soda. Better yet, drink green tea or water flavored with a squeeze of lemon or lime.

7. Start with soup.
Studies show that people who start a meal with soup—especially broth-based soup—end up eating fewer calories by the end of the day without feeling hungrier.

(Continued on page 80)

Tried-and-True Weight-Loss Tricks

1. Keep a diary.

Studies find that people who keep a food diary are more likely to lose weight and keep it off. To make the most of your food diary:

- **Write the whys.** Make a list of all of the reasons you're trying to lose weight. Not just to lower your cholesterol, but so you can live to see your children and their children grow up. So you and your husband can take that cross-country trek when you retire. So you can have the joy of burning the mortgage when it's finally paid off. You get the picture.
- **Write the worries.** What are you worried about in terms of your ability to lose weight? Do you think you won't be able to give up fried chicken or resist your mom's death-by-chocolate brownies? Certain the holidays will derail your efforts? Writing down your worries and developing an action plan to address each one will keep you in control of your goal.
- **Record your triggers.** Every time you eat something you think you shouldn't, document how you felt when you ate it. Soon you'll see patterns, like the fact that you tend to dig into the ice cream when you've just had a fight with your daughter, you hit the drive-through when work gets stressful, or you eat the chips on the restaurant table because everyone else does. You may not be able to eliminate these triggers, but you can change how you react to them.

2. Don't eat like him.

If you're a woman trying to lose weight, one of your biggest roadblocks may be your husband. Studies find that women often put on weight soon after they get married. The reasons are varied. He eats bigger portions and you try to keep up (you only need about two-thirds of what he eats). You're cooking a full dinner every night, whereas in your single days a salad may have sufficed (a large salad with a bit of tuna for protein and an olive oil-based dressing can work well for both of you). Or you eat out more (it's far easier to eat healthfully at home).

3. Downsize your plate.

Start using a salad plate instead of a dinner plate to encourage smaller portions.

4. Use the toothpaste trick.

Brush your teeth immediately after dinner to stave off late-night noshing. (When your mouth feels clean and minty, you're less likely to think about eating.)

5. Feel the difference.

Carry around a 5-pound bag of sugar for a day. Then notice how much lighter you feel when you put it down. That's how you'll feel when you lose 5 pounds.

Continued from page 76

7.6 percent drop in LDL. The way to lose weight is simply by consuming fewer calories, burning more calories through exercise, or both. (See "Winning Weight-Loss Strategies" beginning on page 78 for some tips on how to do it.)

Fat. All it takes is a stroll down any supermarket aisle to notice that we're a nation obsessed with fat. It's amazing that toothpaste isn't labeled low fat—just about everything else seems to be. But as you'll learn later in this chapter, while the amount of fat you eat does matter, the kind of fat you consume is far more important. The Plan calls for you to get about 25 percent of your calories from fat, primarily unsaturated fat. You want to keep saturated fats to less than 7 percent of your total calories, and trans fatty acids (explained on page 86) to, ideally, nothing. By contrast, average Americans get about 34 percent of their calories from fat (13 percent of that fat is saturated and another 2 to 3 percent comes from trans fatty acids).

What amount of fat is 25 percent of your calorie intake? If you're getting about 2,000 calories a day, 25 percent from fat translates to about 56 grams of fat. To figure your target, take the number of calories you want to consume each day, multiply it by .25, and then divide by 9 (there are 9 calories in 1 gram of fat).

> In our view the Atkins, the Zone, or other high-protein diets are not the way to eat for lifelong health.

Protein. In our view the Atkins, the Zone, or other high-protein diets are not the way to eat for lifelong health. The *Live It Down Plan* does include a fairly generous amount of protein—up to 20 percent of calories. But the source of this protein is every bit as important as the quantity. The bulk of it comes from plant foods and fish, with a bit of lean meat thrown in for variety. We'd like you to eat fish as often as three to four times a week and

Chicken and Pinto Bean Tacos
Wish you could eat like this tonight? You can! Chicken breast and beans provide lean protein, and avocados are a great source of unsaturated fat. **Recipe on page 238.**

Bulgur Wheat and Prawn Salad
It's okay to indulge! This elegant salad is chock full of fiber, and the prawns provide heart-healthy omega-3 fatty acids. **Recipe on page 233.**

chicken one to two times a week. We'll tell you how to sneak more beans into your meals (they're a great source of fiber as well as protein). On the *Live It Down Plan* you'll aim to get three to four servings of beans and legumes, including soy, a week. And don't forget about eggs. Egg white is a perfect source of protein, and the cholesterol in egg yolk is probably less damaging to heart health than experts previously thought. If you substitute eggs for some of the high-fat meat in your diet, you're almost certainly lowering your cardiac risk. Enjoy them scrambled, fried, poached, or boiled (just not under hollandaise sauce) two or three times a week.

Carbohydrates. They really should come up with two names for carbohydrates. One would be for simple sugars and starches, like white bread, chips, packaged cakes and cookies, doughnuts, and french fries, which contribute to insulin resistance, pack on the pounds, and leave you hungry a couple of hours after eating. And the other would be for complex carbohydrates, which are full of fiber, vitamins, and minerals and are absorbed slowly by your body, minimizing blood sugar and insulin peaks and valleys while filling you up on less. We're talking about whole grain breads and cereals, brown rice, whole wheat pasta, barley, and oatmeal, as well as fruits and vegetables. You'll get about 55 percent of your daily calories from these foods.

Fiber. When it comes to lowering your cholesterol, fiber is king. Most Americans get only about 15 grams of fiber a day; on the *Live It Down Plan* you'll aim for at least 25 grams a day from foods like vegetables, beans, and whole grains. To help all that fiber pass through your system, you'll need to drink at least eight glasses of water or other noncarbonated, nonsweetened fluid a day (herbal tea works).

Eating: The Sum of the Parts

Maybe you're thinking, "How do I know if I'm getting 25 percent of my calories from fat, let alone what percentage is coming from different types of fat?" It's not as if the turkey sandwich you make for lunch has a nutrition label. Even if it did, you could drive yourself crazy counting every gram of food that passes through your mouth.

Fortunately, you don't have to. If you follow the advice in this chapter and in the 12-week Plan starting on page 206, you'll automatically be getting more or less the right percentages of fat, carbohydrates, and protein. Just be sure to eat small portions of some of the higher-fat foods we recommend, like nuts, seeds, olives, avocados, and olive oil. Fruits and vegetables, which should make up a large portion of your calories, generally have no fat, so you can eat them with abandon.

It's also important to remember that the percent of total calories from fat (or protein or carbohydrates) in your diet is the average of the percent in individual foods. So if most of the foods you choose are high in fat, your diet will be high in fat. If most of the foods are low in fat, your diet will be low in fat.

The best way to get a sense of what you're really eating is to keep a food diary. It will give you a good overview of where your calories are coming from, and also prevent "wishful remembering" about what you've eaten. Swear you got six servings of veggies last Friday? Well, if you're a man, you're prone to exaggerate your consumption of veggies. Swear not a morsel of chocolate passed through your lips yesterday? If you're a woman, you're more likely to underreport eating such high-calorie foods as

Show Kids the Way

As you read in Chapter 1, a shocking number of children are overweight and obese, and doctors are seeing increasingly high levels of cholesterol in children, even those with no family history of high cholesterol. To help your kids maintain a healthy diet and healthy cholesterol levels:

Pack their lunches. That way you can at least try to ensure they get something healthy instead of the fried and starchy foods that dominate most school cafeterias. (The three most common foods ordered in elementary school cafeterias are ground beef, chicken nuggets or patties, and cheese.)

Limit fast-food. Set a cap of no more than one or two fast-food meals a month, and when you do make a fast-food visit, push the salads, plain baked potatoes, and broiled chicken. If the kids must have hamburgers, order them without cheese.

Forget white. White bread, white rice, white pasta, that is. Serve their peanut butter and jelly on whole wheat bread and their meatballs on whole wheat pasta.

Make it easy. Cut up a bowl of fruit and put it before your TV-gazing kids. They'll eat it as if it were popcorn. Better yet, turn the TV off and serve the fruit to them after they've finished a bike ride around the block.

Set an example. The best way to make sure your kids live a heart-healthy lifestyle is to live one yourself. Follow the *Live It Down Plan* and you should see benefits not only to your cholesterol, but to your children's as well.

chocolate and ice cream. In fact, a U.S. Department of Agriculture (USDA) survey released in 2000 found the following:

- All adults believe they ate fewer servings of grains (2 to 3 a day) than they actually consumed (roughly 4 to 6 per day). Still, nearly all ate fewer than the recommended 6 to 11 servings.
- Both men and women say they eat more fruit than they do.
- Women thought they ate about 2.5 servings of veggies a day, but they actually ate just less than 2. Neither men nor women came close to the 3 to 5 servings of vegetables that the government recommends, never mind the 9 servings of fruits and vegetables the *Live It Down Plan* suggests.
- While respondents thought they ate only about 2 servings of fat, oils, and sweets a day, the real number was closer to 4.5.

On the *Live It Down Plan* we'll help you make sure you're getting enough of the types of foods shown to lower your cholesterol. For the "what," "why" and "how," keep reading. You'll also get week-by-week guidance starting on page 206.

Putting the Plan on Your Plate

1. Get Savvy about Fat

For all of the low-fat rhetoric, know this: Without fat in our food, we might as well be eating cardboard. Not only do our bodies need fat to function, but the simple fact is that fat tastes good. It may also trigger chemical receptors in our body that create a feeling of fullness and well-being. So fat isn't all bad. Actually, some types of fat are downright good for your arteries. Get enough of these "good" fats, eliminate enough of the "bad" fats, and watch your cholesterol levels improve and your heart disease risk plummet. This doesn't mean you have free rein when it comes to fat; we still want you to limit your overall intake of fat to about 25 percent of calories. The point is that both quality and quantity count.

Hazards of the Hard Stuff

Butter. Milk. Steak. Hamburgers. Cream. Cheese. You can just taste their richness now, can't you? Well, much of that richness comes from the high level of saturated fats in these foods. Saturated fat is solid at room temperature—picture the congealed grease in the pan after you fry hamburgers. This type of fat raises LDL as surely as an argument with your spouse raises your blood pressure. Even just one meal high in saturated fat (think double-bacon cheeseburger and large fries) can temporarily increase your risk of a heart attack or stroke if you already have heart disease

Salmon with Mango Salsa
A sure way to lower your cholesterol—and your heart disease risk—is to dine on more fish. This dish has it all: fruit, vegetables, and good-for-you omega-3 fatty acids. **Recipe on page 237.**

because it raises triglycerides and reduces nitric oxide production, which, as you read in Chapter 2, plays a vital role in the health of your arteries.

You can't avoid saturated fat altogether; even "healthy" fats like olive and canola oil contain some. But they have far less than other fats, like butter. Most Americans get about 12 percent of their calories from saturated fat; on the *Live It Down Plan* you'll bring that number down to 7 percent or less. To do it you just need to cut out the equivalent of about three pats of butter a day.

What the Eskimos Know

Another type of fat is called polyunsaturated fat. Found in most vegetable oils, fish oils, and oily fish, this fat lowers total blood cholesterol and reduces blood stickiness, thus preventing clotting. It's made up of essential fatty acids, which help your cells communicate, protect you from cancer, and regulate blood sugar.

There are two main types of essential fatty acids: linoleic acid (omega 6) and alpha-linolenic acid (omega 3). Neither one of these can be made by our bodies; we must get them from food.

Omega-6 fatty acids are found in most vegetable oils, like safflower, sunflower, corn, and soybean. Omega-3s are found in most fish and in flaxseed. Most of us get way more omega-6 fats than omega-3s, and that's not good. While omega-6s don't contribute to increased LDL like saturated fats do, they can lower HDL and increase the oxidation of LDL, contributing to the production of cell-damaging free radicals. Omega-3s, on the other hand, lower VLDL (which eventually turn into LDL) and triglycerides. They're the reason Greenland Eskimos have such low rates of heart disease, despite the fact that they have one of the highest-fat diets in the world, get very few vegetables, fruits, or fiber, and they smoke.

Unlike the Eskimos, Americans don't get nearly enough of these valuable fats. Our early ancestors got a nearly perfect 1:1 ratio between omega-6s and omega-3s; today our ratio is closer to 25:1. So the *Live It Down Plan* increases the fish in your diet, adds a fish-oil supplement, and encourages you to sprinkle flaxseed on everything from yogurt to cereal. It also switches you over from the ubiquitous corn oil to more healthful fats like canola and olive oils. Substituting these fats for saturated fats lowers LDL and also increases HDL.

A New Public Enemy

Lurking in french fries and any packaged food with the words "hydrogenated" or "partially hydrogenated" on the label, trans fats (also referred to as trans fatty acids) are often called hidden fats because they masquerade as "healthy" vegetable oil. But their original chemical composition has been changed, resulting in a higher melting point and longer shelf life. Unfortunately, what's good for the food industry is bad for the arteries: Trans fats are at least as harmful to your arteries as saturated fats. In September 2002 the National Academy of Sciences made it official, concluding that these fats were as bad as, if not worse than, saturated fat in raising coronary heart disease (CHD) risk. The only safe amount to eat, concludes the Academy, is none.

Trans fats not only raise LDL more than saturated fats do, but they also lower HDL. Small wonder, then, that Harvard researchers estimate that these fats should be blamed for nearly 30,000 premature deaths every year in the United States.

Major sources of trans fats include:

- Anything made with partially hydrogenated oils, such as crackers, cookies, doughnuts, breads, and frozen waffles.
- Corn puffs, popcorn, chips.
- French fries or chicken fried in hydrogenated shortening.
- Stick margarines and vegetable oil spreads; some tub margarines may also contain trans fats.

In fall 2002 the FDA announced it would require that food producers list the amount of trans fats on product labels, along with other nutrition facts.

One fast-food giant has already made a move against trans fats: In September 2002, McDonald's announced it would reduce the amount of trans fats in its french fries and other fried foods. To do that it switched to a variety of corn and soybean oils high in polyunsaturated fats but lower in saturated and trans fats. Lest you be fooled into thinking french fries have now moved into the "healthy" category on the nutrition chart, think again. The switch doesn't affect calories, which, in a super-sized order of fries equal 610, a whopping 43 percent of them coming from fat. If you eat the whole order of fries solo, you'll get 29 grams of fat—somewhere in the neighborhood of half your entire day's allowance.

2. Factor Out the Bad Fat

Cutting down on "bad" fats and reducing your overall consumption of fat isn't something that's going to happen overnight. But the 12-week *Live It Down Plan* starting on page 206 will help you get there. In addition to making the obvious move of switching to low- and nonfat versions of staples such as milk, mayonnaise, sour cream, and ice cream (doing so can save you anywhere from 1 to 22 grams of fat per serving), try to:

Eat naked chicken. Peel the skin off chicken (either before or after cooking) and cut the visible fat (before cooking) from all meat. If you pop the chicken or meat in the freezer first for about 20 minutes, the fat hardens and is much easier to trim.

Bake your fries. Instead of dunking potatoes in boiling oil or buying frozen fried potatoes chock full of saturated fats, make your own fries the healthy way. Preheat the oven to 425°F. Slice (you don't even need to peel) potatoes into sticks about a

Doing the Fat Math

Nutrition labels list total fat content, but that number may not tell you everything you want to know about the food. For instance, you should take into account:

Percentage of calories from fat. Most labels don't tell you this number. To figure it out, divide the fat calories per serving by the total calories per serving and multiply by 100. So a food that contains 90 calories per serving and has 30 calories from fat would get 33 percent of its calories from fat. A food that gets less than 30 percent of calories from fat is considered a relatively low-fat food; food that gets less than 20 percent of

its calories from fat is considered a low-fat food.

Fat you add. Combination foods and mixes, like Hamburger Helper, often have two sets of numbers on the label—one "as packaged" and one "as prepared." If the "as packaged" numbers are good and you can prepare it with low-fat or nonfat ingredients, the product is a good choice.

Servings per container. Read these carefully; often you may assume a package contains only one serving, when in fact it contains two—and therefore double the fat on the label.

Veggie Burger
Want to eat less fat and more vegetables? Have a burger! A veggie burger, that is. **Recipe on page 244.**

half-inch thick, coat a cooking sheet with cooking spray, put the potatoes on it, then spray the potatoes. Sprinkle with salt and pepper to taste, then bake for 45 minutes or until brown and crisp, turning the slices once midway through.

Don't pour, mist. Get a non-aerosol sprayer (like a Misto) and fill it with your favorite oil, or use a nonfat spray like Pam. Use for flavoring foods, coating pans and grills, or spraying directly on bread or salad (best done with a high quality olive oil in the Misto).

Fake the cream. Instead of heavy cream or half-and-half in recipes, substitute nonfat condensed milk. You'll get the creaminess without the fat.

Bulk up skim milk. Simply switching from whole milk to skim can cut your cholesterol levels 7 percent. But for some people skim is just too thin. To bulk it up, stir 2 to 4 tablespoons of instant nonfat milk powder into each cup of skim milk until it dissolves. Or try a protein-fortified skim milk like Skim Plus. It tastes creamier and thicker than skim, but still has no fat.

Do better than butter. Butter substitutes like Molly McButter really do taste like butter—give them a try.

Go whipped. Hate to give up butter altogether? Try whipped butter. It contains just 60 calories a serving compared to 100 calories for stick butter, and it has 5 grams of saturated fat compared to regular butter's 7. Let it soften before using; it spreads easier, so you'll use less.

Turn to Teflon. Nonstick pans enable you to brown or stir-fry meats and vegetables with far less oil or butter than regular pans require.

Substitute with applesauce. Applesauce substitutes well for some or all of the oil or butter used in muffins and cakes.

Stretch the meat. Add grated vegetables (try carrots or onions) to ground turkey or beef to stretch the meat, reduce the fat in burgers, and add some much-needed fiber. Learn to use soy, beans, lentils, mushrooms, and eggplant as delicious protein sources instead of meat in dishes like stews, spaghetti sauce, and lasagna.

The Pizza Problem

Americans aren't the French, but we still love cheese. From the convenience of American cheese slices and mozzarella cheese sticks to the decadent creaminess of a runny Brie, cheese is hard to ignore. Perhaps that's the reason that between 1975 and 1999, the amount of cheese eaten per person per year doubled, from 15 pounds to more than 30 pounds. Must be all those double cheeseburgers and extra-cheese pizzas.

It could also be a contributing factor to the obesity epidemic. Just 1 ounce of cheddar cheese contains 9 grams of fat, 5 of them saturated. And nonfat cheeses . . . well, let's just say that the wrapping tastes about as yummy. You don't have to throw the baby out with the bathwater, however. Just follow these tips:

Go where the flavor is. Hard, flavorful cheeses like Parmesan and especially Romano (the freshly grated stuff, not the stuff in the green can) pack a wallop of flavor, so you can use less. Two grated tablespoons contain less than 4 grams of fat, about 2 of them saturated. Just a tiny bit of strongly flavored cheese like blue,

Put Your Pizza on a Diet

Americans order 3 billion pizzas a year. That's a lot of cheese! According to the Center for Science in the Public Interest:

- Three slices of Pizza Hut's pan cheese pizza have 12 grams of saturated fat, about the same as three slices of its pan pepperoni pizza. Two slices of the stuffed crust anything have anywhere from 26 grams of fat (12 saturated) to a whopping 44 grams (18 saturated), depending on the toppings.
- Domino's veggie pizza comes with extra cheese. In total, two slices of a medium pizza contain nearly 16 grams of fat (7 saturated) and 439 calories. Two slices of a medium America's Favorite provide 22 grams of fat, 9 of them saturated.

To avoid blowing your fat budget for the day:

- Order half cheese or no cheese.
- Ask for vegetable toppings, with extra vegetables.
- Steer clear of stuffed-crust pizzas.
- If you must have meat on your pizza, make it chicken or ham, not pepperoni. Or try clams, shrimp, or anchovies.

Tuna and Tomato Pizza
Have your pizza and eat it, too, with our special
Live It Down *version.* **Recipe on page 235.**

Stilton, or feta goes a long way crumbled over salads.

Shred 'em. You'll also use less if you sprinkle on reduced-fat shredded cheese instead of layering on slices.

Be a softie. Some soft cheeses, such as ricotta and goat cheese, are often lower in fat than other cheeses.

Go American. American cheese has just 4 grams of fat per slice and 60 calories, which makes it a great alternative to cheddar.

3. Factor In the Good Fat

While you're cutting back on "bad" fats, you'll want to add more of the "good" fats. And so the *Live It Down Plan* will steer you toward fish (rich in omega-3 fatty acids), olive oil, and sterol-based margarine—the kinds of fat that actually help to improve your cholesterol levels.

Fall in Love with Olive Oil

Talk about a great job. Chris Ortiz Temnitzer, president of Oliveoil.com, spends most of the year in Europe, touring the olive groves in the countrysides of France, Italy, Spain, and Greece in search of the ideal olive oils for import to the United States. He conducts about 200 tastings a year, swirling the fragrant oil in a small, blue glass, sniffing, swallowing, and rating. You can bet his cholesterol levels are low.

The generous amount of olive oil consumed by people who live in Mediterranean countries forms the core of the so-called Mediterranean diet, one high in vegetables, fruits, and grains, but also fat—about 40 percent of total calories. People who follow this diet have much lower levels of heart disease than those following the typical Western diet. And the benefits come quickly. One study found that adults who consumed about 2 tablespoons of virgin olive oil daily for just one week had lower LDL and

Spinach, Sweet Potato, and Shiitake Salad
Dressing salads like this one with virgin olive oil is a simple way to lower your cholesterol. **Recipe on page 232.**

higher levels of antioxidants in their blood. Numerous other studies conducted over the past 40 years attest to the oil's heart benefits, including studies finding that olive oil not only lowers LDL but also raises HDL. An added benefit: Studies suggest that olive oil may slow stomach contractions, helping you feel full longer. And when olive oil was offered for bread-dipping in place of butter, people who dipped consumed 52 fewer calories than those who spread the butter.

Don't let this classic oil intimidate you. Here's what you need to know.

Buy the best. Not all olive oils are created equal. A better oil will add better flavor to your food. The main types of olive oil are:

> **Extra virgin olive oil.** Sometimes described as "cold pressed" or "first press," extra virgin olive oil has the lowest acidity of all olive oils and meets the highest taste and aroma standards. It also has the greatest cholesterol lowering benefits and the most antioxidants. (Choose cold-pressed extra virgin for even more.)

> **Olive oil.** Sometimes described as "pure," this is a blend of refined olive oil and extra virgin olive oil. Refining removes color, taste, and some of the nutrients.

> **Light olive oil.** No, it doesn't have fewer calories. It's just refined oil mixed with just enough extra virgin oil to give it a light flavor and color.

Keep it fresh. Look for the date of extraction or use-by date on the label. Unlike wine, olive oil is best used soon after its pressing. All oils oxidize over time and eventually become rancid. Leave a bottle of old oil open in the sun for a week or so and then smell it. You'll never forget the scent of rancid oil. So keep your olive oil in a dark, cool cupboard in dark glass or tin; heat and light are olive oil's enemies. Stored properly, olive oil will last for years. If the oil turns cloudy, its nutritional properties may have changed; it's time to throw it away and buy a new bottle.

Olives: Powerhouse Nuggets

Loaded with monounsaturated fat and heart-healthy phytonutrients, these single-seeded fruits are a delectable treat. To stretch your olive allowance (8 large black ones or 10 stuffed green ones have about 45 calories and 5 grams of fat), make a tapenade spread, dice olives into sauces (puttanesca), or add to salads or tuna. Rinse canned olives to reduce sodium.

For a real treat, consider roasting olives. From the California Olive Industry comes this recipe: Spread olives in a single layer in a baking dish, coat with olive oil (of course!), sprinkle with lemon peel, then bake at 350°F for 45 minutes. Serve as a side dish or over pasta. For more delicious ideas on integrating olives into your daily diet, go to www.calolive.org.

Use it on everything. Don't relegate olive oil to the back of the cabinet. From breakfast through dessert, it works with nearly everything.

- Drizzle it on your morning toast or bagel, or dip hunks of bread into it instead of spreading on butter or margarine.
- Use it to make garlic bread. Brush extra virgin olive oil on both halves of a split loaf of Italian or French bread, sprinkle the bread with chopped garlic, and then broil until lightly browned.
- Baste turkey and chicken with extra virgin olive oil for extra flavor.
- Use extra virgin olive oil to replace smoked meats and sausages typically used to flavor bean and pea soups.
- Sauté nuts in a little extra virgin olive oil for added flavor.
- For a tasty dessert, sauté bananas, apples, pears, or other fruits in light olive oil. Sprinkle with cinnamon and sugar and serve.
- Use the conversion chart below to make the switch from butter and margarine.

At the same time you're making that switch to olive oil in place of other fats, be careful not to go overboard on your overall fat or calorie limits. Too often we're more likely to add rather than substitute.

If recipe calls for this much butter/margarine	Use this much olive oil
1 teaspoon	3/4 teaspoon
1 tablespoon	2 1/4 teaspoons
2 tablespoons	1 1/2 tablespoons
1/4 cup	3 tablespoons
1/3 cup	1/4 cup
1/2 cup	1/4 cup + 2 tablespoons
2/3 cup	1/2 cup
3/4 cup	1/2 cup + 1 tablespoon
1 cup	3/4 cup

Hold a tasting. Like wine tastings, olive oil tastings are a wonderful way to find a brand you really like, for there are nearly as many varieties of olive oil as there are of wine. When Temnitzer conducts tastings, it's a highly stylized ritual complete with covered blue glasses (so he's not influenced by the color of the oil and can swirl the oil to release its aroma and warm it), wool cloths (for breathing into to cleanse the nasal "palate"), and apples (for cleansing the other palate). You don't have to be so precise. Although you can find olive oil tasting kits online (www.oliveoilsource.com/taster_case.htm, www.italiancookingandliving.com/store/olive_oils, or www.oakville grocery.com/html/gifts-ultimate_olive_oil_tasting_box.html), you can do it with a regular glass and, of course, several bottles of quality olive oil. Here's how:

- Start with three or four oils and decant them into small containers. Pour about 2 tablespoons into a small glass. Number the oils or place them on paper mats with numbered circles so that you can easily keep track of them.

Ready? Set? Taste! On the *Live It Down Plan* you'll be consuming plenty of olive oil, so try a few different brands to find one you love.

- Warm the glass by cupping it and swirling it slightly. Then take a brief sniff to get a first impression, followed by a deeper smell.
- Take in a teaspoonful of the oil, roll it around your mouth, and suck air in through clenched teeth.
- Swallow and wait. You should get the oil's aftertaste in a few seconds.
- Make notes throughout the tasting.
- You're looking for a fruitiness, a "green grass" or "leafy" smell, and also some bitterness. In olive oil, bitterness is good. Ideally, you should get a balanced sensation of fruitiness, bitterness, and pungency, which tells you it's a good oil.
- Among the positive words used to describe olive oil: apple, almond, artichoke, astringent (a puckering sensation), banana, bitter, buttery, fresh, fruity, grass, green, green leaf, harmonious, hay, melon, perfumy, musky, nutty, woody, peppery, pungent, and rotund. Avoid oils that taste briny, burnt, coarse, musty, earthy, flat, or winey.
- In the end, says Temnitzer, what's most important is that you like the oil.

The "Other" Olive Oil

Although we talk a lot about olive oil in this chapter, don't think you have to use it exclusively. After all, there are instances—for example, when baking—where olive oil won't do. The best choice in those cases is canola oil. It's the lowest in saturated fat, with a favorable ratio of omega-3 to omega-6 fatty acids, and although it doesn't get nearly as much publicity, it's just as good as olive oil when it comes to lowering your cholesterol. It's also cheaper than olive oil and has very little flavor, making it more versatile. Keep a bottle in your cupboard for any recipe that calls for vegetable oil.

Use a "Magic" Margarine

Margarine isn't exactly good for your arteries—unless it's a special kind of margarine that can actually lower your cholesterol. In 1999 the FDA approved the addition of natural plant chemicals called sterols to margarine. Because sterols have a similar chemical structure to cholesterol, they compete with cholesterol for receptors that facilitate absorption by the body, and they usually win. Studies find that 2 to 3 grams a day of a margarine such as Benecol and Take Control can reduce total and LDL cholesterol levels 9 to 20 percent. If these margarines were widely incorporated into our diets, experts say they could slash the incidence of heart disease by one-third.

Type of fish	Total omega-3 content per 3.5 ounces
Mackerel	2.6 grams
Trout, lake	2.0
Herring	1.7
Tuna, bluefin	1.6
Salmon	1.5
Sardines, canned	1.5
Sturgeon, Atlantic	1.5
Tuna, albacore	1.5
Whitefish, lake	1.5
Anchovies	1.4
Bluefish	1.2
Bass, striped	0.8
Trout, brook	0.6
Trout, rainbow	0.6
Halibut, Pacific	0.5
Pollock	0.5
Shark	0.5
Sturgeon	0.4
Bass, fresh water	0.3
Catfish	0.3
Ocean perch	0.3
Flounder	0.2
Haddock	0.2
Snapper, red	0.2
Swordfish	0.2
Sole	0.1

Source: *The Health Effects of Polyunsaturated Fatty Acids in Seafoods*

One potentially negative side effect is that sterols may reduce your body's ability to absorb certain nutrients from food, specifically beta-carotene and vitamin E. But a daily multivitamin, as recommended on the *Live It Down Plan*, should resolve that problem. Also keep in mind that sterols, even in margarine, are medicine. Don't use more than the recommended amount, about three servings (they're packaged in individual servings) a day.

Embrace Omega-3s

You read earlier about omega-3 fatty acids, which lower your risk of heart disease mainly by lowering triglycerides and countering inflammation. You can find these fats in a variety of sources, including spinach, mustard greens, wheat germ, walnuts, flaxseed (and flaxseed oil), soybean and canola oil, and even pumpkin seeds. But the very best source is fish.

Not all fish is created equal, however. At left is a handy chart to help you choose fish with the highest omega-3 content.

Go Nuts for Nuts

Back in the old days (say, about five years ago), no nutritionist worth her calorie counter would recommend adding nuts to your diet. High in fat and calories, nuts were a definite no-no. Not anymore. Seems there's barely a nut out there whose health benefits aren't being touted these days. That's because while nuts are relatively high in fat, they're high in unsaturated fats, including omega-3s, and also high in fiber. In recent years numerous studies have linked eating nuts to better heart health and improved cholesterol levels.

In August 2002 a study published in *Circulation*, a journal of the American Heart Association, found that when 27 people with high cholesterol ate one or two handfuls of almonds daily for a month, they reduced their LDL levels between 4.4 and 9.4 percent. Another study found that two handfuls of pecans a day for four weeks lowered LDL by 10 percent. And when it comes to walnuts, researchers found that eating 1.6 ounces a day for six weeks lowered LDL and total cholesterol, and also decreased dangerous low-density LDL 27 percent.

Some nuts may be better for lowering your cholesterol than others. Thus far the best evidence of heart-health promoting properties has been generated for walnuts, followed by almonds.

What about the calories? Yes, nuts are calorie-dense. (See the chart on the next page to find out just how many calories different nuts contain.) But studies show that people who eat nuts actually tend to be thinner than those who don't, perhaps because nuts are so filling that eating them helps you eat less of other foods. But don't go overboard. Aim for 1 to 2 ounces of nuts (1 ounce is about 7 shelled walnuts) as a daily average, and try to eat them instead of other sources of calories, rather than as an addition.

Be creative when it comes to nuts. For instance:

● Sprinkle them on salads.

● Toast them to bring out their full flavor.

● Chop them and sprinkle them on cereal or mix them into muffin batter.

● Grind them and use as a coating for cooking salmon or chicken.

● Stir them into ice cream (the low-fat kind, of course).

Date and Walnut Cake
Heart-healthy walnuts, fiber-rich dates—what more could your arteries ask for in a snack? **Recipe on page 249.**

A Guide to Nuts					
Nut	**Fat content per 3.5-oz. serving**			**Calories**	**Keep in mind**
	Fat (g) Mono (%) Poly (%) Sat. (%)				
Chestnuts	2.2	31.0	36.0	16.0	245	Lowest in calories and fat.
Cashews	44.3	61.7	17.7	20.6	573	
Pistachios	46.1	15.9	70.9	13.2	577	
Peanuts (dry roasted)	46.8	52.2	33.3	14.5	567	Really a legume, not a nut. Especially high in protein. Also rich in resveratrol, the same antioxidant found in red wine.
Almonds	49.8	68.1	22.0	9.9	589	More calcium and fiber than any other nut.
Walnuts	53.9	23.6	69.7	6.7	642	Also rich in homocysteine-controlling vitamin B6.
Hazelnuts	59.7	82.2	10.1	7.7	632	
Brazil nuts	63.3	36.4	38.1	25.5	656	Rich in the mineral selenium.
Pecans	64.3	65.6	26.0	8.4	667	Beware of calories.
Macadamias	70.5	82.5	1.9	15.6	702	Highest in fat and calories.

Try the Peanut Butter Solution

There is more fat in a peanut butter sandwich than in a McDonald's cheeseburger; there are about 21 to 27 grams per 3 tablespoons of peanut butter. But peanut butter is no dietary evil. Most of its fat is monounsaturated, and it also provides a good source of protein, vitamin E, and fiber. So don't pass on this childhood treat. (And don't think you're saving calories if you go for the low-fat version; the fat is just replaced with sugar.) Just make sure peanut butter is *replacing* other forms of fat and calories, not adding to them. You can also try other nut butters, like almond, cashew, and macadamia. They usually have a lower percentage of saturated fat than peanut butter.

To enjoy peanut butter wisely, follow these tips:

Take a lick. Take a teaspoon of peanut butter and slowly lick it off the spoon as if it were a lollipop while you watch TV or relax.

Spread it thinly. Use it in place of cream cheese on bagels or butter on toast.

Go natural. To avoid the added salt and sugar in commercial peanut butters, as well as the hydrogenated oils most contain, visit a health food store that lets you make your own, or buy a "natural" brand. Because they contain no hydrogenated oils, these brands will separate, so you'll need to stir them before eating.

Dip in. Peanut butter makes a good dip for apples, celery, carrots, or other fruits and vegetables. Again, limit the portion or you could find yourself eating an entire week's worth of fat calories in one sitting.

4. Up Your Fiber Intake

One of the most striking differences between the caveman's diet and our own is the amount of fiber our ancestors ate: about 100 grams a day, the amount some people in rural areas of the developing world still get. The average American, on the other hand, consumes only about 15 grams of fiber per day, well below the recommended 25 grams. The cavemen didn't know it, but all of that fiber had countless health benefits, from lowering cholesterol to helping control (or maybe prevent) diabetes.

There are two types of fiber. Insoluble fiber, such as wheat bran, helps prevent constipation and may protect against colon cancer. It also fills your stomach, helping to quench hunger without calories. Soluble fiber, found in foods such as fruits, oats, barley, and peas, has more to do with lowering cholesterol. Soluble fiber forms a kind of gel in your intestines that helps reduce your body's absorption of the fat you eat. And if that fat never makes it into your bloodstream, it can't do its damage by raising your blood cholesterol levels.

Studies find that eating 10 to 30 grams of soluble fiber a day—much more than the average American eats—reduces LDL about 10 percent. (Remember, Americans average 15 grams of fiber, including both soluble and insoluble.)

One analysis of 67 different studies concluded that for every gram of soluble fiber you add to your diet, you can expect an LDL decrease of 2.2 milligrams per deciliter (mg/dl). So if you added just 10 grams a day—less than a cup of baked beans—you could see your level drop 20 points.

Start Slow with Fiber

You probably don't want to jump from 10 grams of fiber a day to 25 all at once. If you do you may experience some bloating and flatulence. Instead, aim to gradually add about 4 grams of fiber every other day, cutting back if you experience stomach problems, until you're able to handle larger amounts. Four grams is about the amount of fiber found in a whole apple with skin.

Breakfast Muffins
Wake up and taste the flavor in these cholesterol-busting muffins—designed with your heart in mind. **Recipe on page 231.**

The best fiber-rich foods? Here are our top 10:

1. **Dried beans, peas, and other legumes.** These include baked beans, kidney beans, split peas, dried limas, garbanzos, pinto beans, and black beans.
2. **Oatmeal and bran cereals.**
3. **Vegetables.** Top contenders are fresh or frozen lima beans and green peas, sweet corn, broccoli, green snap beans, pole beans, broad beans, carrots, and Brussels sprouts.
4. **Dried fruit.** Figs, apricots, and dates top the list.
5. **Fresh fruit (with skin).** Particularly raspberries, blackberries, strawberries, plums, pears, apples, and cherries.
6. **Whole wheat and other whole grain products.** These include rye, oats, buckwheat, and stone-ground cornmeal, as well as bread, pastas, pizzas, pancakes, and muffins made with whole grain flours.
7. **Baked potato with skin.**
8. **Greens.** Some of the best include spinach, beet greens, kale, collards, Swiss chard, and turnip greens.
9. **Nuts.** Especially almonds, Brazil nuts, peanuts, and walnuts.
10. **Bananas.**

Fruity Muesli

Cereal doesn't get much more nutritious than this muesli, made with oats, nuts, seeds, and fruit. Enjoy it at breakfast or as a snack. **Recipe on page 230.**

Sit Down to Cereal

So about now you're thinking: "Eat 25 grams of fiber? How do they expect me to do that?" Two words: Eat breakfast. Cereal is perhaps the simplest way to get more fiber into your diet. It may also be a way to lower the fat in your diet. One study found that people who ate two bowls a day of high-fiber cereal cut the amount of fat they ate by 10 percent without even trying.

The only way to know for sure if your cereal is fiber-filled is to read the label. Look for brands that have 5 or more grams of fiber per serving. And ignore claims like "fortified with 11 vitamins and minerals." (The vitamins are usually sprayed on and provide no more benefit than taking a daily multivitamin.) Some cereals that sound fiber-rich, like Rice Chex, have no more fiber than the milk you pour over it. The ones listed below are loaded with fiber.

Cereal	Fiber content (per serving)
Kellogg's Raisin Bran	8 grams
Multi-Bran Chex	8 grams
Shredded Wheat 'N Bran	8 grams
Kashi GoLEAN	10 grams
Kellogg's All-Bran Original	10 grams
General Mills Fiber One	14 grams

Some more breakfast-time tips:

Mix it up. If you think high-fiber cereals taste like the boxes they come in, then mix them with your regular cereal, gradually adding more of the high-fiber cereal and less of the regular stuff.

Go with oats. When researchers at Colorado State University had 36 overweight men eat either an oat or wheat cereal with 14 grams of fiber daily for 12 weeks, those getting the oat cereal had lower levels of the small, very dense LDL cholesterol, and less LDL overall.

Give it a sprinkle. Just 2 tablespoons of ground flaxseed sprinkled on your oatmeal boosts its cholesterol-lowering ability like super fuel in a rocket. One study found that 2 tablespoons of ground flax daily cut total cholesterol 9 percent, and LDL 18 percent. Flaxseed is a powerful laxative, so be sure to use it in moderation.

Don't forgo the bowl. Those cereal bars, says *Consumer Reports*, are generally no more nutritious than oversized cookies. "Most breakfast bars are high in sugar and have very little fiber, basically giving you the equivalent of a sugary cereal without the milk," the magazine wrote in a January 1998 article.

Not All Carbs Are Created Equal

Unfortunately, food labels don't distinguish between complex carbohydrates and simple carbohydrates (like sugar). But you can get a sense of the type of carbohydrate by looking at the grams of fiber. The higher the fiber content, the more complex carbohydrates you're getting. If you don't see a listing for fiber, that's because there is none, period. Aim for at least 3 grams of fiber per serving. And to make sure that a product doesn't derive most of its carbohydrates from sugar, check the ingredients for sugar synonyms, such as corn syrup, sorbitol, dextrose, glucose, fructose, maltose, honey, and molasses.

Don't Let the Label Fool You

Breads that say *multigrain, seven-grain, nutra-grain, cracked wheat, stone-ground wheat,* or *enriched wheat* must fill the bill, right? Wrong. Unless the word *whole* appears in the first ingredient, the bread is lacking some of the vitamins and minerals, not to mention fiber, of whole grains. Even a dark brown bread is no guarantee of whole grain; the color could be the result of molasses or caramel coloring. The bottom line: Make sure that the first ingredient is *whole wheat* or *whole grain*. Now, if we're talking oats, simply *oats* or *rolled oats* will do.

Move Away from White

Another way to boost fiber and complex carbohydrates, the kind the *Live It Down Plan* recommends, is to shun white—white bread, rice, and pasta—in favor of whole grains. More than 25 studies find that people who regularly eat whole grains reduce their risk of heart disease. In the Harvard Nurses' Health Study, which followed 80,000 women for more than 20 years, women who ate at least one serving of whole grain foods daily had about a one-third lower risk of heart disease than women who rarely ate whole grains. It's not just the soluble fiber in whole grains that provides benefit. Other plant nutrients, including tocotrienols (a form of vitamin E not found in most supplements), are also at work. Yet Americans average just one serving of whole grain foods a day. You won't be one of them when you follow the *Live It Down Plan*, which calls for seven to eight servings a day. Here's how to get them:

Broccoli and Pearl Barley Salad
Barley is an excellent source of cholesterol-lowering soluble fiber. Serve this as a light lunch or satisfying side dish. **Recipe on page 245.**

Brave the brown. In one intriguing study, when a group of men swapped 220 calories of white rice for 220 calories of mostly whole grains, after 16 weeks their levels of homocysteine and oxidized LDL dropped nearly one-third. cutting their risk of heart disease significantly. Go brown by opting whenever possible for whole wheat bread instead of white, brown rice instead of white, and whole wheat pasta instead of regular. Stick with regular pasta and you're getting about the same amount of fiber as you'd get in chocolate or beer. Choose whole wheat pasta and triple the amount you get.

Be exotic. For a real fiber bang, explore shelves at your grocery store that you usually ignore. Those are the ones stocked with such "exotic" grains as amaranth, bulgur, whole wheat couscous, and wheatberries. Most are as simple to fix as rice, yet are packed with fiber and other nutrients. Mix in some steamed carrots and broccoli, toss with olive oil and a bit of Parmesan or feta cheese, maybe throw in a can of tuna or a couple of ounces of diced chicken, and you've got dinner.

Bargain on barley. Just a cup of cooked pearled barley (which doesn't require any soaking) contains nearly 10 grams of fiber. Mix it with a lamb-and-vegetable stew for dinner, sweeten it with raisins, eat it with sliced apples and cinnamon for breakfast, or serve it with chopped vegetables and an olive oil dressing for a lunch salad.

Opt for oats. There's a reason oat manufacturers are allowed to boast about the grain's cholesterol-lowering benefits. Oats are to cholesterol what a drought is to a pond. They contain a soluble fiber called beta glucan, which numerous studies find lowers cholesterol levels. In 1997 the FDA concluded that getting at least 3 grams a day of beta glucans from oats (about 1½ cups of cooked oatmeal) reduced total cholesterol. Many people will see drops in LDL of 12 to 24 percent, depending on where they start. Choose quick-cooking or old-fashioned oats over instant oatmeal; it would take three packets of most instant oatmeal to get the obligatory 3 grams, and they're often loaded with sugar. Or try uncooked oatmeal in place of bread crumbs in meatloaf made with ground turkey, use it to make a crispy coating for oven-fried chicken, and mix it into baked goods (remember the oatmeal cookies of your youth?).

5. Become an Opportunist

Think fast: How many servings of vegetables have you had today? One? None? How about fruit? If you're like many Americans, you miss plenty of opportunities for getting them—like ordering a veggie topping for your pizza or adding raisins to your oatmeal. On the *Live It Down Plan* you'll become a fruit-and-veggie opportunist. Not only are these foods loaded with cholesterol-lowering soluble fiber, they also contain other artery-friendly compounds, such as cholesterol-reducing sterols and antioxidants. You'll aim for nine servings a day; most Americans get fewer than four.

Best for Cholesterol

All fruits and vegetables have health benefits to offer. But some are especially good for your arteries. Among the best:

Avocados. Although this is one of the few fruits high in fat, it's mainly mono-unsaturated fat. Several studies find that eating one avocado a day can lower your

Counting to Nine

Hearing you need to get nine or more servings of fruits and vegetables can be daunting. But consider the definitions of a serving (below) from the National Cancer Institute. All varieties of fruits and vegetables—fresh, frozen, canned, dried, and 100 percent juice—count.

- One medium-size fruit (apple, orange, banana, pear).
- 1/2 cup of raw, cooked, canned, or frozen fruits or vegetables.
- 3/4 cup (6 ounces) of 100 percent fruit or vegetable juice.
- 1/2 cup of cut up fruit.
- 1/2 cup of cooked or canned legumes (beans, peas).
- 1 cup of raw, leafy vegetables (lettuce, spinach).
- 1/4 cup of dried fruit (raisins, apricots, mango).

LDL as much 17 percent while raising your HDL. Try them in salads and sandwiches or mashed with a bit of lemon juice, onion, and chopped tomato as a topping for baked potatoes. Just don't go overboard; one avocado has about 340 calories.

Garlic. Garlic can lower cholesterol modestly as well as prevent blood from becoming sticky and forming dangerous clots. The compound most studies focus on, allicin, is the same one that gives garlic its distinctive odor. In one analysis of five trials in which participants received either garlic supplements or a placebo, the authors concluded that you could lower your total cholesterol about 9 percent with the equivalent of 1 1/2 to 3 cloves of garlic daily for two to six months.

You need to crush, chop, or otherwise bruise the cloves to release the allicin. For a sweet way to get your garlic, remove the loose paper covering from a head of garlic, cut off the tops of the garlic, drizzle olive oil on it, wrap in foil, and bake in a 350°F oven until soft, about an hour. Then squeeze the heads of the cooked garlic onto toasted bread and spread.

What if you don't like garlic, also known as the "stinking rose"? Can you get the same benefits from a garlic pill? Maybe, if you choose the right one. A study by ConsumerLab.com found that 7 of 14 garlic supplements tested contained less of the active ingredient (allicin) than researchers say is necessary for a therapeutic effect. Those doses include 3,600 to 5,400 milligrams of allicin, while the doses in the products tested ranged from 400 to 6,500 milligrams. The products that met or exceeded recommended doses included Garlinase 4000, Nutrilite Garlic Heart Care Formula Dietary Supplement, Spring Valley Enteric Coated Odor-Free Garlic 1,200 milligrams equivalent per tablet, and Kyolic Aged Garlic Extract.

Oranges. Think of your morning orange juice as cholesterol medicine in a glass. After drinking three glasses of orange juice a day for four weeks, 25 participants in a

Canadian trial increased their HDL levels 21 percent and lowered their LDL/HDL ratio 16 percent. Of course, if you're watching your calorie intake, three glasses of juice is a lot; you'll probably want to stick to a glass or two a day.

Prunes. Prunes (dried plums) contain a special kind of soluble fiber called pectin, which forms a gel in your intestines that sops up cholesterol before it hits your bloodstream. Blend cooked prunes with water into a puree that can replace oils and fats in baking, add dried prunes to stews for a delicious sweetness, or chop and sprinkle over salads, yogurt, cottage cheese, or cereal.

10 Fast Fruit and Veggie Ideas

Struggling to get your fill of fruits and vegetables? Try these 10 tricks:

1. **Start with vegetables.** Before you put anything else on your plate, start with a salad, a heap of green beans, or a stalk of broccoli. After you've eaten your vegetables, add the other components of the meal. Since you're eating your veggies first, when you're hungry, you're likely to eat more.

2. **Make a super salad.** One 7-ounce bag of washed lettuce equals a bit more than one serving. Add a sliced tomato, a diced apple, and a quarter cup of raisins and you've just increased that to four servings.

3. **Keep it convenient.** Either slice vegetables yourself and keep them in the fridge in ice water or buy precut vegetables. Don't shun canned fruits, either. If they're packed in unsweetened syrup, they provide a quick, convenient way to get a serving or more. Try canned peaches on ice cream or mandarin orange segments in salads. Frozen vegetables are another excellent shortcut. Throw them into soups or stews without defrosting. Buy bags of frozen chopped onions and peppers for quick starts to dinners.

4. **Drink them.** Although you don't get the same amount of fiber in canned fruit or

Couscous Casablanca
Give this recipe a "10" for its more than 10 different vegetables! It's so hearty and flavorful, you'll never miss the meat. **Recipe on page 242.**

vegetable juice as you do in the whole fruit, it's still a good way to get a serving or two a day. Add a small can of V-8 or tomato juice to your afternoon snack, or throw a banana, a cup of berries, and a container of nonfat yogurt into your blender for a three-fruit-servings smoothie. Sprinkle flaxseeds on top for even more cholesterol-lowering power.

5. **Get them on pizza.** Forget the pepperoni. Order a vegetable pizza. You'll get sweet, roasted vegetables with every slice.

6. **Hide them.** Add grated carrots to lasagna or spaghetti sauce. And use potato puree to thicken soups in place of cream.

7. **Use them as condiments.** Salsas are all the rage these days. Don't stop with tomato salsas. Fruit salsas (pineapple, onion, and mint, or cantaloupe, balsamic vinegar, and brown sugar) make wonderful accompaniments to pork, fish, and chicken. Try jarred chutneys for an easy option.

8. **Give 'em a roast.** Roasting vegetables such as onions, carrots, turnips, bell peppers, eggplant, and even asparagus is a wonderful way to bring out their natural sweetness. Just spray the vegetables and pan with cooking spray, or drizzle on a bit of olive oil, then roast in a hot oven (450°F) until done. (Different vegetables require different cooking times.) Check often, and turn midway through. Grilling is another way to bring out the flavor in vegetables; try zucchini strips at your next backyard cookout.

9. **Get them in burgers.** Veggie burgers, that is.

10. **Plan an adventure.** Buy one exotic fruit or vegetable on your next trip to the grocery store. Here are some to try (and some ways to try them):

Carambolas (star fruit). Ripen at room temperature (the ribs on the skin will turn brown) then refrigerate. To serve, cut into star shapes with the skin. They're a great complement to meat in stir-fries.

Plantains. Available year-round, this slightly acidic fruit tastes a bit like squash. Try green plantains peeled and chunked in stews.

Tomatillos. Available year-round from Mexico and California, these small fruits resemble green tomatoes and have a slight, sweet apple or plum flavor. They're the basis of green salsa and are loaded with vitamins A and C.

Belgian endive. This type of lettuce has a mild, slightly bitter flavor, and it's packed with fiber, iron, and potassium. Use it in salads and substitute it for crackers with vegetable dips.

Jicama. Known as the Mexican potato, jicama (HE-cah-ma) is a root tuber, like potatoes. Buy it smooth and firm with unblemished roots. Serve it cold and raw, or in soups, stews, or salads. It's great as a substitute for water chestnuts.

Bok choy. An Asian cabbage, bok choy is excellent chopped and stir-fried in a bit of peanut oil and soy sauce, or throw it into soup just before serving.

6. Pick the Right Protein

We are not going to tell you to avoid red (or white) meat entirely on the *Live It Down Plan*. But we are going to help you find healthier alternatives to hamburgers. For, as the Center for Science in the Public Interest (CSPI) notes: "Ground beef adds more fat—and more artery-clogging saturated fat—to the average American's diet than any other single food. Plus, you can't trim away fat from ground meat like you can with steak or pork." And don't think you're safe if you stick with "lean" or even "extra lean" ground meat. The USDA allows ground beef that is up to 22.5 percent fat to be called "lean," even though most other foods labeled "lean" must contain no more than 10 percent fat. One 4-ounce serving of lean ground beef still contains 16 grams of fat, 7 of them saturated.

Chose Your Cuts Carefully

Beef and pork per se are not bad. Today's pork, for instance, is much leaner than it used to be, containing on average 31 percent less fat, 14 percent fewer calories, and

Country Captain Chicken
Think chicken isn't as tasty without the skin? Think again. Bursting with the flavors of curry, garlic, tomatoes, and apricots, this dish will become a favorite. **Recipe on page 238.**

10 percent less cholesterol than just 20 years ago. Today's beef is 27 percent leaner than 20 years ago, with more than 40 percent of beef cuts having no external fat at all. And although beef, pork, and lamb are high in saturated fat, about 30 percent of that fat comes from stearic acid, a type of saturated fat that does not appear to have the same heart-damaging effects of most saturated fat; some studies even suggest it can lower cholesterol.

One study compared the effects of the National Cholesterol Education Program's Step Diet, which eliminated all beef and pork in favor of chicken and fish, to a diet that included 6 ounces of lean red meat five to seven days a week. The result? Both groups saw their total cholesterol drop 1 percent and their LDL 2 percent, while their HDL increased 3 to 4 percent.

While lean meat is no bad guy, you don't want meat to make up most of your meals. Why not? Because that would mean you're not getting as much fish or plant-based protein from foods like beans, which have clear cholesterol-lowering benefits. So on the *Live It Down Plan* you don't have to scratch meat off your shopping list, but you'll be limiting your consumption in order to make room in your diet for other heart-healthy foods.

Here is a chart to help you choose the leanest cuts. Remember to watch your portion size: 3 ounces of meat is about the size of a deck of cards or a computer mouse.

Cut of meat (3 ounces)	Total fat (grams)	Saturated fat (grams)
Chicken breast	3.0	0.9
Pork tenderloin	4.1	1.4
Extra lean top round	4.2	1.4
Extra lean eye round	4.2	1.5
Mock tender steak	4.7	1.6
Shoulder pot roast, boneless	5.7	1.8
Boneless pork sirloin chop	5.7	1.9
Round tip	5.9	2.0
Shoulder steak, boneless	6.0	1.9
Pork loin roast, boneless	6.1	2.2
Top sirloin	6.1	2.4
Bottom round	6.3	2.1
Pork top loin chop, boneless	6.6	2.3

Go Wild for Game

If you're a meat lover, give some of the wild game meats turning up in grocery stores a try. Grain-fed beef (which includes practically any beef you buy in the supermarket) has as much as 36 percent fat, while game meats such as bison, wildfowl, and venison have about 3 to 4 percent, like most fish. A 3-ounce serving of venison, for instance, contains 2.7 grams of fat, none of it saturated, while a 3-ounce serving of buffalo has just 2 grams of fat, less than 1 gram saturated. And game meats also contain more omega-3 fatty acids.

To get the most out of game:

- Marinate meats in low-fat marinades and sauces to improve tenderness.
- When sautéing add a little olive or canola oil for tenderness and flavor.
- Some game meats taste, well, "gamey." If that doesn't appeal to you, first try small amounts as part of stir-fries, casseroles, and rice dishes. See which meat suits your taste buds before stocking up your freezer.

Get Hooked on Fish

Not only are fish and seafood wonderful, low-fat replacements for higher-fat meats, but as we mentioned earlier, they're the best source of omega-3 fatty acids you'll find. On the *Live It Down Plan* you'll be aiming to eat fish and seafood three to four times a week. (People who absolutely can't stand fish and those who are allergic to shellfish can substitute other lean forms of protein.)

You don't have to get fancy; tuna—even canned—is perfectly fine. In fact, in one study published in the *New England Journal of Medicine*, people who ate 8 ounces or more of fish per week—mostly from canned tuna—lowered their risk of a having a fatal heart attack by 40 percent over those who didn't eat fish regularly. But buy your tuna packed in water; when you drain oil-packed tuna, you also drain as much as one-quarter of the omega-3 fatty acids; draining water-packed tuna removes just 3 percent.

Fish en Papillote
For a quick and easy weeknight meal, serve fish cooked in a foil packet. **Recipe on page 236.**

And don't worry about the cholesterol in shellfish. When 18 men with normal cholesterol levels replaced the animal protein in their diet with protein from shellfish (oysters, clams, crabs, and mussels), their LDL/HDL ratios either dropped or remained the same, and their VLDL, triglycerides, and total cholesterol dropped.

If eating three to four fish servings a week seems impossible, check out these simple ways to "go fishing":

Can it. Canned tuna is terrific, but there are also canned salmon and sardines to consider. Sardines provide calcium from the easily digestible bones they include. Mix sardines with low-fat mayonnaise and spread on whole wheat crackers for a great snack or light lunch.

Get fresh. The flesh of fish should spring back when pressed, its surface should glisten, and it shouldn't smell fishy. Frozen is generally a good bet, since it's often flash-frozen on docks or on the fishing boats themselves.

Eat the "other" steak. Salmon can be broiled, pan-fried, or grilled just like a steak, only much quicker. If you're grilling salmon fillets, place them on aluminum foil and cook them skin-side up; the fat under the skin will bathe the fish beneath, which will add flavor and moisture.

Be a poacher. To poach fish, heat a quarter-inch of liquid (broth, wine, or even water flavored with a crab boil like Old Bay seasoning) in a pan, add the fish and gently simmer for 10 minutes or so.

Anchovies, anyone? Order them on pizza (and ask for less cheese). Mashed anchovies form the flavorful base for numerous Mediterranean inspired sauces, such as puttanesca, clam sauce, and even Caesar salad dressing.

Go clamming. Clams are packed with those sterols we talked about earlier, chemicals that prevent your body from absorbing cholesterol. Enjoy them in clam chowder, use canned clams for a quick seafood stew, or mix them with nonfat sour cream for a low-fat veggie dip. And don't forget about clam sauce over whole wheat linguine.

About shrimp. No need to shy away from this crustacean. Although shrimp are relatively high in cholesterol, they're very low in saturated fat and are also an excellent source of omega-3 fatty acids. So enjoy them in stir-fries, chopped over a salad, or thrown into that seafood chowder you're making. Just skip the scampi style, which is usually laden with butter.

Meatless Meals

Let's say you're eating fish two nights a week. (Congratulations!) And perhaps you're choosing lean cuts of meat to cook on three nights. What do you do on the other two? Try going vegetarian. Now before visions of rabbit food or bulgur meatloaf swim through your head, rest assured: You can make a hearty and satisfying meal by using meat substitutes like the ones below. Besides adding diversity to your menus, they

Teriyaki-Style Noodles with Tofu
*Embark on a tongue-tingling trip to Japan tonight. With zero saturated fat and plenty of protein,
this meal-in-a-bowl is one stop on the road to clearer arteries.* **Recipe on page 243.**

also bring cholesterol-lowering benefits all their own. Here are some ideas:

Soy. Okay, tofu may not top your list of favorite foods, maybe because you think it has no taste, or perhaps you don't like the texture. We can solve both problems. If you think you don't like tofu, it's worth giving it another try—it's an excellent meat substitute, and it will even help lower your cholesterol on its own if you eat enough of it. A word to the wise: Don't buy tofu sold loose in open containers, as it may be contaminated with bacteria. Instead, buy packaged tofu in the refrigerated section of your grocery store.

Here are some tasty ways to try soy:

- Add firm tofu to stir-fries. The tofu will soak up the flavors you cook with and taste delicious.
- Stir soy crumbles (found in the frozen food section) into spaghetti sauce or vegetable stews. They'll provide some meat-like texture without altering the taste.
- Try steamed edamame, the actual soybean, sprinkled with a bit of salt. Or look for roasted soy nuts, which make a fun, healthy snack and provide the perfect crunch to salads.

Eggs: Setting the Record Straight

Remember when eggs were off limits because of their cholesterol content (one large whole egg contains about 213 grams)? Well, not only are eggs back—with studies finding that even two eggs a day have no effect on cholesterol—but certain eggs are actually beneficial.

That's because some farmers have begun producing so-called "designer" eggs, extra high in omega-3 fatty acids. They do this by adding flaxseed to chicken feed. The label will clearly indicate this with wording like "omega-3 enriched" or "high in omega-3 fatty acids." You can find these eggs in most groceries. Eggs are an ideal source of protein. And while one egg contains 4.5 grams of fat, half of that fat is unsaturated.

- Add tofu and some fresh spinach to chicken broth and a bit of miso (fermented soybean paste, available in the Asian foods section of the grocery store) for a quick, light soup.
- Try a soy burger. Some really do taste like meat.

Beans. Loaded with soluble fiber, beans are a powerful way to cut your cholesterol. How powerful? When one researcher had 20 men with high cholesterol eat about 1½ cups of pinto and navy beans a day, their total cholesterol dropped an average of 56 points, and their LDL an average of 51 points. There are countless ways to make beans part of your meals. For lunch, try black bean or lentil soup, or toss garbanzo beans over a hefty salad. For dinner, make vegetarian chili or add a can of rinsed white beans to pasta dishes.

Eggplant. Few other vegetables can fool the palate and eye as well as eggplant. This fibrous purple vegetable soaks up flavoring like a sponge. (Unfortunately, it also soaks up oil the same way, so avoid frying it.) And eggplant is very filling, with virtually no fat. Try making eggplant Parmesan by baking slices of bread crumb-encrusted eggplant (instead of frying them) and covering with skim mozzarella cheese; using eggplant in place of meat in lasagna; and sautéing eggplant with tomatoes, onions, squash, and garlic and serving over brown rice for a delicious ratatouille.

Portobello mushrooms. These have a surprisingly meaty texture that is good enough to substitute for burgers on buns or beef in wraps. Grill them with a brushing of olive oil and balsamic vinegar and use them anyway you like. Several studies have found that mushrooms, high in fiber and plant sterols, can help lower cholesterol.

7. Eat More Antioxidants

The diet described thus far in this chapter will help you lower your LDL. But certain foods can also make the LDL you do have less dangerous.

As we talked about in Chapter 1, LDL is a bigger threat when it becomes oxidized. This happens because of exposure to free radicals, highly reactive molecules that are byproducts of bodily functions involving oxygen (which is just about all of them). When LDL is oxidized it becomes stickier and therefore more likely to form plaque. If LDL can be prevented from oxidizing, your arteries are less likely to become clogged.

How do you prevent LDL from becoming oxidized? With antioxidants—which many of nature's best-tasting foods happen to include. That's one of the reasons you're going to eat less meat on the *Live It Down Plan*: so that you can make more room for fruits and vegetables.

Antioxidants in a Cup

Fruits and veggies aren't the only way to get your antioxidants. Tea, whether black or green, caffeinated or decaffeinated (herbal teas don't count), has spectacular antioxidant capabilities owing to large amounts of substances called flavonoids. In addition to preventing oxidation, flavonoids may have an anticlotting effect.

One study found that among people who'd had heart attacks, those who drank 14 or more cups of tea a week were 44 percent less likely to die in the 3½ years following their heart attacks than those who didn't drink any tea. In another study people who drank about 1½ cups of tea daily had roughly half the risk of heart attack of those who didn't drink tea. An added bonus: A cup of black tea has less than half the caffeine of coffee; green tea has even less. Some tea tips:

Bag it. When *Consumer Reports* tested the antioxidant

Blueberry Cranberry Crunch
Berries add antioxidant power to this sweet and crunchy morning treat. **Recipe on page 230.**

Power-Packed Produce

Which fruits and veggies pack the most powerful antioxidant punch? Researchers at the Human Nutrition Research Center on Aging at Tufts University figured it out by measuring various fruits and vegetables for their "oxygen radical absorbance capacity," a fancy way of saying their antioxidant power. Here are the top 10 performers in each category:

Fruits

Prunes

Raisins

Blueberries

Blackberries

Strawberries

Raspberries

Plums

Oranges

Red grapes

Cherries

Vegetables

Kale

Spinach

Brussels sprouts

Alfalfa sprouts

Broccoli flowers

Beets

Red bell peppers

Onions

Corn

Eggplant

punch of 15 brewed, bottled, and instant teas, it found most teas brewed from tea bags scored highest in antioxidant content. In fact, the magazine reported, "Brewed tea appears to have more antioxidant action than almost any whole fruit or vegetable—and more than most commercial fruit or vegetable juices, too." But iced teas from mixes and bottle are a decent second choice; they contain a "good deal" of antioxidants, according to the magazine. Just watch the sugar content.

Dunk the bag. Continuously dunking the tea bag as the tea steeps seems to release far more antioxidant compounds than simply dropping it in and leaving it there.

Add lemon. One study found that the addition of lemon to plain tea increased its antioxidant benefits. That make sense, since lemon itself contains antioxidants.

Brew a batch. To make a day's supply of iced tea, bring 20 ounces of water to a boil, then remove from the heat. Drop in three tea bags, cover, and steep for 10 minutes. Remove tea bags and refrigerate.

Try green tea. Because it isn't fermented, green tea has even more antioxidant power than black tea does. It also has less caffeine. And it may provide some protection against certain cancers. Experiment with brands until you find one you like. Don't let green tea steep for more than a couple of minutes or it may become bitter.

Chocolate's Secret Health Benefits

Remember that scene in the Woody Allen movie *Sleeper* in which Woody, who has been frozen for 200 years, wakes up to find that chocolate and banana crème pie are now health foods? Well it's not so far-fetched. Chocolate is chock full of potent antioxidants called phenols, the same as those found in wine. In fact, a 1.5-ounce chocolate bar has as much antioxidant power as a 5-ounce glass of red wine. (White chocolate, which doesn't contain any cocoa solids, doesn't count.) And contrary to popular belief, chocolate contains only a very small amount of caffeine.

More good news: One-third of the fat in chocolate is a cholesterol-friendly fat called stearic acid, and another third is an unsaturated fat called oleic acid. When Pennsylvania researchers (including some from the Mars candy company) had 23 people follow either the average American diet or the same diet supplemented with 22 grams of cocoa powder and 16 grams of dark chocolate, they found that the chocolate diet reduced LDL oxidation. If you're going to indulge:

Choose dark. Dark chocolate contains more phenols than other forms of chocolate. Milk chocolate contains milk fat (palmitic acid) that is highly saturated. Semi-sweet chocolate has less fat than milk chocolate.

Kill two birds. Dip strawberries into melted chocolate for a high-antioxidant snack that can easily satisfy one or two fruit servings. An easy way to get melted chocolate is to simply microwave semi-sweet chocolate chips on medium for about 30 seconds. Be sure the strawberries are complete dry before you dip.

Go for quality. Buy the richest, creamiest chocolate you can afford. You'll be more satisfied with one piece of the good stuff than five pieces of the mediocre stuff.

Chocolate Cake with Raspberries
Go ahead! Chocolate and raspberries team up to provide twice the antioxidant power in this guilt-free treat.
Recipe on page 248.

What About Alcohol?

By now the "French Paradox" is old news. The phrase refers to the fact that despite eating lots of saturated fat and cholesterol (read: cheese, butter, and cream), the French have a relatively low incidence of heart disease. A major reason, researchers suspect, is the generous amount of wine that the French drink. Although the very existence of the paradox itself is currently under question—some researchers believe the French underreport heart disease—the evidence in support of wine and other forms of alcohol is not.

Dozens of studies on white wine, red wine, beer, and hard liquor attest to the heart-protective effects of alcohol. (That's right, it's not just wine that's good for you.) In fact, 60 to 80 percent of the population could benefit from moderate drinking, said Harvard researcher Eric Rimm, Ph.D, during a briefing sponsored by the National Beer Wholesalers Association in 2002. In a study of more than 80,000 American women, those who drank moderately had only half the heart attack risk of those who did not drink at all, even if the teetotalers were slim, eschewed tobacco, and exercised daily.

How does alcohol help? To start with, it raises HDL. This is true no matter what type of alcohol you drink. One study found that drinking half a bottle of white wine per day for six weeks increased HDL 7 mg/dl—a significant jump—in 12 healthy women and men, all of whom had otherwise normal cholesterol levels. Even significantly less alcohol was found to increase HDL up to 2 mg/dl in other studies. Recent research suggests that the heart-health benefit of alcohol is increased if moderate consumption is also consistent—three to seven times per week, rather than sporadic.

Red wine has additional benefits, some of which can be ascribed to powerful antioxidants. Because the skin of the grapes used to make red wine stays in contact with the juice as the wine ferments, more antioxidants, in the form of flavonoids, leach into the wine. (The skins are removed when white wine is made, thus the lower flavonoid content.) Red grape juice also contains flavonoids, but not as much: only about one-fourth to one-third of that found in red wine.

How much is enough to gain heart protection? In one study of 353 men aged 40 to 60 who had had a heart attack, two or more glasses of wine each day reduced their risk of another heart attack by more than half compared to nondrinkers.

Everything in Moderation

Of course, go overboard with alcohol and the risks quickly outweigh the benefits, particularly in women, who don't metabolize alcohol as well as men. As little as two drinks a day in women could lead to liver disease. And studies find that daily drinking could increase a woman's risk of breast cancer 30 percent. (Keep in mind, however, that far more women die each year from heart disease than breast cancer. Also, a

Continued on page 116

Learning the Lingo

Wine scares many people. They envision snobbish wine store clerks, $200 bottles, and the need to know whether there are hints of chocolate, raspberry, or dirty old socks in the "bouquet." The truth is that you don't need to know much about wine to enjoy it; just find out which types of wines you like, then buy them. It may be handy when shopping at the wine store to know how to describe your preferences. Here are some words that can help:

Body: The viscosity of the wine (a wine can be as thin as water or as thick as cream).

Big: High in alcohol.

Buttery: Having an aroma of butter or butterscotch.

Crisp: High in fruit acidity (in a positive way).

Fat: Full-bodied.

Flabby: Not enough acid.

Finish: The wine's aftertaste.

Fruity: The fruit the wine is made from (the grape) or another fruit flavor is perceptible.

Hard: Too tannic (astringent and bitter due to a high level of compounds called tannins).

Light: Light-bodied.

Oaky: Can taste the oak imparted from aging in an oak barrel.

So which wines do you drink with which foods?

Forget the old "rules" about white with fish and red with meat. If it works, it works. Here are some guidelines, courtesy of wineanswers.com:

- Match light wines with light foods (this can either be a light white or a light red wine).
- Try highly acidic wines with acidic or tart foods.
- Try a wine with just a touch of sweetness (called off-dry wine) with savory foods that have a bit of sweetness to them or spicy foods for balance.
- Aim for less tannic wines with bitter foods and more tannic wines with astringent foods.

Consider Israeli Wine

Who says white can't be red? Scientists at the Technion-Israel Institute of Technology created a kosher white wine with all of the beneficial health effects of red wine by adding skins of chardonnay or Muscat grapes (which are white or yellow) to the alcohol for the flavonoids. The wine is available under the Binyamina Winery label. They also found that Israeli wines overall contain a higher content of flavonoids than French wines. One reason may be that the intense Israeli sunlight spurs the grapes to produce more flavonoids. The result? Studies find that Israeli red wine reduces cholesterol oxidation twice as much as French wines.

Continued from page 114

30 percent increase for a woman at low risk of breast cancer amounts to a change in risk from 10 in 100,000 to 13 in 100,000.) Too much alcohol can also increase the risk of a rare type of stroke called hemorrhagic stroke (involving a burst blood vessel), and binge or heavy drinking can actually damage the heart.

Women should limit themselves to no more than one drink a day; men, no more than two. One drink is 4 ounces of wine, 12 ounces of beer (a bottle or can), or 1 ounce of hard liquor.

Eating Out on the *Live It Down Plan*

The typical American eats out about four times a week. Think that sounds too high? If you include everything from the muffin and coffee you grab on your way to work to the lunch you eat in the company cafeteria to stops at drive-through joints, you can see how quickly it adds up. The problem with eating out is that, with the ironic exception of fast-food restaurants, there's rarely any nutritional information available on menus. And most restaurant food isn't as healthful as what you'd prepare at home. Nutrition researchers at the University of Memphis found that women who ate out 6 to 13 times a week consumed about 300 more calories, 19 more grams of fat, and 400 more milligrams of sodium than women who ate out five times a week on average. Another survey found that those who dined out ate up to 25 percent fewer fruits and vegetables than those who ate at home.

That doesn't have to happen to you. The *Live It Down* eating strategy translates easily enough to dining out. But you'll need to navigate the menu carefully.

Conquering the Chains

From Applebee's to Red Lobster, the chaining of American eateries has taken hold across the country. The advantage: You can plan ahead in terms of what you'll order. That's a good thing, since many of these restaurants seem to specialize in fried foods. Even a seemingly innocuous Chinese chicken salad often comes with chunks of fried chicken. Considering a patty melt? Assuming it comes with a side of fries, you could be getting an astounding 2,000 calories along with more than 50 grams of fat, more than 25 of them saturated. And you know those trendy blooming onions served at many steakhouses these days? The CSPI found they contain an astounding 2,100 calories and 18 grams of trans fats.

> A survey found that people who dined out often ate up to 25 percent fewer fruits and vegetables.

Another major minefield is portion size. A CSPI survey found that restaurants often serve two to three times more than food labels list as a serving.

Here are the top five points to keep in mind if you want make it through your dining-out meal with your arteries intact:

1. **Ask for a doggie bag when you place your order.** Put half in the box, close it up, and dine happily on the rest with the knowledge that you've now got lunch or dinner for tomorrow. Or split an entrée.

2. **Read between the lines.** Any menu description that uses the words *fried*, *creamy*, *breaded*, *crisp*, or *stuffed* is likely loaded with hidden fats—much of it saturated or hydrogenated. Also skip anything sautéed in butter or served with a cream or cheese sauce (*au gratin*). And stay away from anything fried. Chances are it's fried in partially hydrogenated vegetable oil, which translates to trans fats. Choose items that are baked or grilled instead.

3. **Practice safe salads.** Salads are a great way to get your vegetables at a restaurant, but many are loaded with hidden hazards: creamy dressings, bacon bits, fried noodles, etc. The typical Caesar salad in most restaurants (the one topped with chicken or shrimp as well as fried croutons and plenty of cheese and mayo in the dressing) contains 36 grams of fat. The solution? Ask for a salad with an oil-based dressing on the side, then spoon the dressing on yourself. Better yet, dip your fork in the dressing, then spear a piece of lettuce.

4. **Change the menu.** Don't be afraid to ask the waiter for a change in how your food is prepared. For instance, request that the salmon be grilled with a brushing of olive oil instead of butter, or ask for your pasta with steamed vegetables and a bit of olive oil instead of the cream sauce. If your meal comes with fries, ask for a side of steamed vegetables or wild rice instead.

5. **Find the vegetables.** It's all too easy to get through an entire restaurant meal and realize you haven't eaten a vegetable or fruit (and no, we're not going to count the french fries or onion rings). So make sure you get a salad (some are so large you could get four or five servings of vegetables from one salad), stir-fry, or other entrée that includes veggies or fruit.

Eating Out Ethnically

Nowhere is the melting pot of America more obvious than in our restaurants. From Greek to Indian to Chinese to Mexican, family-owned to chain, the ethnic food choices are endless. And most ethnic restaurants have plenty of minefields of their own, as well as ways to a heart-healthy meal. To *Live It Down* no matter what country you're dining in, follow these recommendations.

If you're eating Chinese:
- Avoid the fried noodles on the table.
- Order fewer dishes than there are people at the table.
- Start with soup to fill you up.
- Avoid fried appetizers (this means no egg rolls).
- Opt for steamed rice, not fried. If the restaurant serves brown rice, ask for it.
- Use the 2:1 ratio: two times as much rice to main dish.
- Avoid menu items described as *crispy* or *golden brown*. They're all deep-fried.
- Choose dishes rich in vegetables, and order at least one vegetarian entrée.

If you're eating Italian:
- Split and share. One order of pasta is usually enough for two people, especially if you also share a salad.
- Pick tomato-based sauces: marinara, Bolognese, red clam, puttanesca. Avoid cream-based sauces: Alfredo, primavera (while the veggies are great, the sauce is usually loaded with butter and cream).
- Skip the garlic bread or breadsticks and ask for plain bread and a dish of olive oil for dipping.
- Go with fagioli—Italian for "bean."

If you're eating Mexican:
- Keep your hands away from the fried tortilla chips. Instead, ask for a soft tortilla to scoop up the healthy salsa and get a couple of vegetable servings under your belt even before the main meal arrives.
- If a salad comes in a fried tortilla bowl, don't eat the bowl.
- Choose beans to fill your burrito instead of beef or cheese.
- Ask for black beans, not refried.
- Nix the sour cream.
- Go for soft tortillas instead of fried tacos.
- Avoid chimichangas (fried) and dishes labeled *grande* or *supreme*.

If you're eating Indian:
- Skip the appetizers (most are fried).
- Avoid the papadum, chapati, nan, kulcha, or roti breads, which have all been fried or soaked in fat.

- Order side dishes with vegetables, beans, or peas, such as dahl or chutney.
- Choose tandoori. Tandoori foods are oven-baked and usually include little or no added fat.

If you're eating Thai:
- Start with a broth-based soup, not one made with coconut milk.
- Go light on any dishes made with coconut milk. Coconut milk is loaded with saturated fat—45 grams in 1 cup.
- Choose dishes that have been stir-fried, grilled, or steamed.
- Here's a good way to get your soy: steamed or baked tofu (make sure it's not fried) and vegetables.

If you're eating diner food:
- Choose Canadian bacon instead of regular bacon.
- Skip the fries. Ask for a side salad or order of vegetables instead.
- Forgo tuna and chicken salads; they're likely loaded with mayo. Instead, order a turkey, roast beef, or even ham sandwich—plain or with mustard or horseradish—and remove some of the meat if it's piled too high.
- If you order a salad, ask for no croutons and get the dressing on the side.

Mexican Pork with Salsa

For tasty Mexican fare that's far better for your heart than the food at your local Mexican joint, try this succulent dish made with pork tenderloin. **Recipe on page 239.**

Best Bets in Fast Food

It's challenging, but not impossible, to eat heart-healthy meals at fast-food restaurants. Everything on this list, unless otherwise noted, gets 25 percent or less of its calories from fat. (The exception is Taco Bell. None of the items on that restaurant's menu gets less than 30 percent of its calories from fat, but we've included some of the healthier menu choices for your information.)

This is not a comprehensive list; Subway, for instance, has numerous sandwiches and salads with less than 25 percent fat. Most fast-food restaurants can provide you with a brochure that contains nutritional information, and many list that data on their Web sites. You can also log onto www.fatcalories.com for detailed nutritional information on a number of chains.

Item	Calories	Total fat	Saturated fat
Arby's			
Side salad*	25	0	0
Caesar side salad	45	2	1
Sourdough with bacon	420	10	2.5
Sourdough with ham	390	6	1
Light grilled chicken sandwich	280	5	1.5
Light roast chicken deluxe sandwich	260	5	1
Light roast turkey deluxe sandwich	260	5	0.5
Grilled chicken salad	210	4.5	1.5
Roast chicken salad	160	2.5	0
Garden salad	70	1	0
Burger King			
Garden salad	25	0	0
Chicken Whopper Jr. (without mayo)	270	6	1.5
BK veggie burger	330	10	1.5
Chicken Whopper (without mayo)	420	9	2.5
KFC			
Mashed potatoes and gravy	120	6	1
Corn on the cob	150	1.5	0
Mean beans	70	3	1
BBQ baked beans	190	3	1
Honey BBQ flavored chicken sandwich with sauce	310	6	2

Item	Calories	Total fat	Saturated fat
McDonald's			
Fruit and yogurt parfait	380	5	2
Fruit and yogurt parfait without granola	280	4	2
Chicken McGrill (without mayo)	300	6	1.5
Plain hotcakes	320	8	1.5
Low-fat apple bran muffin	300	3	0.5
Chef salad	150	8	3.5
English muffin	150	2	0.5
Grilled chicken Caesar salad	100	2.5	1.5
Subway			
Sweet onion chicken teriyaki on wheat (6-inch)	366	4.5	1
All salads	120 or fewer	3	1.5 or fewer
6-inch roast beef sub	264	4.5	1
6-inch ham sub	261	4.5	1.5
6-inch turkey sub	254	3.5	1
6-inch roasted chicken breast sub	311	6	1.5
6-inch club sandwich	294	5	1.5
6-inch veggie delite	200	2.5	5
Club salad	145	3.5	1
Ham deli salad	194	3.5	1
Turkey breast deli salad	200	3.5	1
Taco Bell			
Soft taco, steak	190	7	3
Soft taco, chicken	180	8	4
Pinto and cheese soft taco	180	8	4
Bean burrito	370	12	3.5
Fiesta burrito, steak	370	12	4
Fiesta burrito, chicken	370	13	4
Wendy's			
Side salad	35	0	0
Frozen dessert, medium	440	11	7
Baked potato, sour cream and chive	370	5	4
Baked potato, plain	310	0	0
Grilled chicken sandwich	300	7	1.5
Frosty dairy dessert, junior	170	4	2.5
Soft bread sticks	130	3	.5
Mandarin chicken salad	150	1.5	0
Caesar side salad	70	4	2

Salads do not include dressings

The Art of Change

Changing ingrained habits is one of the most difficult things to do. And the changes probably feel most overwhelming in the eating arena. But relax. We don't expect you to institute them all at once. Just doing one new thing at a time—switching from 2 percent milk to skim, substituting a salmon steak for a sirloin, or changing the brand of cereal you eat every morning—will eventually add up to big benefits. Within a few weeks that initial change that felt so strange will feel as familiar as your own bed.

To help you get into the new habits we've recommended in a relatively painless manner, we've developed a three-month, week-by-week Plan starting on page 206 that introduces a few manageable changes at a time. By the end of 12 weeks you'll find the *Live It Down Plan* has become a regular part of your life.

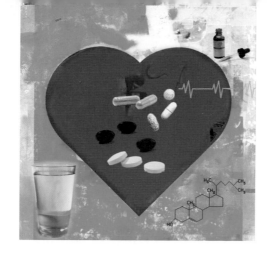

Live It Down | Supplements

According to one definition, the word "supplement" means "something added to complete a thing, to extend or strengthen the whole." And that's just what the supplement portion of the *Live It Down Plan* is intended to do—strengthen your efforts to lower your cholesterol and improve your overall heart health.

The supplements we outline in this chapter serve different purposes. Some make blood platelets less sticky, reducing your risk of artery-blocking clots; some prevent the oxidation of LDL, making it less likely to lead to plaque; others help minimize certain side effects of cholesterol-lowering drugs; still others act as alternatives to prescription drugs. Some of the supplements in this chapter won't be right for you. Others will—especially the two we advise everyone on the Plan to take.

In addition to these two, we list seven supplements that, since they have the strongest evidence behind them in terms of lowering cholesterol or protecting you from heart disease, we think you should consider. (We also mention a handful of supplements at the end of the chapter that, while we aren't recommending as part of the Plan, are worth watching.) For each supplement we tell you whom it's appropriate for. Chromium, for instance, is best used by people with metabolic syndrome. And red yeast rice extract is only for people whose cholesterol levels are high enough to qualify them for medication. Finally, we explain any contraindications or warnings for each supplement. Because as with drugs, all supplements pose potential risks. Before you start taking any of the supplements in this chapter, check with your doctor. Turn the page for more specific advice on using supplements safely and effectively.

A Few Words to the Wise

Before reading on to find out which supplements you should consider taking, keep two pieces of important advice in mind:

"Natural" doesn't mean "safe." Just because a supplement may be natural doesn't mean taking it is completely without risk. Many, if not all, supplements have the potential to interact with prescription or over-the-counter drugs, cause harmful side effects if taken inappropriately, or even make existing medical conditions worse. That's why it's critical that you tell your health care providers about any supplements you take. In a University of Michigan study one-third of the patients taking supplements were using ones that could interact with their heart medications. Be especially cautious if you're taking blood-thinning medication like aspirin, Coumadin (warfarin), or Plavix (clopidogrel); many supplements, such as ginkgo biloba, ginseng, garlic, vitamin E, fish oil, and coenzyme Q10, also have blood-thinning properties, and the combined effect could lead to dangerous bleeding.

Also, just because the label may say "natural" doesn't mean that supplements are any safer than pharmaceutical drugs. They still include chemicals that have an effect on your body; that's why they work. So don't exceed the recommended dose, and don't take any supplement longer than advised. If you are pregnant or nursing, be doubly sure to check with your doctor before taking any supplements.

Know what you're getting. The FDA subjects prescription and over-the-counter drugs to rigorous testing and manufacturing standards, but vitamins, minerals, herbs, and enzymes don't have to be proven safe or effective before they're sold. In fact, there's no guarantee that the supplement you buy even contains what the label says it contains. So one brand of coenzyme Q10, for instance, could have very different properties than another.

To get the facts, rely on ConsumerLab.com, which independently tests supplements and provides information on hundreds of brands on its Web site, www.consumerlab.com. (Some of the information on the site costs money to view.)

The Live It Down Plan
♥ Supplements

- Everyone on the Plan will take a multivitamin/multimineral and 2 grams of fish-oil supplements daily.
- Depending on your health profile, you may also consider taking gugulipid (especially for people with cholesterol in the "gray" zone), red yeast rice extract (as an alternative to cholesterol-lowering drugs), chromium (especially for people with metabolic syndrome), coenzyme Q10 (especially for people taking statins), psyllium (for extra soluble fiber), arginine (if your diet is less than ideal), and hawthorn (to improve blood flow and reduce LDL oxidation). Don't take any of these without first checking with your doctor.

On product labels look for "USP," which stands for U.S. Pharmacopeia. The USP is a nonprofit organization that promotes public health by establishing standards to ensure the quality of medicines and other health care technologies. If a label says USP it means the product meets the standards for measures such as strength and purity of ingredients and degree of absorption by the body. If a label doesn't say USP, however, it doesn't necessarily mean the product is inferior. For some supplements, there are no USP standards. And some brand-name manufacturers, for whatever reason, choose not to perform the tests necessary to garner USP approval.

Also, look for products produced under good manufacturing practices (GMP). These are regulations that describe the methods, equipment, facilities, and controls required for producing quality products. A trade group called the National Nutritional Foods Association (NNFA) operates a GMP certification program that includes inspections of manufacturing facilities to determine whether products meet GMP standards. Once certified, manufacturers can use the NNFA's GMP seal on their products.

Two Supplements Everyone Should Take

The seven supplements you'll read about later in this chapter are intended for people who fit certain health profiles. But the *Live It Down Plan* includes two supplements that everyone should take every day: a daily multivitamin/multimineral (which we'll call a "multivitamin" from here on for the sake of simplicity) and fish oil. They're safe, they're inexpensive, and they offer significant health benefits for all adults.

A Multivitamin

More Americans take a daily multivitamin than any other supplement. You will too on the *Live It Down Plan*. It's an easy, safe way to get numerous benefits from a variety of nutrients without having to pop a handful of pills every day. Taking a daily multivitamin is especially important for older adults because as we age, our bodies become less efficient at absorbing vitamins and minerals from food. And if you follow a vegetarian diet, you may not be consuming enough of certain vitamins and minerals to begin with.

When choosing a multivitamin, pick a brand with high quality control, high reported bioavailability (this means your body can absorb the vitamins), and few additives. These include multis by Thorne, PhytoPharmica, and Vital Nutrients. Don't choose a multi that contains iron unless you're a woman who is still menstruating or your doctor has recommended that you take additional iron.

A Multitude of Benefits

Multivitamins got a boost in June 2002, when the *Journal of the American Medical Association* published two articles by Harvard doctors on their benefits. The doctors recommended that everyone, regardless of age or health status, take one. We agree. Among the heart-related benefits you might reap are a lower homocysteine level and less oxidation of LDL. Some of the nutrients most likely responsible include:

B vitamins. One of the best reasons to take a multivitamin every day is to be certain to get your fill of B vitamins. This family of vitamins—thiamin, riboflavin (B_1), pyridoxine (B_6), niacin (B_3), pantothenic acid (B_5), cobalamin (B_{12}), folic acid, biotin, choline, inositol, and para-aminobenzoic acid—plays a critical role in every function inside your body. But the vitamins really shine when it comes to your heart. You already know from Chapter 2 that folate, B_6, and B_{12} help prevent a dangerous buildup of the amino acid homocysteine. If homocysteine levels rise too high, they damage endothelial cells (which line the arteries), blocking the production of nitric oxide and leaving arteries more prone to plaque buildup. Keeping homocysteine in check is a good enough reason by itself to take a multivitamin.

Another B vitamin, choline, helps your body process cholesterol. And Vitamin B_5 can actually lower LDL and triglycerides and raise HDL, at least at high doses. The vitamin apparently works by reducing the amount of cholesterol your liver makes.

Generally, a multivitamin will give you all of the B vitamins your body needs. But if you have elevated homocysteine levels, talk to your doctor about taking an additional B vitamin supplement. Should you decide to do so, don't exceed the recommended dosages. Because they are fat soluble, many of these vitamins can build up in the body to toxic levels.

Vitamin E. Vitamin E is a powerful antioxidant. Whether or not it can help protect you against heart disease is a matter of great controversy. When researchers looked at large populations, it appeared that people who got the most vitamin E through their diets and/or supplements had significantly lower rates of heart disease. But in three large studies in which vitamin E supplements (in doses ranging from 400 International Units, or IU, to 800 IU) were pitted against placebos (dummy pills), the vitamin disappointed—there was no effect on heart disease risk. Some studies even found that high doses of vitamin E could actually encourage the oxidation of LDL cholesterol.

But many researchers still believe in vitamin E, in part because the disappointing studies may have been less than perfect. Problems may have included the type of vitamin E used (the most common form is alpha-tocopherol, but a growing body of research suggests that gamma-tocopherol is more potent and should be used together with alpha-tocopherol), the dose, and the participants themselves. Some participants may have neglected to take the vitamin daily, and others may not have taken it with food, which greatly facilitates absorption. (One study found that vitamin E supplements taken with food were four times more powerful at preventing oxidation than vitamin E taken on an empty stomach.)

And there is some compelling evidence for the vitamin's effects on cholesterol and plaque. A 2000 study from Rome that focused on stroke victims and patients with high cholesterol found that those who took large doses (1,350 IU) of vitamin E daily not only experienced less severe artery blockages, but their cholesterol levels dropped to nearly normal. Further, a study published in September 2002 in the *American Journal of Clinical Nutrition* found that healthy women with no history of heart disease who ate few vitamin E-containing foods were more than twice as likely to have signs of plaque in their arteries than those who ate more vitamin E-filled foods. The researchers concluded: "Low vitamin E intake is a risk factor for early atherosclerosis."

> Among the heart-related benefits you might reap from a multivitamin are a lower homocysteine level and less oxidation of LDL.

Based on the current state of the research, we don't think you need to take a separate vitamin E supplement. If your multi contains 100 to 200 IU, that's sufficient—and not unimportant. Our ancestors got about 100 IU of vitamin E through food, but it's difficult to get even that modest amount from diet alone. (Even olive oil, one of the best sources of vitamin E, has just 1.74 IU per tablespoon. To get 100 IU, you'd need to drink 3.5 cups a day!)

If you do decide to take a separate vitamin E supplement, look for one labeled "assorted" or "mixed" tocopherols, usually available only at health food or specialty stores. The body absorbs mixed tocopherols better than alpha-tocopherol. Because vitamin E has blood-thinning properties, check with your doctor if you're also taking a daily aspirin or other blood-thinning medication.

Vitamin C. Vitamin C is another powerful antioxidant with mixed results when it comes to heart disease and cholesterol. Studies found no link between the vitamin C in people's diets and their heart disease risk. But of the small handful of studies focusing on vitamin C supplements, some have found promising results.

In one study 10 women who took 1,000 milligrams of vitamin C daily for four weeks saw their LDL levels drop an average of 16 percent and their HDL levels improve slightly. A much larger study with 256 men and 221 women showed similar results. Vitamin C seems to have similar effects even at lower doses.

Vitamins E and C seem to work best in conjunction with one another, another reason to get these vitamins as part of a multivitamin. Look for one with 200 to 500 milligrams of vitamin C. (Most vitamins are measured in milligrams, but fat-soluble vitamins such as E and A, measured in IU, are exceptions.)

Fish-Oil Supplements

The *Live It Down Plan* calls for eating fish several times a week. But believe it or not, eating fish regularly is still not enough to give you the amount of omega-3 fatty acids that,
according to the latest research, can lower triglycerides, counter inflammation, reduce blood stickiness, and provide other heart benefits. That's why everyone on the Plan will also take a daily fish-oil supplement. (And if you don't like fish and aren't planning to make it a regular part of your diet, it's especially important that you take this supplement.) Fish oil may have other benefits as well, such as strengthening immune function, staving off depression, helping with allergies, countering inflammation in people with conditions such as rheumatoid arthritis and Crohn's disease, and possibly helping stave off certain cancers.

If you're worried about having to swallow a yucky-tasting oil every day (maybe you're remembering taking castor oil as a kid), you'll be happy to learn that fish-oil supplements are available in capsules.

A Whale of a Good Idea

Fish oil wields amazing power to protect your heart, mainly because it's an easily available and inexpensive source of omega-3 fatty acids, which you read about in Chapter 4. Fish oil may even improve your LDL/HDL ratio in addition to potentially lowering your triglyceride level.

In a 2001 Israeli study 52 patients who were taking cholesterol-lowering drugs received either 7 grams of a dietary spread containing omega-3 fatty acids or an olive oil spread. The participants were also asked to limit the amount of omega-6 fatty acids (found in most vegetable oils) in their diet. Overall, the patients using the omega-3 spread saw their total cholesterol levels drop an average of 12 percent, their LDL levels plummet nearly 17 percent, and their triglyceride levels plunge an impressive 36 percent. The group getting the olive oil spread found their LDL levels dropped an average of about 15 percent, but they didn't have any significant changes in either their HDL or triglyceride levels.

Shopping for Fish Oil

Fish-oil supplements are an easy way to add more omega-3 fatty acids to your diet. The translucent, gelatin capsules are odorless, tasteless, and easy to swallow, even though they are large. And they're also relatively inexpensive—you can get 100 1,000-milligram softgels for under $3. (As a reminder, 1,000 milligrams equal 1 gram.)

Just be sure to look for a brand with the USP label (see page 125) verifying that the supplement contains the level of ingredients the label claims. When ConsumerLab.com, an independent company that evaluates dietary supplements, tested fish-oil supplements, it found that one-third of the 20 brands tested did not contain the levels of EPA and DHA advertised. Two of the products that failed even stated on their labels that they had been tested or verified for potency. Among the brands that passed the test: Nutrilite Omega 3 Complex Dietary Supplement and Puritan's Pride Inspired By Nature Salmon Oil.

Some other benefits worth noting:

- Studies find that taking 2,000 milligrams or more of fish oil daily can lower triglyceride levels, slow blood clotting, and reduce blood pressure.
- Combining fish oils with statin drugs may help stave off type 2 diabetes in obese people with high cholesterol. (Statins by themselves have little effect on triglycerides, which play a distinct role in the development of diabetes.)
- Fish-oil supplements appear to help regulate your heart's electrical activity, lowering the risk of heart attack or sudden cardiac death from arrhythmias, or irregular heart beats.

What to Take, and How Much

Two main types of omega-3 fatty acids make up fish oil: EPA and DHA (don't worry about the full scientific names). Look for a product that contains both. One product we like is Max EPA. Take 1,000 milligrams twice daily. If you already have heart disease, talk to your doctor about taking higher doses. If you're a vegan (someone who does not eat any animal products or fish), consider taking flaxseed oil instead of fish-oil supplements. Flaxseed and its oil are excellent sources of omega-3 fatty acids. Take a tablespoon a day in either capsule or oil form, or use in salad dressings and cooking. Just don't take both fish oil and flaxseed oil, since both have blood-thinning effects.

Because fish-oil supplements can reduce the time it takes blood to clot, talk to your doctor before taking them if you're also taking blood-thinning medications like Coumadin (warfarin) or are at high risk for bleeding disorders.

Seven Other Key Supplements

Everyone on the *Live It Down Plan* will take a daily multivitamin and a fish-oil supplement (or flaxseed oil for vegans). But some may benefit from additional supplements. Next we outline the strongest candidates and who should consider them. Remember to check with your doctor before deciding to take any supplement.

Guggul

Guggul, short for guggulsterone (also known as gugulipid), is an extract derived from the resin of the mukul myrrh tree, which grows in India. It has more than 3,000 years of history behind it in treating a variety of 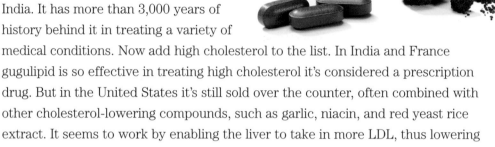 medical conditions. Now add high cholesterol to the list. In India and France gugulipid is so effective in treating high cholesterol it's considered a prescription drug. But in the United States it's still sold over the counter, often combined with other cholesterol-lowering compounds, such as garlic, niacin, and red yeast rice extract. It seems to work by enabling the liver to take in more LDL, thus lowering the amount circulating in the blood. It may also stimulate the thyroid gland, which is involved in cholesterol metabolism (recall from Chapter 2 that hypothyroidism is a leading cause of high cholesterol).

What the research shows: In studies conducted in India, 205 people with high cholesterol took 500 milligrams of gugulipid a day. After 12 weeks 70 to 80 percent of the patients saw their cholesterol drop an average of 24 percent and their triglycerides drop an average of 22.6 percent. It took about three to four weeks before cholesterol began dropping, the researchers reported. Additionally, in 60 percent of those who responded to the gugulipid therapy, HDL levels increased.

Who should take it: Anyone with high cholesterol who is looking for an alternative to a prescription drug, particularly if your cholesterol is still in a "gray" zone in which medication isn't specifically recommended.

Recommended dose: An effective dose is 75 milligrams of guggulsterones, the active ingredient in gugulipid, taken in divided doses (25 milligrams three times a day). Read the label carefully to make sure you're getting the right dosage and a standardized product.

Warnings/contraindications: Gugulipid may interfere with some medications, such as Inderal (propranolol) and Cardizem (diltiazem). Don't take it if you have liver disease or inflammatory bowel disease.

Red Yeast Rice Extract

Red yeast, grown on fermented rice, has been used in China for more than 1,000 years to improve heart function (and give Peking Duck its red color). It works by blocking an enzyme necessary in the formation of cholesterol and by speeding the removal of LDL from the blood. Think of it as nature's statin drug. It is so similar to statins, in fact, that the FDA pulled one brand of red yeast rice extract, Cholestin, from store shelves in the summer of 2002, saying it contained natural lovastatin, the same compound synthetically produced and sold as the prescription drug Mevacor. Cholestin's manufacturer quickly reformulated the product using policosanols (see page 137), and it's still sold under the same brand name.

Other forms of red yeast rice extract continue to be available over the Internet and through specialty health food stores, individual physicians, and alternative health care providers. Although they haven't been as closely studied as Cholestin, these alternatives still have some cholesterol-lowering effects and may cost as little as one-fifth the price of prescription statins.

What the research shows: Researchers at the University of California, Los Angeles, studied the benefits of red yeast rice extract on 83 healthy adults with high LDL levels. For 12 weeks the participants received either the extract or a placebo and followed a low-fat, low-cholesterol diet. In the supplement group total cholesterol dropped an average of 46 points after eight weeks. There was no significant decrease in the placebo group. In a larger study conducted at 12 medical centers throughout the United States, 187 men and women with high cholesterol levels took Cholestin for eight weeks. Their total cholesterol dropped an average of 16 percent, from 242 milligrams per deciliter (mg/dl) to 204 mg/dl. Four weeks after they stopped taking the supplement, their counts rose again to prestudy levels.

Who should take it: Anyone with cholesterol levels high enough to require drug treatment, but who doesn't want to take a prescription drug, should consider it.

Recommended dose: Follow the manufacturer's directions.

Warnings/contraindications: Because red yeast rice extract is a natural form of statin, it may have the same side effects as statins, including heartburn, dizziness, muscle weakness, and a very slight chance of liver damage. Don't mix it with other statin-type cholesterol-lowering medications, although it can be safely combined with niacin supplements. Consider supplementing with coenzyme Q10 (more on this on the next page) if you do decide to take red yeast rice extract. Since the extract is a statin, albeit a naturally occurring one, it can have the same lowering effects on coenzyme Q10 as any of the pharmaceutical statins.

Chromium

Chromium is an essential trace mineral first discovered in 1955. Although our bodies contain only a few milligrams, even this tiny amount is critical for regulating insulin and blood sugar levels, as well as activating enzymes essential for energy production.

We get chromium through food, primarily yeast, grains, nuts, prunes, potatoes, and seafood. But we don't get enough overall; many Americans are deficient in chromium. One reason is that diets high in refined sugar leach chromium right out of us.

Recent studies find that supplementing with chromium may not only lower cholesterol but also help stabilize blood sugar levels and improve insulin sensitivity. Thus, it may be particularly beneficial to people with metabolic syndrome or diabetes.

What the research shows: In one small study of 28 people, those taking 200 micrograms of chromium daily for 42 days had significant decreases in both total cholesterol and LDL, decreases that didn't occur when they took a placebo. At least eight other studies have found that chromium supplementation improved cholesterol. And numerous studies found supplementing with at least 400 micrograms of chromium improved fasting glucose levels, a sign of improved insulin sensitivity. Be aware that chromium may take several weeks or even months to yield results.

Who should take it: People with metabolic syndrome or diabetes, as well as anyone susceptible to chromium deficiency (including athletes, the elderly, and people who follow diets high in refined sugar).

Recommended dose: 200 to 400 micrograms a day in divided doses for people with insulin resistance; 400 to 1,000 micrograms a day in divided doses for people with diabetes. Use chromium picolinate as your source. For everyone else the amount in a multivitamin should be sufficient.

Warnings/contraindications: If you have diabetes, check with your doctor; taking chromium may alter your requirements for insulin or other diabetes medication.

Coenzyme Q10

Humans naturally produce the vitamin-like compound known as coenzyme Q10, or CoQ10. In fact, it's found in every cell in your body. And you get more of this powerful antioxidant through food, primarily red meat, nuts, dark green vegetables, and vegetable oils. It provides energy for every cell, particularly the heart. Without it your heart wouldn't have the wherewithal to beat. No surprise, then, that the heart contains higher concentrations of CoQ10 than any other tissue, or that people with heart disease have up to 25 percent less CoQ10 than their heart-healthy counterparts. Doctors in other countries commonly prescribe this supplement for heart disease patients.

Working together with vitamin E, CoQ10 piggybacks on LDL particles as they travel throughout the body, helping to protect them from oxidation. You may remember from Chapter 1 that LDL becomes much more dangerous to your arteries once it has been oxidized, the biological equivalent of rusting.

Levels of CoQ10 naturally decline as we age. But studies also find that cholesterol-lowering statin drugs like Lipitor (atorvastatin) and beta-blockers like Inderal (propranolol) deplete CoQ10 by interfering with the body's ability to make the compound. This may be one reason for the muscle weakness sometimes associated with statins.

What the research shows: While CoQ10 doesn't appear to have any effects on cholesterol levels per se, it may help prevent LDL oxidation. At least that's what one rabbit study suggests. Two groups of rabbits were fed a diet rich in trans fatty acids to raise their cholesterol and triglyceride levels. Then one group received CoQ10 in its rabbit chow. The result? That group had significantly less arterial plaque than the control group. Moreover, the plaque that was present was more stable—that is, less likely to burst and cause a heart attack.

Who should take it: Anyone with a high LDL level and anyone taking a statin drug might consider supplementing with CoQ10 if they can afford it   this supplement isn't cheap. CoQ10 may also be helpful for people with high blood pressure or congestive heart failure.

Recommended dose: 100 milligrams in divided doses (50 milligrams twice a day). Take it with food to enhance absorption.

Warnings and interactions: Some literature suggests CoQ10 may interact with blood-thinners such as Coumadin.

Psyllium

This source of soluble fiber—the outer coating of the psyllium seed—has been marketed as a laxative for more than 60 years under the brand name  Metamucil. But now we know it also has amazing cholesterol-lowering properties. Just 10 grams a day can lower your total cholesterol 5 percent and your LDL 9 percent. Ideally, on the *Live It Down Plan* you'll be getting all the soluble fiber you need through fruits, vegetables, and beans. But if you don't feel you can consistently eat foods rich in soluble fiber, try a psyllium supplement.

What the research shows: In an analysis of eight different studies, University of Kentucky researchers found that taking about 10 grams a day of psyllium for eight weeks reduced LDL 7 percent.

Who should take it: Anyone who isn't getting at least 25 grams of dietary fiber a day.

Recommended dose: 10 grams a day of an over-the-counter psyllium supplement, such as Metamucil, Citrucel, or Fiberall.

Warnings/contraindications: Take with plenty of water to reduce bloating and gas and prevent constipation.

Arginine

Arginine, or l-arginine, is eventually converted to nitric oxide in your body. Nitric oxide, you may recall from Chapter 2, is produced mainly in the blood vessel walls. It keeps the  endothelium, or artery lining, smooth and slick, helping to prevent the buildup of plaque. Dietary sources of arginine include oats, eggs, and soybeans.

What the research shows: When John P. Cooke, M.D., Ph.D., associate professor of cardiovascular medicine at Stanford University, gave 43 volunteers large doses of l-arginine (6 to 21 grams a day), blood flow and artery flexibility improved significantly after one week. Cooke also found supplementing with arginine can reduce the stickiness of blood platelets, white blood cells, and even the artery walls in people with high cholesterol. Less stickiness means less likelihood of plaque and clots.

Who should take it: Anyone with impaired endothelium function would likely benefit from taking extra arginine. But since there's currently no easy way for you to tell if your endothelium function is impaired, consider taking arginine if you have existing heart disease or multiple risk factors for heart disease, and your diet is less than ideal. (If you eat plenty of oats, eggs, or soy, you probably don't need it.)

Recommended dose: 2 to 3 grams daily in divided doses.

Warnings/contraindications: Side effects may include stomach upset, diarrhea, headache, or shingles. Don't use it with Viagra since it may cause a dangerous drop in blood pressure. It's also not recommended for people with cancer or a history of cancer, serious infections, or inflammation.

Hawthorn

Hawthorn is a spiky bush or tree found in Europe, northwestern Africa, and western Asia. It's considered an extremely valuable medicinal herb,  used since the Middle Ages as a remedy for many conditions. Its medicinal properties may be due in part to its high concentration of antioxidants called flavonoids.

What the research shows: Studies suggest that this herb can help reduce angina attacks by improving blood and oxygen supply to the heart by dilating blood vessels. It also guards against LDL oxidation.

Who should take it: We aren't ready to put everyone on the *Live It Down Plan* on hawthorn supplements because the evidence of its benefits isn't yet definitive. But if you already have heart disease, or you have high blood pressure or high cholesterol, and you want to do everything you can to lower your risk, it's probably a good idea.

Recommended dose: 100 to 300 milligrams standardized extract daily.

Warnings/contraindications: Don't take this if you're taking a vasodilator. Hawthorn may lower blood pressure and prevent blood clotting. If you are taking any prescription or over-the-counter medications that also have these effects, make sure you talk to your doctor before starting hawthorn.

Other Promising Supplements

You've just read about the supplements we recommend or think you should consider based on a significant body of research. But evidence is also mounting in favor of other supplements that may prove to help lower cholesterol. While the evidence isn't strong enough yet for us to recommend taking them regularly, here are eight to keep an eye on. One among them—calcium—is a mineral just about everyone should be taking anyway to protect their bones. That evidence is clear!

Dried artichoke extract. Artichokes contain plant chemicals that appear to decrease the amount of cholesterol the liver makes and also help convert cholesterol into less dangerous bile acids. In one German study published in 2000, researchers gave 143 people with high cholesterol either 450-milligram tablets of dried artichoke extract or a placebo for six weeks. Those taking the supplement saw their LDL levels drop an average of 22.9 percent, compared to a 6.3 percent drop for the control group.

Blue-green algae. Blue-green algae, or cyanobacteria, are among the most primitive life forms on Earth. Africans and Native Americans used to store dried algae for year-round use and trade. It is a nutrient-dense food, chock full of valuable amino acids and minerals, including zinc, selenium, and magnesium. It's also rich in antioxidants as well as polyunsaturated fatty acids. Most of the research demonstrating its ability to lower cholesterol has been conducted in animals.

Calcium. As little as 1,000 milligrams of calcium citrate taken daily could lower your LDL level and increase your HDL level … at least that's what Australian researchers learned during a study that had absolutely nothing to do with cholesterol. The study was designed to assess the effects of calcium on the incidence of bone fractures. A group of 223 women received either calcium citrate or a placebo for one year. Those receiving the calcium saw their cholesterol ratio improve more than those in the placebo group. The main reason for the ratio improvement? An average increase in HDL levels of 7 percent. Then, of course, there is calcium's benefit to your bones, and

Continued on page 137

Drugs vs. Supplements

How well do some of the supplements in this chapter really work? See for yourself how well six of them stand up against four prescription drugs. (Keep in mind that in some cases you may be taking both a supplement and a prescription drug.)

	Average cholesterol reduction (percent)	Average LDL reduction (percent)	Average HDL increase (percent)	Average triglyceride reduction (percent)	Best for	Potential side effects
Drugs						
Bile acid sequestrants	Up to 15	15–30	5	Variable; may raise levels	Lowering LDL	Gastrointestinal complaints
Fibrates	Up to 20	Variable to 10–15 decrease	5–20	20–50	Lowering triglycerides and raising HDL	Gastrointestinal complaints, increased risk of gallstones
Nicotinic acid (niacin)	Up to 20	20–30	15–35	20–50	All lipid abnormalities	Flushing, liver damage (in sustained-release form), gout, gastrointestinal complaints
Statins	Up to 40	20–60	5–15	10–40	Lowering LDL; Zocor (simvastatin) is also approved for raising HDL	Liver damage, muscle weakness, loss of libido
Supplements						
Chromium	Not significant	Not significant	Not significant	17	Lowering triglycerides	None
Fish oil	12	17	Not significant	36	Preventing LDL oxidation and improving heart function	Has blood-thinning properties; use with care if you're taking other blood-thinners
Gugulipid	25	16	Not significant	18	Lowering LDL and triglycerides	Gastrointestinal upset, nausea, headache, diarrhea
Pantethine (vitamin B_5)	13.5	13.5	10	13–30	Lowering LDL and triglycerides and raising HDL	None
Psyllium	7	7	Not significant	Not significant	Lowering LDL	Bloating, gas, and abdominal discomfort
Red yeast rice extract	16–20	21–25	Less than 5	6–15	Lowering LDL and triglycerides	Gastrointestinal discomfort, rash, headache

Continued from page 135

it also helps regulate blood pressure. So if you're worried about either your bones or your blood pressure (as most people should be) in addition to your cholesterol, you should be taking a calcium supplement. (Most multivitamins don't contain as much as you need.) Postmenopausal women and men over 65 need 1,500 milligrams; everyone else needs 1,000 to 1,200 milligrams. It's best to take it in divided doses twice a day.

Fenugreek. This Indian herb is often used to help nursing mothers produce more breast milk (as well as to flavor curries). According to several studies it may also be effective in lowering cholesterol. In one small study of 20 people, participants dropped their LDL cholesterol an average of 21 percent by mixing 18 grams of fenugreek powder into their food every day.

Licorice. An ingredient in licorice called glabridin delays LDL oxidation, a main contributing factor to plaque buildup. This may be one reason for low rates of athero-sclerosis in Asian countries like Mongolia and Vietnam, where people commonly chew licorice. Chewing licorice releases enzymes that break down the glabridin, enabling the body to absorb it. In one Israeli study, after 20 medical students took 100 milligrams of licorice extract tablets daily for two weeks, the LDL in their blood was 80 percent more resistant to oxidation than that of a control group. Don't try to get your glabridin from licorice whips, however. It's found in the parts of the root thrown away after the candy is made. Instead, look for extracts, capsules, or wafers labeled DGL, or deglycyrrhizinated. This means the product has been stripped of a compound in licorice that raises blood pressure.

Plant phytosterols. You may remember reading in Chapter 4 about cholesterol-lowering margarines that contain plant-based sterols (phytosterols). Sterols are so similar in chemical structure to cholesterol that they occupy the receptors for cholesterol in the intestine, blocking the absorption by the body of the cholesterol you eat. If you're not interested in sterol-based margarine spreads, you might consider taking phytosterol supplements, available as powders, capsules, or oils. Brands include Basikol, Kholesterol Blocker, Cholesterol Success, Cholestain, and Phytosterol Complex. Keep in mind, however, that as with sterol spreads, you should consider these medication and follow the dosage instructions carefully. In one small pilot study conducted by Mary McGowan, M.D., medical director of the Cholesterol Management Center at the New England Heart Institute, five patients (two of whom were also taking a statin drug) took 800 milligrams of Basikol twice daily with a meal. Total cholesterol fell an average of 13.2 percent, with a range of 6 to 24 percent, while LDL fell an average of 20 percent, with a range of 10.5 to 32 percent.

Policosanol. The latest cholesterol-lowering substance to hit the medical journals is a mixture of alcohols, purified either from sugar cane or beeswax. A group of Cuban researchers has published the bulk of the studies on policosanol, finding that at doses of 10 to 20 milligrams per day, policosanol lowers total cholesterol 17 to 21 percent and LDL 21 to 29 percent, while raising HDL 8 to 15 percent. In studies daily doses of only 10 milligrams a day were as effective in lowering total cholesterol or LDL as the same dose of Zocor (simvastatin) or Pravachol (pravastatin). The supplement appears safe, given evidence from people who have used it for more than three years.

Pycnogenol. This substance, found in pine bark, works as an antioxidant, neutralizing free radicals and thus preventing the oxidation of LDL. In one study 40 patients with chronic venous insufficiency (a condition that leads to swelling of the legs) were treated daily with either 600 milligrams of horse chestnut extract or 360 milligrams of pycnogenol for four weeks. The pycnogenol significantly decreased total cholesterol and LDL blood levels without affecting HDL levels.

Supplements, Not Cure-Alls

In the next few years you're bound to hear more and more about natural alternatives for lowering cholesterol and protecting the heart. But before you jump on any bandwagons, take heed: No supplement is a substitute for the lifestyle changes you'll be making on the *Live It Down Plan*, particularly the new eating habits you'll adopt. The fact is that scientists will probably never be able to duplicate the complex effects and myriad health benefits of foods like fruits, vegetables, and whole grains with a pill. And of course, lowering your cholesterol with supplements such as guggul while eating steak and ice cream with abandon, or taking hawthorn or CoQ10 to lower your blood pressure while doing nothing to alleviate the stress caused by your nerve-racking job, won't do your heart or your arteries much good in the end.

Finally, don't forget the three golden rules for taking supplements:

- **Don't keep it a secret.** Tell your doctor what you're taking.
- **More is not better.** Follow dosage directions.
- **Know what you're getting.** Look for USP and GMP labeling.

Next you'll read about another "supplement"—something you'll add to your life that's more important to your heart than any supplement in this chapter. It doesn't come in a pill or an extract, and it will take more than a few minutes to "swallow." But we guarantee it will make you feel more energetic, be happier, and sleep better. And of course, it will slash your risk of having a heart attack.

Live It Down | Exercise

When's the last time you changed the channel without using the remote? Walked to the store for milk instead of driving? Took the stairs instead of the elevator, or parked at the far end of the parking lot instead of circling around for five minutes looking for a closer space? If you're like most Americans, it's been awhile.

Desk jobs, television addiction, and convenience devices like remote controls and riding lawn mowers, coupled with our fixation on cars, have created a sedentary nation, with more than 6 of 10 American adults either inactive or underactive. Small wonder that this country is in the midst of an obesity epidemic.

What does this have to do with your heart? Everything. Moderate exercise alone isn't going to lower your cholesterol significantly, but it will help you avoid a heart attack—most likely the reason you wanted to lower your cholesterol in the first place. Exercise is a virtual panacea for the cardiovascular system, lowering blood pressure, reducing resting heart rate (so your heart doesn't have to work so hard to pump blood), making the blood less likely to form dangerous clots, and slightly dropping LDL and increasing HDL. It also helps your body utilize insulin and glucose, so you're less likely to develop metabolic syndrome or diabetes.

The link between exercise and heart disease has been clear for years, with lack of physical activity running second only to cigarette smoking as a risk factor for coronary heart disease. But a Duke University Medical Center study published in the November 7, 2002, *New England Journal of Medicine* showed for the first time that exercise by itself has beneficial effects on cholesterol, even without any accompanying weight loss. In the study the participants did the caloric equivalent of walking briskly or jogging 12 or 20 miles a week, exercising either vigorously or moderately. In terms of cholesterol benefits, the intensity made no difference; what was important was the amount of exercise. The more participants moved, the larger and fluffier their cholesterol particles became. Recall that it's the smaller, denser LDL particles that are most likely to burrow into the lining of the artery wall and cause plaque.

You simply cannot follow the *Live It Down Plan* without exercising because exercise is so vital to the overall health of your heart and blood vessels. It also facilitates weight loss, which reduces your triglyceride level. Even if you don't lose weight, physical activity can still help you live longer. Research from the Cooper Institute in Dallas found that being physically fit significantly protects against premature death, regardless of your weight. In fact, it showed that obese people who were fit had one-third the risk of premature death as their heavy but unfit counterparts—roughly the same risk as fit, lean men.

The Live It Down Plan
♥ Exercise

- At least 30 minutes of moderate exercise most days of the week. To help you reach this goal you'll use a pedometer to track your steps, aiming for 50,000 steps a week by the end of 12 weeks.
- Strength training to maintain muscle mass and boost metabolism. You can choose from our 10-Minute Tune-Up or 30-Minute Total Body Toner.
- Stretching to maintain flexibility. Our Clean-and-Stretch Series is so simple you can even do it in the shower.

Equally important are the benefits of physical activity to your mental state. Numerous studies point to aerobic exercise (like walking) as one of the best remedies for anxiety and depression, capable of boosting mood, self-esteem, and mental functioning. It can also help you deal with stress, which, as you'll find out in Chapter 7, is important to controlling your cholesterol and avoiding a heart attack. On the *Live It Down Plan* you won't have to train for a marathon or even join a gym. All the exercise we recommend—at least 30 minutes of walking on most days (more if you need to lose weight), plus a little strength training to keep your body toned and rev your metabolism—can be done with little or no equipment. The key is to get moving, feel better, have more energy, and become less susceptible to stress.

A few words of caution before you read further: If the most exercise you've gotten in the past year was running through the airport to catch a plane after standing in the security checkpoint for two hours, give your doctor a call. You need to get medical clearance before starting any program that increases your level of physical activity, as the *Live It Down Plan* will do. The same applies if you already have heart disease or any other chronic illness.

And start slow. Some of the main reasons people quit exercising are they overdo it early on, get injured, or become frustrated when they don't see quick results. So pace yourself—this is a lifelong proposition. And listen to your body. If it hurts a lot the next day, you've overdone it. If you get dizzy or feel nauseous, stop. The idea here is to improve your health, not harm it.

Your Walking Plan

To get your heart pumping hard enough to provide cardiac benefits, all you need is a decent pair of walking shoes. According to the Harvard Nurses' Health Study, which followed 80,000 women for more than 20 years, just a half hour of brisk walking a day—that's 30 minutes, or the time it takes to watch one sitcom—can slash your risk of a heart attack by 30 to 40 percent.

There are many reasons we chose walking as the core of the *Live It Down* exercise plan. Among them:

Walking is safer than jogging. Because a walker lands with just one-fifth the force of a runner, walking is much easier on your joints and ligaments.

Anyone can walk. It's a good option even for people who are pregnant, have arthritis, have heart disease, or are just recovering from a heart attack.

It's inexpensive. A pair of shoes and socks are all you need. (Well, you should wear clothes.)

You'll stick with it. Only 25 percent of people who walk for exercise quit, compared to 50 or 60 percent of those who start other exercises.

You can do it anywhere, anytime. Bad weather? Walk in the mall. On vacation? Walking is a great way to see the sites. Overdue for an outing with friends? Schedule a scenic hike.

It's easy to vary the intensity. To work harder, walk faster or walk up and down

Your Target Heart Rate

To get the most from aerobic exercises such as walking, the American College of Sports Medicine suggests maintaining a heart rate between 60 and 80 percent of your maximum heart rate for at least 20 minutes of exercise. Your maximum heart rate is 220 minus your age. Unless you're wearing a heart-rate monitor, you'll need to stop exercising to take your pulse. To do it quickly, count the pulses in 10 seconds, then multiply by 6. There's no need to do this every time you exercise, just now and then to make sure you're working at the right intensity level.

Age	Target heart rate	
	60% of max.	80% of max.
30	114	152
35	111	148
40	108	144
45	105	140
50	102	136
55	99	132
60	96	128

stairs or hills. Feeling tired or recovering from an illness? Slow it down.

On the *Live It Down Plan* we want you to build you way up to walking at least 30 minutes a day (60 if you need to lose weight) on most days. On top of that you'll look for opportunities to fit walking into the rest of your day.

Before you begin, find out where you stand now in terms of aerobic fitness. Walk a mile (that's four laps around a high school track). Record how long it takes you and what your heart rate, or pulse, is immediately after you finish. Try this again in four weeks. Chances are your time, heart rate, or both will have improved. (If you walk faster as you get fitter, your heart rate may not decrease.) To take your pulse, place two fingers on your wrist near your thumb, or on the side of your neck just below your Adam's apple. Adjust your fingers until you feel a strong pulse. Count the number of pulses in 30 seconds, then multiply by 2. (For an even quicker pulse check, see the box at left.)

The Little Gadget that Could

Who would have thought that something smaller than a deck of cards and cheaper than a pair of sneakers could make all the difference when it comes to getting yourself to walk more? We're talking about a pedometer, a device that senses your body motion and counts your steps, then converts that number into distance based on the length of your stride. On the *Live It Down Plan* we encourage you to buy a pedometer and keep track of the steps you take every day, aiming for a goal of 50,000 steps a week by the end of 12 weeks.

"We have found inexpensive, electronic step-counters to be a fabulous tool for motivating people to increase physical activity," says James O. Hill, Ph.D., director of the Center for Human Nutrition at the University of Colorado Health Sciences Center in Denver. The Center is working to get people throughout the entire state of Colorado to track their steps as they walk their way to fitness.

While pedometers have just begun to take off in the United States, they've been popular in Japan for more than 30 years, and the average Japanese family owns 3.2 of them. Pedometers make physical activity fun, and they tap into our competitive

Pick the Right Pedometer

Pedometers have gone upscale. Today they can read your pulse, estimate the calories you've burned, time your activity, and estimate your speed, as well as provide music to move you along on your walk. With literally hundreds of brands and styles out there, it can be daunting to choose the right one. Here are six of our favorites. All require you to enter your stride length, which is easy enough to do. Just walk 10 steps, measure the distance in feet, and divide by 10.

Brand	Features	Price
BodyTrends Full Function Pedometer	• Automatic start/stop records time only while in motion. • Calculates average speed. • Counts number of steps up to 99,999. • Belt clip.	$21
Brunton's Digital Pedometer with Alarm	• Calorie counter. • Built-in panic alarm. • Backlit digital crystal display.	$30
New Lifestyles Digiwalker SW-401	• SW series often used by researchers in scientific studies. • Distance meter. • Security strap.	$30
Oregon Scientific's PE316FM	• FM radio. • Digital 12/24 hour clock. • Miniature earphone buttons.	$30
Sportline's Fitness Pedometer 360	• Measures calories burned. • Digital seven-day walking log. • Odometer. • Automatic start; stops after four minutes of stillness.	$40
Sportbrain	• Comes with cradle for uploading data to www.sportbrain.com Web site, where you can track your fitness.	$99

streak by enabling us to compete against ourselves or others. On average, sedentary people take only 2,000 to 3,000 steps a day. But studies find that taking 6,000 steps a day significantly reduces the risk of death. Adding 2,000 steps, or about 1 mile a day, will help you maintain your current weight and stop gaining weight. That takes only about 15 to 20 minutes, which you can spread over the course of your day.

Tricks of the Trade

Walking is a gentle sport, but you do need to pay attention to your form and protect your body from any strains or injuries. It's not difficult—just follow these tips:

Stretches for Walkers

Every time your foot strikes the ground, your muscles and joints receive a load roughly 1.5 times your body weight. To prevent injuries, walk in place for a few minutes to warm up your muscles, then do these four stretches before setting out. After stretching one side, switch sides and repeat. Stretch several times on each side.

1 Calf stretch
Stand about 2 feet from a wall and place your hands on the wall. Extend your right leg about 2 feet behind you. Bending your left leg, lean forward while keeping your right heel on the ground.

2 Achilles stretch
Place your right leg in front of the left and bend the left knee toward the ground, keeping your heel on the ground. This stretches the Achilles tendon and the soleus muscle, which lies underneath the calf.

- When possible walk on a soft surface such as a running track, dirt road, or grass, instead of a hard sidewalk or road, to cushion the impact on your joints.
- Increase your mileage or time in small increments. In other words, don't go from 0 to 5 miles in two days.
- Keep your arms bent at a 90-degree angle.
- Hold your body fully upright, with your shoulders pulled slightly back and pushed down, not rounded. (Try to squeeze or pinch your shoulder blades together.) Don't thrust your head forward; keep your ears aligned with your shoulders. Your hands should be slightly clenched.

3 Hamstring stretch

Place your left foot on a curb or bench. Keeping the heel of your right foot on the floor, slowly lean forward, without rounding your back, until you feel the stretch in your hamstring (the back of the leg from behind the knee up to the buttock).

4 Lower back stretch

Lie on your back with your knees bent and your arms away from your body. Keep your knees and ankles together throughout the stretch (imagine a piece of rope is tied around your ankles). Slowly let your legs drop to the left. (In the beginning your knees may not touch the floor.)

The exercise routines in this book were developed by exercise physiologist Michael Wood, C.S.C.S., director of the Sports Performance Group in North Attleboro, Massachusetts.

- Bring your hands no higher than shoulder height in the forward motion, and keep them by the side of your body in the backward motion. This is especially important if you're using hand weights for added resistance. And stay away from ankle weights while walking; using them can throw off your natural gait, which may lead to injuries.

Walk in the Right Shoes

While you can walk in any pair of sturdy, comfortable shoes, you may want to invest in a pair of sneakers specifically designed for walking. If you do, follow these tips:

Start with socks. While you're at the shoe store, buy some new socks, too. Look for padded socks made of acrylic. Acrylic tends to wick away perspiration—which active feet can produce from 250,000 sweat glands at a rate of 4 to 6 ounces a day—better than cotton or wool.

Get the timing right. Try shoes on in the afternoon, since your feet swell enough during the day to affect your shoe size. Make sure to try them on with athletic socks.

Go for a three-way fit. The longest of your toes should clear the end of the shoe by about one-half inch (about the width of your thumb). The ball of your foot should fit comfortably into the widest part of the shoe. And the heel of your foot should fit snugly in the back without any slippage.

Replace shoes often. Trade in your shoes when you've walked 350 to 550 miles in them. If you're logging about 15 miles a week (2 to 3 miles a day, five days a week), that means replacing them about every six months. Once your shoes have covered that much distance they will have lost their shock-absorption capacity and some of their stability. To see if it's time for a new pair, place your shoes on a table and look at them from behind. Check for wear and tear of the sole. If they're leaning to one side, the midsole cushioning is probably shot. The next time you're in a shoe store, try on a new pair of the model that you are currently wearing. If the cushioning in your shoes feels dead in comparison, it probably is.

Hitting Your Stride

Your goal is to walk for at least 30 minutes on most days of the week and also to look for other opportunities during the day to be active so you can log 50,000 steps on most days by the end of the 12 weeks. Keep your pedometer on all day to encourage yourself to walk when you might otherwise drive or sit still. (The 12-week Plan starting on page 206 will ask you to write down the number of steps you take every day.) If you take an hour-long walk, you're almost there. If you take a 30-minute walk, you'll need to fit more walking into the rest of your day. Here are some ways to do it:

- Park as far as possible from entrances at work, shopping centers, or restaurants.
- If you take the bus, get off a stop or two early and hoof it the rest of the way.

- Pace instead of standing while talking on the phone or waiting for the elevator.
- Take the stairs rather than the elevator.
- Hide the remote and use commercials as your signal to get up and walk up and down the stairs or circle your house until the program comes back on.
- Return the shopping cart all the way into the store.
- Get a dog and do not fence your yard. You'll have no choice but to walk Rover at least three times a day. (Rover will love you for it.)
- Can't get a dog? Volunteer to walk a neighbor's pooch or the dogs at your local animal shelter.
- Get up and talk to your coworkers instead of e-mailing them.
- Use the rest room, copy machine, or water fountain farthest from your work area.
- Find a walking buddy. Studies show that people are more likely to stick with an exercise program if they're doing it with someone. Invite a neighbor, relative, or coworker to hit the ground walking.
- Get a freezer or refrigerator for the garage or basement and keep some staples there. It forces you to walk back and forth several times a day.

Other Cool Gadgets

In addition to pedometers, there are numerous other accessories to help you track your activity and measure your results. While you don't *need* any of them, some might help with that most important component of exercise: motivation.

Walking speedometer. As if knowing how far you're going wasn't enough, now you can track your speed and even your position on the globe. Some walking speedometers include global positioning system (GPS) technology, which maps your location. Most attach to your shoe. Prices vary considerably. A basic model will cost about $125; one with GPS can be upwards of $200.

Heart rate monitor. Most look like wristwatches, but instead of telling time, they tell your heart rate, beeping when it gets too high or too low. Some models also calculate calories burned as you exercise. Cost is $60 and up. For a good selection check out www.heart-rate-monitor.com.

Personal pulse meter. The low-cost alternative to the heart rate monitor, this gadget—worn on your wrist or around your neck—uses a finger pad pulse sensor to deliver quick readings of your heart rate. It includes a timer and clock and costs about $20.

Digital wrist blood pressure monitor. About the size of a wristwatch, these monitors include memory to store and review findings. Cost is about $70.

Body fat monitor. These come in two main styles: a scale you step on or a small, handheld device. Cost is between $60 and $90.

A Strong Case for Strength Training

Undoubtedly the best workouts for your heart are aerobic activities like walking, running, swimming, biking, dancing, or really vigorous housework or yard work. But aerobic exercise isn't the only kind shown to help your heart. Strength training—the type of exercise that builds muscle mass—may also be important to your heart (and it's certainly important to the rest of your body).

In a study published in the *British Journal of Sports Medicine,* strength training lowered total cholesterol 10 percent and LDL cholesterol 14 percent, and also reduced body fat in 24 women who worked out for 45 to 50 minutes three times a week. Strength training also guards against osteoporosis, helps protect your joints, and revs your metabolism, since muscle tissue burns calories much faster than fat tissue does. And of course being strong lets you put more muscle behind everyday tasks like carrying groceries and grandkids, so you'll tire less easily and be less prone to injury. A side benefit: When you tighten up sagging muscles, you look better!

Muscle mass peaks around age 30 and then gradually declines until your fifties, when it tends to go downhill fast. And while walking is terrific for your heart and your legs, it doesn't work the rest of the body very hard. So we're going to ask you to do a bit of strength training in addition to your walking.

If you picture weight lifters heaving hundreds of pounds over their heads or gym fanatics pushing themselves to the limit when you imagine strength training, take heart: We don't have anything like that in mind for you. Just some simple moves that you can do in the comfort and privacy of your own living room. Most of them don't even require dumbbells. And don't worry about "bulking up" too much. It takes hours of work a day to build big muscles; it won't happen by accident.

So how much do we want you to do? How does 10 minutes a day sound? If that's all the time you can spare, or you're out of shape now, start with our 10-Minute Tune-Up beginning on page 149. Try to do it four times a week. Once you master these moves and your body is ready for a slightly more challenging workout, try the 30-Minute Total Body Toner starting on page 153. Aim to do it at least twice a week.

Perform the exercises slowly and deliberately; there's no sense rushing through them—you'll only be courting injury. To protect your back, keep your stomach muscles tensed throughout these exercises.

10-Minute Tune-Up

Perform one set of 8 to 12 repetitions (on each side of the body, where appropriate) for all exercises in this group except the wall sit (below); hold the wall sit for 20 to 30 seconds. All movements should be performed in a slow and controlled manner.

1 Wall sit

Muscles worked: thighs, hamstrings, and buttocks

In a standing position, put your back against a wall with your feet approximately 18 inches from the wall and shoulder-width apart. Now slowly lower yourself as if you're going to sit in an invisible chair, keeping your back against the wall, until your knees are bent almost at a 90-degree angle. If your knees extend beyond your toes, move your feet further from the wall.

(Continued)

10-Minute Tune-Up *(continued)*

2 Outer leg lift
Muscles worked: hips

Lie on your left side, supporting your head with your left hand and your body with the right, as shown. Tighten your abdominal muscles, lift your right leg 45 degrees, then lower. Remember to keep your top hip aligned over your bottom hip; in other words, don't lean back while performing the exercise.

3 Inner leg lift
Muscles worked: inner thighs

Lie on your left side as in the exercise above. Keeping your left leg straight, cross your right leg over your left leg. Grab your right ankle for support. Tighten your stomach muscles, raise your left leg approximately 30 to 45 degrees, then lower.

4 Modified push-up
Muscles worked: arms and chest

Start on your hands and knees, your arms straight, and your hands under your shoulders and slightly wider than shoulder-width apart. Slowly lower your body until your upper arms are parallel with the floor. Return to starting position. When performing this exercise keep your back flat. Inhale on the way down and exhale on the way up.

5 Hip extension
Muscles worked: buttocks
Start in a kneeling position with your forearms on the ground. Bring the sole of your right foot toward the ceiling, keeping your leg bent at a 90-degree angle. Return to starting position.

(Continued)

6 Crunch
Muscles worked: abdominals

Lie on your back with your knees and hips at a 90-degree angle, as shown. Raise your chest toward your thighs until your shoulder blades clear the floor. Keep your thighs vertical; they shouldn't move forward. Return to starting position.

7 Superman
Muscles worked: lower back, buttocks, and hamstrings

Lie on your stomach with your arms stretched in front of you. Keep your hips in contact with the floor throughout the exercise. Simultaneously raise one leg and the opposite arm. Lower and then immediately repeat on the other side.

30-Minute Total Body Toner

For some of these exercises you'll need a pair of light hand weights. (The dumbbells pictured are 8-pound weights.) Perform each exercise 8 to 12 times (on each side of the body, where appropriate) or as noted. Work through the exercises with minimal rest in between. Then rest for three to five minutes, and perform the entire routine one more time. To protect your back and make sure you're working the right muscles, keep your stomach muscles tensed throughout each exercise.

1 Lunge
Muscles worked: quadriceps, hamstrings, and buttocks
Take a giant step forward with your right foot, planting the foot firmly in front of you. As you step, keeping your upper body straight, bend your right leg at a 90-degree angle. (Don't extend your knee past your toes.) You'll end up on the ball of your left foot. Hold the position briefly, then press back up to starting position.

(Continued)

30-Minute Total Body Toner *(continued)*

2 Bent row

Muscles worked: back and posterior shoulders

For this exercise you'll need a bench or table. From a standing position, support your upper body with your left arm as shown. Hold a dumbbell in your right hand, with the arm hanging directly below your shoulder. Pull the weight upward to your underarm, keeping your elbow close to your side. Work on pulling the weight from your elbow rather than from your hand. Slowly return to starting position.

3 Upright row

Muscles worked: forearms, shoulders, and upper back

Start with weights resting on your thighs while you're standing up. Pull weights up toward your chest, keeping your elbows higher than your hands. Pause and return to starting position.

4 Push-up

Muscles worked: chest and arms

Start with your arms fully extended, as shown. Lower yourself down until your upper arms are parallel with the floor. Inhale on the way down and exhale as you return to starting position. Keep your abdominal and buttock muscles tensed throughout the exercise.

(Continued)

30-Minute Total Body Toner *(continued)*

5 Push press
Muscles worked: shoulders and arms

Hold a dumbbell in each hand at shoulder height, as shown. Begin with your knees slightly bent and your abdominal muscles tensed. Press the weights over your head until your arms are almost straight, simultaneously straightening your legs. Return to starting position and repeat.

6 Opposite arm/opposite leg
Muscles worked: lower back, posterior legs, and shoulders

While on all fours, raise your right leg and left arm parallel to the floor as shown. Pause for 2 to 3 seconds, return, then immediately repeat on the other side.

7 The bicycle

Muscles worked: abdominals

Lie on your back with your knees bent and your hands on the sides of your head (not behind your head). Raise your feet and shoulders off the floor. Bring your right knee toward your chest and your left elbow toward your right knee. Return to starting position and repeat on the opposite side. Keep your shoulder blades off the floor throughout the exercise. Perform 16 total repetitions.

Stretching Your Limits

Chances are it's been years since you could touch your toes. You're not alone. The trouble with losing your flexibility as you get older is that you lose your full range of motion, and that poses a problem if you want to be active (or, frankly, even if you don't). Flexibility protects you against injuries and pain. It can also help you maintain good posture. But it won't happen naturally, given today's sedentary lifestyles. You have to work at it.

The Clean-and-Stretch Series

Here's a great stretching routine that's so simple you can even do it in the shower. Just make sure you have a slip-free shower mat and you're careful not to fall. If you're at all unsteady in the shower, or you get dizzy, do these stretches on dry land.

1 Calf stretch
Stand several inches from the back wall of the shower (or another wall). Place your forearms on the wall. Extend your right leg about 2 feet behind your left. Lean forward, bending your left knee and keeping the heel of your right foot down. Repeat on the other side.

2 Quadriceps stretch
Relax your lower back. With your left hand on the shower wall for balance, bend your right knee, grab your foot, and pull it toward your buttock until you feel a gentle stretch along the front of your thigh (quadriceps). Do not try to touch your foot to your buttock, and do not pull the foot to either side. Repeat on the other side.

It doesn't take much—just a few simple stretches performed once or twice a day. Not only does stretching help keep your body limber, it's a terrific way to relax and relieve tension. Our stretching routine is so simple that you can even do it in the shower. (It's best, and safest, to stretch muscles when they are warm—as they are in the shower or after physical activity.) Stretch to the point of tension but not pain. And never bounce while stretching; instead, move into the stretch slowly, and hold the position for 30 seconds.

4 Shoulder stretch

While standing, grab your right elbow with your left hand and pull it straight across your chest until you feel a gentle stretch in the back of your shoulder.

3 Hamstring stretch

Place your right foot several inches in front of your left. Keeping the heel of your left leg on the floor, slowly lean forward, without rounding your back, until you feel the stretch in your hamstring.(You may want to put your hands on the wall for support.) Switch legs and repeat.

5 Neck stretch

Keeping your head in line with your shoulders (in other words, don't bend it forward or backward), slowly bend your neck to the side until you feel a gentle stretch along the opposite side of your neck. Repeat on the other side.

Other Ways to Get Your Exercise

Variety is the spice of life, and exercise comes in as many varieties as you could want. Whether it's walking, tai chi, tennis, gardening, or swimming, the key is to find something you enjoy and keep doing it. (Having a few options to choose from so you can vary your routine helps.) Here are a few fun, inexpensive ideas to try:

Exercise Balls

One of the hottest exercise trends to hit the country in recent years involves nothing more than a brightly colored, oversized plastic ball. Physical therapists have been using these giant balls for years; finally they're available to the rest of us. The balls are used in a variety of exercise moves and routines to improve your balance, coordination, strength, flexibility, and posture, primarily by helping you strengthen your body's core muscles: the abdomen, back, and sides.

The balls trump other exercise routines for numerous reasons, says Liz Applegate, Ph.D., author of *Bounce Your Body Beautiful: Six Weeks to a Sexier, Firmer Body.* They're portable—you can even deflate one and bring it with you when you travel; they are attractive, so you don't have to "hide" it in the basement; and they're efficient. For every exercise you do, the rest of your body also gets a workout. They're also inexpensive, starting at around $25. You can buy your ball from sporting goods stores, shop online at sites such as www.balldynamics.com, or call 800-752-2255.

Pilates

If you're looking to simultaneously strengthen your muscles, become more flexible, and improve your posture, look to Pilates. One of the latest fitness trends, Pilates is embraced by movie stars and professional dancers, who value its integration of mind and body and its ability to help them maintain a lean shape. It was developed by a German man named Joseph Pilates in the early 20th century as a way to regain his strength after he spent much of his childhood as an invalid. It focuses on using the body's core muscles to support you as you move through large ranges of motion.

Many Pilates exercises require only an exercise mat, although some utilize large pieces of equipment involving pulleys. (For access to these, you'll need to sign up for a class. Look for a certified Pilates instructor—many are not certified—by logging onto www.pilates-studio.com.) The "mind" portion of Pilates comes with the intense concentration on the quality of the highly controlled movements. For a Pilates workout you can do at home, check out these videos:

- "Pilates for Dummies," with Michelle Dozios. A good, basic workout for beginners.
- The Method, with Jennifer Kries. This is a series of videos, both for beginners and those who have done Pilates before.

160

- "Stott Pilates —Advanced Matwork," with Moira Stott-Merrithew, one of the gurus of the Pilates movement. This is for a more advanced participant, although Stott-Merrithew also makes a video for beginners.

Resistance Bands

Remember as a kid how you would stretch a rubber band against your index finger and fling it across the room at your brother? Well, the same concept is at work with exercise resistance bands, only there's no flinging involved, and it's not your index finger that gets the workout but nearly every other muscle in your body. Resistance bands use your own body weight instead of dumbbells to provide resistance.

Generally, you slip a band around your foot or arm and lift or extend the limb, working against the band's resistance. You can also secure the band to a door or bar. The bands are not only portable, they're cheap: You can find them in sporting goods stores for under $15. They come in different lengths and degrees of resistance. The shorter bands are used to strengthen hips, ankles, wrists, and hands, while longer bands are best for legs and arms. Both are usually color coded: Yellow provides the least resistance, followed by green, red, blue, and black. For a good video introduction to using the resistance bands, check out "Denise Austin—Pilates for Every Body." (The makers of the video call it a Pilates workout, but true Pilates does not involve resistance bands.) A number of other toning and strengthening videos incorporate resistance band exercises into their routine.

Exercise Your Options

On the *Live It Down Plan* we recommend at least 30 minutes of brisk walking on most days of the week, but you can substitute any of the following activities. They are all considered moderate exercise—defined by the U.S. Surgeon General as anything that burns an average of 4 to 7 calories per minute.

Washing and waxing a car for 45–60 minutes.
Washing windows or floors for 45–60 minutes.
Playing volleyball for 45 minutes.
Gardening for 30–45 minutes.
Wheeling self in wheelchair for 30–40 minutes.
Bicycling 5 miles in 30 minutes.
Dancing fast (social) for 30 minutes.
Raking leaves for 30 minutes.
Water aerobics for 30 minutes.
Swimming laps for 20 minutes.
Basketball (a game) for 15–20 minutes.
Bicycling 4 miles in 15 minutes.
Jumping rope for 15 minutes.
Shoveling snow for 15 minutes.
Stair-walking for 15 minutes.

Source: Surgeon General's report on Physical Activity and Health, 1996

Moving Without Exercising

Exercise doesn't have to involve equipment or even a special time set aside in your day. Any kind of movement that increases your heart rate provides benefits. That includes everything from house cleaning to dancing to gardening, as long as you accumulate at least 30 minutes of such activity per day.

If your hobby involves being physically active, perfect! Just consider the workout you get from gardening. Between edging and raking the lawn, walking back and forth to the mulch pile, pulling weeds, digging holes, and planting seeds, gardening uses all of the major muscle groups. And half an hour of general gardening burns about 202 calories in a 185-pound person. One study even found that gardening could reduce insulin resistance, a condition that could lead to metabolic syndrome or diabetes, both of which significantly increase your risk of heart disease. It's even been suggested that urban gardens be used to improve public health, not only by providing fresh produce, but also by providing exercise. To get the most out of gardening, nix the gadgets that make it easier, such as electric weed-whackers.

In addition to gardening, simply eschewing convenience devices like remote controls and garage-door openers can make a big difference in terms of the calories you burn and your overall amount of physical activity.

Putting it All Together

No matter what type of exercise you choose, remember that the goal isn't to add exercise to your life but to make it a permanent part of your life, along with eating, sleeping, and brushing your teeth. So build walks into your schedule and let your family and friends know those outings aren't expendable. If you're having trouble fitting walking—or any other exercise—into your day, make it the first thing you do in the morning so it won't get "bumped" by work, chores, or other activities. On days when you don't walk, don't just sit there—rake the lawn, wash the car, pop in an exercise video, or go for a bike ride. Remember, the goal is to be physically active for at least 30 minutes a day on most days of the week.

Once your body gets used to moving, you may actually start to crave exercise because it simply feels good. People who exercise sleep better and have more energy and a brighter outlook on life. And there's another benefit: Even one walk or workout can blast away stress. That's important because, as you'll read in the next chapter, stress is a major contributor to heart disease and heart attacks. Read on to find out more—but first, get up, lace your shoes, and take your first steps toward a healthier heart and a more active life!

Live It Down | Stress

In 1983 *Time* magazine declared that stress was "the epidemic of the
'80s." What does that say about us now? In the two decades since that
declaration, we've welcomed into our lives cell phones, beepers, the
Internet, 24-hour news, and self-managed retirement plans. The workplace has been revolutionized—a few times. So have the financial markets.
Shopping choices have proliferated (funny how tomatoes now come in
grape, cherry, plum, and pear variations), meaning decision-making is
harder than ever. Beyond our control are the more insidious concerns of
terrorism, a one-world economy, and global warming. If someone asked
you to describe life today in one word, it's a pretty good bet that word
wouldn't be "calm," "serene," or "tranquil."

Given its profound influence on our physical and mental well-being, stress may well
be America's No. 1 health problem. The American Institute of Stress estimates that
75 to 90 percent of all visits to primary care physicians are for illnesses caused or
made worse by stress. Included in that category are high cholesterol, high blood
pressure, and heart disease. That's why the *Live It Down Plan's* stress-reduction
component is so important. If you can learn how to relax and be more sanguine
about the "24-7" world we live in, you can make major progress in lowering your
heart attack risk and improving your life.

What Is Stress?

According to the *Encyclopedia of Stress*, "stress" is one of the most frequently used but ill-defined words in the English language. We say we're stressed when we're late for work and when we can't pay our bills. We laugh about the stress of the holidays and cry over the stress of a divorce. Even an ostensibly happy occasion—such as the birth of a child—can be stressful.

The encyclopedia defines stress as a "real or interpreted threat to the physiological or psychological integrity of an individual that results in physiological and/or behavioral responses." In other words, stress is any change in your world that evokes some reaction from you. If you're a neatness nut, having 10 people staying in your house for a long weekend could be incredibly stressful; but if you don't mind chaos and clutter, then let the fun begin. If you thrive on to-do lists and deadlines, a week with absolutely nothing to do and nowhere to go could make you crazy; another person might feel positively reborn.

"People talk about stress as though it's a bad thing," says stress researcher Catherine M. Stoney, Ph.D., a psychology professor at Ohio State University, "but stress exists inside us. It's really the interaction between what's in our environment and how we cope and deal with it."

Stress is often linked to a short-lived event, such as an argument. But it can be prolonged as well. In fact, the persistent yet subtle pressures of modern-day living are an ever-increasing—yet harder to diagnose—cause of stress. Doctors identify three main classes of stress:

Acute stress. This is the most common form, stemming from the demands and pressures of the recent past and the anticipated demands and pressures of the near future, such as a fast-approaching deadline. Acute

How Stressful Is Your Job?

What makes one job more stressful than another? The National Institute for Occupational Safety and Health lists several stress-causing workplace conditions, including these:

Design of tasks. Heavy workload, infrequent breaks, long hours, shift-work, hectic and routine tasks that have little inherent meaning and provide little sense of control.

Management style. Lack of participation by workers in decision-making, poor communication in the organization, lack of family-friendly policies.

Interpersonal relationships. Poor social environment and lack of support from coworkers and supervisors.

Work roles. Conflicting or uncertain job expectations, too much responsibility, too many "hats to wear."

Career concerns. Job insecurity, lack of opportunity for growth, advancement, or promotion; rapid changes for which workers are unprepared.

stress is the kind you encounter when you first find out you or someone you love has cancer; when you have a brand new baby; or when you first read a notice from the IRS asking about last year's taxes. It's what happens to your body when you swerve to avoid hitting a car or rush across town because you're late to an appointment.

Episodic acute stress. People in this category move from one episode of acute stress to another. Typically they live lives filled with chaos and crisis. They take on too much, they're always running late, and their homes are filled with clutter. They never seem to slow down, are quick to anger and, not coincidentally, have higher rates of heart disease. Some are worrywarts, who see disaster around every corner and who live their lives in a constant state of high anxiety.

Chronic stress. This is the subtler, prolonged stress—often linked to large life issues—that wears you down every day. It exists in the background of your daily routine. You become so used to it, you don't even know it's there anymore. It's caring for an aging parent or disabled child, working a job in which you have little control, trying to support your family on a salary that never seems to stretch far enough, or coping with a chronic illness like diabetes or heart disease. It's being trapped in a bad marriage, living in a war zone, or coping with a dysfunctional family.

Genetically, we're relatively well equipped to deal with acute stress. When we're confronted with a stressor—such as when someone suddenly shouts at you, or you're driving in the car and you have to swerve to avoid a collision—the body kicks into gear, releasing a flood of hormones such as adrenaline and cortisol, known as stress hormones. These, in turn, direct a well-orchestrated response throughout the body. Blood sugar level rises and metabolism speeds up to make more energy readily available. Breathing rate and oxygen consumption also increase, and blood flow changes, with blood being pulled from nonessential areas (like the digestive tract and the small muscles in the fingers and toes) and sent to the brain and major muscle groups that you use to fight or flee, primarily the arms, legs, and chest. Even the blood itself is affected, with clotting time decreasing so you're less likely to bleed to

---

The Live It Down Plan
 Stress

- Practice deep breathing to reduce your physical reactions to stress. This, in turn, reduces your risk of heart disease.
- "Spin" stressful or upsetting situations to help you view the world in a more positive light. You'll learn to handle the stressful events of everyday life with more aplomb and calm.
- Actively embrace the things that bring you pleasure, be they friends, hobbies, or spiritual pursuits.
- Each day try out one of the "20 Simple Ways to Get Happy" from the list of ideas that begins on page 177.

death if you're wounded. Meanwhile, the immune system goes dormant because it's not immediately critical to survival.

This fight-or-flight response enabled our ancestors to deal with a more hostile, physically demanding world of hunting, fighting, and surviving. All well and good for those instances when quick thinking and quick feet are necessary. But when stress hormones are continually released, when your body is continually in fight-or-flight mode, and yet you have no physical release for these surges of energy and hormones, then damage can occur.

Fitting Together Stress, Cholesterol, and Heart Disease

When researchers at Duke University Medical Center in Durham, North Carolina, asked women to recall a situation or event in their lives that made them angry, not only did the women's stress hormone levels spike, so did their cholesterol levels. And when researchers in Dr. Stoney's lab at Ohio State University studied male and female airline pilots, they found pilots' LDL levels rose about 5 percent during times of high occupational stress.

While the reasons for the stress-cholesterol connection are still under study, researchers have some theories. One is that stress hormones send a message to your body fat to give up some fatty acids—a way of ensuring you'll have enough energy if you have to move quickly. (This, of course, is an evolutionary response to the fact that our cave-dwelling ancestors were physically threatened quite often.) With that release—as well as the release of triglycerides from the liver—you have more fatty acids circulating in your blood for conversion to cholesterol, says Edward Suarez, Ph.D., associate professor of medical psychology at Duke.

But stress has heart-related effects far beyond cholesterol. Stress increases blood pressure, affecting the health of your arteries. And Dr. Stoney has found that even mild stress can increase blood levels of the amino acid homocysteine, which is a

Can Stress Trigger a Heart Attack?

The answer is yes—if you're already vulnerable to begin with. Here's how: A stressful situation raises blood pressure and heart rate, mimicking the effects of physical exertion. If you have plaque obstructing your arteries, the additional blood pressure can rupture the plaque. Stress also makes blood "stickier" and more likely to clot. Once blood cells begin sticking to the exposed plaque and blocking blood flow, you're in heart attack territory.

major contributor to heart disease. Stress can even affect how well you respond to medication if you already have heart disease.

In the long term stress can wreak havoc in another way. When you're stressed, notes Dr. Suarez, you're less likely to live in a healthy manner. If you're constantly busy, intense, or harried, you're more apt to grab a bag of chips or a fast-food meal than sit down to a salad and steamed fish. You're probably skipping your daily walk, maybe taking up smoking again, or overdoing the wine. And if you need comforting, well, which are you going to choose: the gallon of premium ice cream or the apple?

Stress can also affect you cognitively, altering the way you view and react to the world around you. For instance, when chronically stressed you're more likely to forget things, overreact to little annoyances (think road rage), or expect negative things to happen to you. You're less likely to shine at work, you may find yourself unusually impatient or argumentative, or you may have problems relating to friends or family. You're also more likely to become depressed, and as you read in Chapter 2, depression itself is a risk factor for heart disease.

Lower Your Cholesterol, Improve Your Mood

Lowering your cholesterol can improve your mood. When Canadian researchers compared mood changes in 212 patients being treated for high cholesterol, they found that people who reduced their levels of total cholesterol and LDL also reported feeling less anxious, with women showing the greatest improvement. There has always been a thread running through medical literature suggesting a correlation between mood and cholesterol levels. The reason for these findings, researchers speculate, may simply have to do with the mental boost you get when you improve your health.

Hostility and Heart Attacks

Everyone experiences stress now and then, but some people take stress a step further. Surely you're familiar with the classic Type A personality—the person who interrupts while you're speaking, tailgates the car in front, gives new meaning to the word "impatient," and is quick to snap when things go wrong. For years researchers knew that such people were more likely to have heart disease and heart attacks. Now they're learning why. A principal culprit, it seems, is hostility. At Dr. Stoney's lab, researchers are focusing on a particular kind of hostility called aggressive responding. Aggressive responders tend to have a tough, somewhat cold-hearted view of the world and people around them. They agree with statements like, "I don't blame anyone for grabbing everything he can in this world," and, "I don't try to cover up my poor opinion or pity of another person."

The same researchers also found that people with a trait called cynical hostility were more likely to show areas of dead tissue, or evidence of small heart attacks, in their heart. These people would agree with statements like, "Most people would lie to get ahead," and, "People seek friends who are likely to be useful to them."

Hostility may be so physically damaging that, according to a study published in the November 2002 issue of *Health Psychology*, it may trump overweight, cigarette smoking, and even high cholesterol as a predictor of heart disease. In the study, which looked at 774 men with an average age of 60, the researchers found that the more hostile the men were, the more likely they were to suffer from heart disease—regardless of any other risk factors, including high cholesterol.

Live It Down Stress Solutions

The reality is that you can't completely eliminate stress from your life—nor would you want to. Boredom can be just as stressful in its own way as racing to mail your taxes at 11:50 p.m. on April 15. But you can change the way you react to stress. And that's what counts. When researchers look more closely at the stress-heart disease connection, they find it isn't the stressor itself that's responsible for the negative health effects, Dr. Suarez says, but how much emotion that stressor arouses. The rest of this chapter, then, will focus on techniques for coping with stress in new, healthier ways.

1. Learn A Better Way to Breathe

As babies we instinctively know how to breathe properly. But as adults we tend to forget. Babies breathe with their whole bodies, their stomachs puffing out every time they breathe in and collapsing when they breathe out. Now check your own breathing. Place one hand on your chest and the other on your stomach, then take a normal breath. Which hand moved more? If you're like most people, neither moved much, but the hand on your chest probably moved a bit more. That's the habit of shallow breathing that most of us have acquired—and it's why we use barely 20 percent of our lungs' capacity when we breathe (even less when we're stressed). It's small wonder that scientists used to think anxiety and hysteria were essentially respiratory problems in nature and that they could be brought about by faulty breathing.

> You can use deep breathing to counter the fight-or-flight reaction any time you feel stressed.

While that may not be true, it is true that you can use deep breathing to counter the fight-or-flight reaction any time you feel stressed—whether you're seething in a traffic jam, worrying about a deadline, or replaying in your mind that fight with your spouse. "When you're stressed, you may be sitting on the outside but running on the inside," says Robert Fried, Ph.D., director of the Stress and Biofeedback Clinic at the Albert Ellis Institute and a senior professor of psychology at Hunter College, both in New York City. "Deep breathing for stress reduction means you're sitting on the outside and you're reposing on the inside."

Once you've learned to do deep breathing, says Dr. Fried, author of *Breathe Well, Be Well*, it takes less work to breathe, thus reducing the amount of work your body has to do and sending a message to your brain that you're inactive. After a while your body gets the signal and your heart rate and oxygen consumption slow.

Believe it or not, some people actually pay "breathing coaches" to help them breathe properly. But you don't have to do that. Instead, follow Dr. Fried's breathing exercise below to still your pounding heart, soothe your churning stomach, and send a signal throughout your body to slow down.

Rapid Alert Relaxation

This exercise combines deep breathing with mental imagery to help you feel relaxed yet alert. The results are immediate, so you can pull out the technique any time you need to feel calmer and more in control. Dr. Fried has used it in treating everything from tension and anxiety to burnout syndrome, panic disorder, agoraphobia, depression, tension headache, and high blood pressure.

A few notes of caution (yes, even something as seemingly innocuous as deep breathing isn't entirely risk-free—a testament to its power to effect change in the body). If you're not used to deep breathing, your diaphragm muscle will need time to adjust and become toned, so start slowly. If you experience cramps while doing the exercise, stop. Also, deep breathing may cause a significant decrease in blood pressure, so if you suffer from low blood pressure or fainting, be cautious when trying it. Check with your doctor before doing this exercise if you have a condition in which you may need to hyperventilate, such as diabetes or kidney disease. (Under certain circumstances hyperventilation may be the body's protection against diabetic acidosis.) And diabetics, take note: The sudden reduction in blood levels of certain stress hormones has been demonstrated to reduce the need for insulin and may cause your blood sugar to drop.

Abdominal breathing. Sitting comfortably, place your hands on your knees and relax. Now place one hand on your chest and one on your stomach. Breathe so that only the hand on your stomach moves.

Day 1. First, seat yourself comfortably, with your back supported by the back of the chair. Loosen any tight-fitting clothing and place your hands on your knees. Let yourself relax. Now you're ready to begin.

- Close your mouth and breathe through your nose only.
- Put one hand on your chest and the other on your stomach. As you inhale, hold your chest and don't let it rise. Let the hand on your abdomen rise as the air fills your lungs.
- Exhale slowly, pulling your abdomen back as far as it will go without letting that raise your chest in the process.

Spend a minute or so on this exercise. If you feel dizzy, you are working too hard. Stop and rest a little until the dizziness passes, then make the motions a little more subtle.

Day 2. Follow the same routine you followed yesterday, but practice the exercise for two to three minutes.

Day 3. Breathe for four minutes, and try the exercise without your hands. You should now be noticing that your inhale and exhale are approximately the same duration. There should be no pause before or after inhale or exhale—just one smooth motion. Your breathing rate may range between three and seven breaths per minute.

Day 4. Today you introduce imagery. Sit in your chair as before. Now:

- Close your eyes.
- Picture a very specific scene—the beach in July, a cool pine forest, swimming underwater. Try to put yourself in the scene—hear the sounds, feel the air (or water), smell the scents.
- As you focus on this scene, begin your deep breathing. Each time you inhale, imagine that you are breathing in the air of your scene, saying to yourself, "I feel awake, alert, and refreshed." And as you breathe out, feel the tension in your body flow out with your breath as you say to yourself, "I feel relaxed, warm, and comfortable."

Do this for four breaths, then stop. After a few minutes of rest, repeat the exercise. Try the routine once in the morning and once in the evening. After about three weeks, Dr. Fried recommends that you do the exercise in rounds of three: Four or five breathing cycles and a few moments of rest, followed by a second round of four or five breathing cycles and a few moments of rest, and finally a third round of four or five breathing cycles.

Once you've mastered deep breathing you can pull it out of your relaxation arsenal whenever life gets tense. Not only will it help slow your body down, but it may also, in effect, slow down time, providing those critical moments that are often the difference between exploding and maintaining your cool. As you breathe in and out,

Tracking Your Breathing

If you're serious about using slower, deeper breathing to help you destress and even lower your blood pressure, consider investing in a biofeedback device called RespeRate. The size of a paperback book, it analyzes your breathing via a sensor buckled around your waist, then plays a series of musical tones to guide you to a lower breathing rate. Several clinical studies published in peer-reviewed journals find that RespeRate lowers blood pressure, and the FDA approved it for over-the-counter sales in July 2002 for just that purpose. The $299 device is available online at www.resperate.com or by calling 1-877-988-9388.

release the physical tension and then ask yourself the following questions:

- Is the way I'm reacting to this situation increasing my tension?
- Is this reaction logical and reasonable?
- Is this reaction realistic?
- Is there another way to view the situation?

The answers may enable you to "spin" the stressful situation from the negative to the positive, or at least to the neutral. Read on to learn more about spinning as a powerful antistress strategy.

2. Practice the Art of Spinning

When you discovered you had high cholesterol, how did you react? Did you panic and begin picturing your own death from a heart attack? Or did you take a deep breath and view the diagnosis not as terrible news but as a kick in the pants to finally make some healthful lifestyle changes? If it's the latter, congratulations—you're a positive person, able to take potentially negative experiences and put a positive spin on them. If it's the former, well then, you're like all too many Americans these days … focusing more on the doom and gloom.

If you tend to view the glass as half empty, don't despair. A growing movement called "positive psychology" is identifying ways that even the most negative-minded people can reframe, or spin, their outlooks on events. Remember, it's not a stressful event that is detrimental to your heart, it's your reaction to it. So learning to think positively may be one of the best things you can do to lower your heart disease risk. Numerous studies find that optimistic people get fewer illnesses and recover better from coronary bypass surgery and cancer. Optimism may even protect older men against heart disease, according to one study.

> Learning to think positively may be one of the best things you can do to lower your heart disease risk.

Of course, optimism is not a new concept; even Virgil wrote of it in the *Aeneid* 2,000 years ago when he penned: "They can because they think they can." That can be a difficult outlook to maintain in today's stressful, complicated world. But a little practice goes a long way. The next time an event or situation starts to raise your ire or your anxiety level, keep in mind the following tips:

Don't take it personally. Rather than viewing setbacks as signs of their own incompetence, optimists view them as flukes or signals that a new approach is needed.

Take a tax audit, for example. Instead of whining about how it's just one more example of his lousy luck, an optimist would view it as a good opportunity to put his financial affairs in order, perhaps even winding up with some money back as errors in his favor are discovered. This doesn't mean, however, that you never accept blame for something that is your fault. But if you're an optimist, you accept the blame, learn from your mistake, and move on, rather than dwelling on the experience.

Maintain realistic expectations. There's no greater path to disappointment and frustration than setting your expectations too high. So if you expect that the cruise you're taking to the islands will be entirely trouble-free for the whole nine days, that every person you meet will become a new best friend, and that you definitely won't exceed the tight budget you have in mind, you're probably setting yourself up for some disappointment. Instead, stroll on board with the understanding that things

Write Your Way to Better Health

Sometimes the simple act of writing things down can help you clarify your feelings and render them less emotionally and physically stressful. Some studies even find that by reducing stress, keeping a journal can improve medical conditions such as asthma.

Simply venting on paper probably isn't enough, though. The key is not only to write about how you feel but to try to make sense of your emotions and learn from them. That's the finding of a study from the University of Iowa published in the August 2002 issue of the *Annals of Behavioral Medicine*. In the study, people who wrote about a negative life experience in just this way were more aware of benefits in their life following the event, such as improved relationships, greater personal strength, spiritual development, and a greater appreciation for life.

Journaling for stress relief doesn't mean writing down everything that happens to you every day. It means using your journal—whether it's on paper or on your computer—to write your emotions and your reactions to what's going on in your life. Sometimes your entries may take the form of a letter to a person with whom you're having a problem. Other times it may just be free-flow writing, with no stopping for spelling, punctuation, or grammar. The key is knowing that no one but you will see it and giving yourself permission to be totally honest in whatever you say. Then go back and read what you've written. Only by learning from the past will you be able to change in the future.

may not go exactly according to plan, but a cruise in the sunshine in February still beats sloshing through the snow at home.

Worry concretely. Just because you're trying to have a positive attitude doesn't mean you don't have worries. The key is how you handle those worries. Write them down, talk about them with a friend, and put them into form and shape, as in, "I'm worried that my husband will lose his job because his plant is having layoffs," rather than suffering with an amorphous sense of financial doom. Worrying about something

Scour Your Arteries with Meditation

Learning to meditate could actually help your body clean out its arteries, according to a study published in *Stroke*, a journal of the American Heart Association. The researchers assigned 60 African American men and women with high blood pressure to either a transcendental meditation (TM) program or a control group. The TM group practiced meditation 20 minutes twice a day. After seven months researchers found that the people in this group lowered their plaque levels (measured by carotid intima-media thickness, or IMT, which reflects the level of fatty substances deposited on the artery walls), reducing their overall heart attack risk up to 11 percent and their stroke risk up to 15 percent. The other group had no reduction; in fact, their plaque levels increased.

"Cardiovascular disease is associated with psychological stress," explained Amparo Castillo-Richmond, M.D., the study's lead author. "Previous research has found that the TM program decreases coronary heart disease risk factors, including hypertension, oxidized lipids, stress hormones, and psychological stress." Moreover, according to the researchers, the state of "restful alertness" brought on by meditation may trigger the body's self-repair mechanisms.

A later study found that when it comes to reducing atherosclerosis, the overall effectiveness of a program that involved meditation and yoga along with a high-fiber, low-fat diet, aerobic exercise, and antioxidant supplements was even greater than in studies involving cholesterol-lowering drugs.

specific is less consuming and less damaging than general anxiety. Anxiety that's unfocused can lead to less logical, less effective responses.

Act happy. "We can act ourselves into a frame of mind," says David Myers, Ph.D., a professor of psychology at Hope College (yes, *Hope* College) in Holland, Michigan. "Manipulated into a smiling expression, people feel better; when they scowl, the whole world seems to scowl back." So as the song goes, put on a happy face. Talk as if you feel positive, outgoing, and optimistic. Going through the motions often can help trigger the emotions.

Understand that enduring happiness doesn't come from wealth. It's one of the great myths of our time: Being rich, famous, or powerful automatically makes you happy. In fact, there are those who would argue the opposite, that too many people at the higher rungs of success have lost their perspective, their humanity, their values—and thus, their happiness. Doubtful? Listen to this: Studies find that everyday people who win the lottery are no happier a year later than they were before they won. The lesson: Tend to the things that make you happy and don't use other people's measures to define yourself.

Take control of your time. Happy people feel in control of their lives. They learn how to say no to activities they either don't want to do or don't have the time to do.

Reframe your perceptions. If you're faced with 20 guests for Thanksgiving dinner (tomorrow) and your dishwasher just broke, instead of panicking about having to wash dozens of dishes, consider it a good excuse to use fancy paper plates—and not wash any dishes at all.

Learn to forgive. Studies find that simply letting go of a grudge has numerous health benefits. In one study researchers found that people showed more signs of stress, including higher blood pressure and a faster heart rate, when they reflected on hurtful memories and grudges than when they imagined granting forgiveness to real-life offenders. In addition to the physical benefits of forgiveness, the act has emotional benefits. Once people truly forgive those who have hurt them, they often speak of feeling a weight lifted, feeling "lighter" and at peace. In one study people who attended a six-week forgiveness program were significantly more optimistic and willing to use forgiveness as a coping strategy months after the training ended than people who had been randomly assigned to a control group.

Read a book. Stress is a big issue for our society, and many savvy doctors, therapists, and spiritual leaders have written books on the topic. There are books that offer daily motivations, 12-week "happiness" programs, tips and advice, or merely reassurance. There are books on coping with grief, depression, lousy bosses, bad marriages, financial problems, and challenging kids. Rest assured that if you go into a bookstore, you'll probably find a book that speaks to whatever problem is causing you stress. Buying it could be an excellent investment in your well-being.

3. Go with the Flow

Creating a sense of peace and calm in your life means more than just coping with stress as best you can; it also means actively embracing those things that bring pleasure and satisfaction. A big part of doing this is finding work and hobbies that challenge you without overwhelming you.

Have you ever been so engrossed in an activity that you forgot to worry about your problems? "Happy people often are in a zone called 'flow,'" Dr. Myers says. That's when two hours fly by in two minutes because you're so involved in what you're doing. In one study researchers gave volunteers a pager and had them note what they were doing and how they felt every time they were beeped. They found people usually felt happier if they were mentally engaged by work or active leisure than if they were just sitting around. Ironically, the less expensive a leisure activity is, the more absorbed and happy people often are while doing it, Dr. Myers says.

Hobbies are not only soothing (for instance, more than half of women who crochet or knit say they do these activities to relax), they can provide a big dollop of self-esteem-boosting satisfaction at a job well done. Don't have a hobby? Not sure what to do with your spare time? To discover which activities are most satisfying to you—and to find new ones—try the following:

Track your time. For one week write down everything you do and rank it on a scale of 1 to 10 in terms of what gives you the most pleasure. The following week try to make sure the scales tip in favor of those things that satisfy you, even if it means giving up a chore or activity you think you have to do (but really don't).

Recall your youth. What did you love to do most when you were a child? Was it coloring? Then why not sign up for a drawing class? Helping your mom cook? Maybe you should spend more time in the kitchen. Making up plays and games? Consider joining a theater group. Riding your bike around the neighborhood? Bike riding is certainly an easy—and heart-healthy—activity to take up.

Explore your community. Too many of us live in ignorance of the many activities going on in our own backyards. So as you search for new experiences to embrace, look in your own community. Check out the course offerings at the local college or high school (some offer continuing education courses). Get on the mailing list for arts groups and concert halls. Scan the meetings and events notices on the bulletin board at the public library.

Schedule some fun. Just as you schedule dentist appointments, schedule some fun time. Try to plan a pleasurable activity at least once a week. And don't forget to put vacations—large or small—on the calendar a few times a year.

20 Simple Ways to Get Happy

Happiness is ephemeral, subject to the vagaries of everything from the weather to the size of your bank account. We're not suggesting that you can reach a permanent state called "happiness" and remain there. But there are many ways to swerve off the path of anxiety, anger, frustration, and sadness into a state of happiness once or even several times throughout the day. Here are 20 ideas to get you started. Choose the ones that work for you. If tuning out the news or making lists will serve only to stress you further, try another approach.

1. Practice mindfulness. Be in the moment. Instead of worrying about your checkup tomorrow while you have dinner with your family, focus on the here and now—the food, the company, the conversation.

2. Laugh out loud. Just anticipating a happy, funny event can raise levels of endorphins and other pleasure-inducing hormones and lower production of stress hormones. Researchers at the University of California, Irvine, tested 16 men who all agreed they thought a certain videotape was funny. Half were told three days in advance they would watch it. They started experiencing biological changes right away. When they actually watched the video, their levels of stress hormones dropped significantly, while their endorphin levels rose 27 percent and their growth hormone levels (indicating benefit to the immune system) rose 87 percent.

> Studies find music activates parts of the brain that produce happiness—the same parts activated by food or sex.

3. Go to sleep. We have become a nation of sleep-deprived citizens. Taking a daily nap or getting into bed at 8 p.m. one night with a good book—and turning the light out an hour later—can do more for your mood and outlook on life than any number of bubble baths or massages.

4. Hum along. Music soothes more than the savage beast. Studies find music activates parts of the brain that produce happiness—the same parts activated by food or sex. It's also relaxing. In one study older adults who listened to their choice of music during outpatient eye surgery had significantly lower heart rates, blood pressure, and cardiac workload (that is, their heart didn't have to work as hard) as those who had silent surgery.

5. Declutter. It's nearly impossible to meditate, breathe deeply, or simply relax when every surface is covered with papers and bills and magazines, your cabinets bulge, and you haven't balanced your checkbook in six months. Plus, the repetitive nature of certain cleaning tasks—such as sweeping, wiping, and scrubbing—can be meditative in and of itself if you focus on what you're doing.

6. Just say no. Eliminate activities that aren't necessary and that you don't enjoy. If there are enough people already to handle the church bazaar and you're feeling stressed by the thought of running the committee for yet another year, step down and let someone else handle things.

7. Make a list. There's nothing like writing down your tasks to help you organize your thoughts and calm your anxiety. Checking off each item provides a great sense of fulfillment.

8. Do one thing at a time. Dr. Suarez's research finds that people who multitask are more likely to have high blood pressure. Take that finding to heart. Instead of talking on the phone while you fold laundry or clean the kitchen, sit down in a comfortable chair and turn your entire attention over to the conversation. Instead of checking e-mail as you work on other projects, turn off your e-mail function until you finish the report you're writing. This is similar to the concept of mindfulness.

9. Garden. Not only will the fresh air and exercise provide their own stress reduction and feeling of well-being, but the sense of accomplishment that comes from clearing a weedy patch, watching seeds turn into flowers, or pruning out dead wood will last for hours, if not days.

10. Tune out the news. For one week go without reading the newspaper, watching the news, or scanning the headlines online. Instead, take a vacation from the misery we're exposed to every day via the media and use that time for a walk, a meditation session, or to write in your journal.

> People with pets had significantly lower heart rates and blood pressure levels when exposed to stressors than those without pets.

11. Take a dog for a walk. There are numerous studies that attest to the stress-relieving benefits of pets. In one analysis researchers evaluated the heart health of 240 couples, half of whom owned a pet. Those couples with pets had significantly lower heart rates and blood pressure levels when exposed to stressors than the couples who did not have pets. In fact, the pets worked even better at buffering stress than the spouses did.

12. Scent the air. Research finds that the benefits of aromatherapy in relieving stress are real. In one study people exposed to rosemary had lower anxiety levels, increased alertness, and performed math computations faster. Adults exposed to lavender showed an increase in the type of brain waves that suggest increased relaxation. Today you have a variety of room-scenting methods, from plug-in air fresheners to essential oil diffusers, potpourri, and scented candles.

13. Ignore the stock market. Simply getting your quarterly 401(k) statement can be enough to send your blood pressure skyrocketing. In fact, Chinese researchers found a direct link between the daily performance of the stock market and the mental health of those who closely followed it. Astute investors know that time heals most financial wounds, so give your investments time—and give yourself a break.

14. Visit a quiet place. Libraries, museums, gardens, and places of worship provide islands of peace and calm in today's frantic world. Find a quiet place near your house and make it your secret getaway.

15. Volunteer. Helping others enables you to put your own problems into perspective and also provides social interaction. While happy people are more likely to help others, helping others increases your happiness. One study found that volunteer work enhanced all six aspects of well-being: happiness, life satisfaction, self-esteem, sense of control over life, physical health, and depression.

16. Spend time alone. Although relationships are one of the best antidotes to stress, sometimes you need time alone to recharge and reflect. Take yourself out to lunch or to a movie, or simply spend an afternoon reading, browsing in a bookstore, or antiquing.

17. Walk mindfully. You probably already know that exercise is better than tranquilizers for relieving anxiety and stress. But what you do with your mind while you're walking can make your walk even more beneficial. In a study called the Ruth Stricker Mind/Body Study, researchers divided 135 people into five groups of walkers for 16 weeks. Group one walked briskly, group two at a slow pace, and group three at a slow pace while practicing "mindfulness," a mental technique to bring about the relaxation response, a physiological response in which the heart rate slows and blood pressure drops. This group was asked to pay attention to their footsteps, counting one, two, one, two, and to visualize the numbers in their mind. Group four practiced a form of tai chi, and group five served as the control, changing nothing about their lives. The group practicing mindfulness showed significant declines in anxiety and had fewer negative and more positive feelings about themselves. Overall they experienced the same stress-reducing effects of the brisk walkers. Better yet, the effects were evident immediately.

18. Give priority to close relationships. One study of more than 1,300 men and women of various ages found that those who had a lot of supportive friends were much more likely to have healthier blood pressure, cholesterol levels, blood sugar metabolism, and stress hormone levels than those with two or fewer close friends. Women, and to a lesser extent men, also seemed to benefit from good relationships with their parents and spouses. Studies also find that people who feel lonely, depressed, and isolated are three to five times more likely to get sick and die prematurely than those who have feelings of love, connection, and community.

19. Take care of the soul. In study after study, actively religious people are happier and cope better with crises, according to Dr. Myers. For many people faith provides a support community, a sense of life's meaning, feelings of ultimate acceptance, a reason to focus beyond yourself, and a timeless perspective on life's woes. Even if you're not religious, a strong spirituality may offer similar benefits.

20. Count your blessings. People who pause each day to reflect on some positive aspect of their lives (their health, friends, family, freedom, education, etc.) experience a heightened sense of well-being.

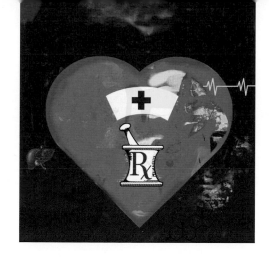

Live It Down | Drugs

Ideally, the *Live It Down Plan* is all you need to bring your cholesterol levels into the "safe" zone and reduce your risk of heart disease. But for some people it won't be enough. If your doctor suggests that you take a prescription drug, don't get upset. It doesn't mean you've failed, nor does it mean you should stop following the *Live It Down Plan*. Rather, it means you need a bit of help. Maybe you have a genetic predisposition to high cholesterol. In that case, making dietary changes, getting more exercise, and even taking supplements simply might not do the trick. So be thankful for the cholesterol-lowering drugs now available.

One major reason people live longer today than they did 50 years ago is the plethora of safe, effective medications at our disposal. True, all drugs have potential side effects, but so does crossing the street. Chosen wisely, medication is much more likely to contribute to your health, well-being, and longevity than to cause harm.

However—and this is critical—taking medication doesn't give you permission to dump the *Live It Down Plan* and start living on steak and potato chips. One major study found that only half of those people taking a cholesterol-lowering drug alone reached their cholesterol goals, compared to 80 percent of those who followed a diet and took medication. (Imagine the percentage if the researchers had also considered weight loss and exercise!) Also continue taking your supplements (make sure your doctor knows what you're taking). Depending on the supplements you're using and the medication prescribed, you may be able to get by with a lower dose of the drug.

Medication: For You? For Life?

As we talked about in Chapter 3 (remember the quiz beginning on page 65?), your levels of cholesterol, combined with your other risk factors for heart disease, determine your need for medication. Your doctor will likely recommend prescription medication if your LDL level remains between 160 and 189 after three months on the *Live It Down Plan* and if you have none of the following risk factors:

- A history of coronary heart disease (CHD), diabetes, or hypertension, or a family history of premature CHD.
- Smoking.
- An HDL level below 40 milligrams per deciliter.

If you don't have any of these risk factors and your LDL level is more than 190, your doctor will likely recommend that you start on medication at the same time that you begin following the Plan. But it's worth noting that the use of medication doesn't have to mean a permanent commitment. If you improve your diet and increase your activity level, in the process you may reduce your cholesterol enough to get off the medication and stay off it.

If you do have any of the above risk factors, your doctor will likely recommend medication even when your LDL level is lower. Once you start on a cholesterol-lowering medication, you may need to remain on it for the rest of your life. These drugs don't "cure" your high cholesterol; they merely prevent your body from producing or absorbing cholesterol while you're taking the drug. Once you stop, your cholesterol levels will return to their premedication levels, unless the lifestyle changes you've made have had an impact.

If You're Given a Prescription ...

Ask your doctor the following questions:
- What is this medicine for?
- What are the potential side effects, and what should I do about them?
- Are there any potential interactions with food, other prescription drugs, or over-the-counter drugs?
- How much should I take?
- When should I take it (for instance, with or without meals?)
- Will I need periodic blood testing?
- What if I forget to take a dose?
- Can I be confident that the likely benefits for me outweigh any risks?

About Safety and Side Effects

So you've left your doctor's office with a prescription. All of the advice and warnings went in one ear and out the other. Now you're worried about the side effects of this medication. It's a valid concern. Every drug—even aspirin—has risks. But keep in mind that if your doctor prescribes a medication, it's because the benefit outweighs the harm. And, frankly, in most cases the harm is relatively slight. Millions of people take cholesterol-lowering drugs with few or no problems. Many of the drugs in use today have been used for 15 or more years.

The most common side effects with most of these drugs are gastrointestinal problems, like nausea or stomach upset. Tell your doctor about any problems you're having, particularly if they persist. You may be able to change the dose or switch to a different medication—there's no reason to suffer.

There's also a very slight risk of liver problems, because cholesterol drugs are processed in the liver, which puts additional stress on the organ. That's why your doctor will take blood tests to measure liver enzyme levels, a kind of snapshot of your liver's health, before starting you on a cholesterol medication. Six to eight weeks after starting the medication you'll undergo another test to make sure your liver is handling the drug all right. Even if your liver enzymes are slightly elevated, don't panic. Quite often they return to normal within a few weeks, even while you continue to take the medication.

The Live It Down Plan
♥ Drugs

- Some people on the Plan will need cholesterol-lowering medication if they don't respond to lifestyle changes after 12 weeks.
- Some people will need to start on cholesterol-lowering drugs even as they start the Plan.
- Refer back to the quiz beginning on page 65 to see which category you likely fit.
- Most people on the Plan will benefit from taking a baby aspirin (81 milligrams) every day. Check with your doctor.

Statins: The New Wonder Drugs

This class of drug, which also goes by the tongue-twisting name HMG-CoA reductase inhibitors, has revolutionized the treatment of high cholesterol more than any other medication. In use for more than a decade, the drugs are sold under the brand names Lescol (fluvastatin), Lipitor (atorvastatin), Mevacor (lovastatin), Pravachol (pravastatin), and Zocor (simvastatin). Additionally, an extended-release form of lovastatin, called Altocor, was approved in 2002. It needs to be taken only once a day; most statins must be taken more often. To prevent confusion, we're going to stick to the brand names throughout this chapter.

Statins work by partially blocking an enzyme called HMG-CoA, which controls how quickly your body produces cholesterol. (Remember that your body makes about three or four times more cholesterol than you eat.) By blocking this enzyme, statins put the brakes on cholesterol production. They also increase your body's ability to remove LDL from your bloodstream and bring it to the liver, where it's broken down and eventually excreted. While statins aren't as good as some other drugs at raising HDL levels or lowering triglycerides, they do have some positive effects in those areas.

Statins aren't perfect, however. They don't work very well at transforming small, dense LDL particles (which are more likely to burrow into artery walls) into larger, fluffier particles, or lowering lipoprotein (a)—Lp(a)—another particle that may contribute to blood clots and plaque formation. So even if you're taking a statin, your doctor may prescribe additional medications, depending on your other coronary risk factors.

How Well Do They Work?

Overall, studies find that statins can lower LDL levels from 10 to 60 percent, depending on the drug and dosage used. One landmark study completed in 1994, the Scandinavian Simvastatin Survival Study, found deaths from heart disease plummeted 42 percent, and deaths from all causes 30 percent, over five years in patients with heart disease who took Zocor. Several other studies found that Pravachol reduced heart attacks, surgical bypass, and angioplasties in patients without heart disease by lowering LDL levels. And one study found the drug reduced overall deaths in patients who had had a previous heart attack but who had cholesterol levels that were more or less average for the general population. New statins currently under development can lower LDL levels even more—up to 80 percent in some cases—garnering them the moniker "super statins."

Given their tremendous success, it's no wonder that statins are among the most frequently prescribed drugs in the United States (Lipitor is prescribed more than any other drug in America). Approximately 12 million Americans take statins. That's a small fraction of the estimated 36 million that doctors believe are eligible for the drugs based on guidelines set by the National Institutes of Health. In fact, some experts suspect that within a few years, half of all American adults will be taking statins, which some call the "drug of the century."

Treating High Cholesterol in the Elderly

The next 30 years will see the graying of America as the baby boomers move into their senior years. The number of people 65 and older will double, growing to 70 million. And, since coronary heart disease (CHD) accounts for 70 to 80 percent of deaths in this age group, reducing CHD risk factors will become an even more critical agenda. Unfortunately, clinical trials find that many older patients with confirmed CHD don't receive therapies shown to help. And two studies conducted in the mid 1990s found that many older patients who were candidates for cholesterol-lowering drugs weren't prescribed them. This despite the fact that four major studies suggest treatment with cholesterol-lowering drugs can have a significant effect in reducing death and heart disease incidence in people 65 and older.

Such faith in the drugs is fueled in part by a British study, published in the medical journal *Lancet*, which concluded that just about anyone, of any age and at any risk for heart disease, could benefit from statins. And as you'll see in a minute, researchers are finding a plethora of benefits to statins that extend far beyond your cholesterol level. Statins, the researchers wrote, are the "new aspirin."

> Some experts suspect that within a few years, half of all Americans will be taking statins, which some call the "drug of the century."

Statins generally take between four to six weeks to reach their maximum effectiveness. Dosages for statins vary depending on the drug, but at least one dose will be taken at dinner or bedtime because the body manufactures more cholesterol at night than during the day.

Stick with It

Just because your cholesterol readings drop doesn't mean you can stop taking a prescribed statin without your doctor's say-so. Yet 25 percent of people 65 and older stop taking statins within the first six months, against their doctor's orders. This is a bad idea for several reasons, not least of which is that statins can't keep your cholesterol under control if you don't take them. Moreover, some studies suggest that abruptly stopping the drugs could result in problems, including an increased risk of heart attack, unstable angina, and stroke. Studies in rats found that stopping the drug suddenly dried up production of nitric oxide, the compound responsible for keeping artery walls smooth and flexible and helping to make blood platelets less sticky.

Following the *Live It Down Plan* may enable you to take fewer prescription drugs, or even stop taking them altogether eventually. But don't taper off or forgo your medication without first talking to your doctor.

Paying for Statins

The cost of statins varies widely—from about $55 a month to more than $200 a month (without insurance)—depending on the drug and the dosage. If your insurance plan doesn't cover prescription drugs, the cost can be quite onerous. But there are ways to spend less. For instance, because drugs are sold by the pill, not by the strength, you can ask your doctor to prescribe double the strength you need (80 milligrams rather than 40 milligrams, for example), then buy a pill-splitter and cut the pills in half. Grapefruit juice increases absorption of statins. If you take your medication with grapefruit juice, let your doctor know; you may be able to get by with a lower dose.

Expect prices to begin dropping since the first generic statin—lovastatin—was approved in 2001. At about $1 a pill, it costs about half as much as its branded version, Mevacor. In coming years more generic statins will become available and may significantly reduce overall prices in this class of drug.

Let your doctor know if you're having trouble paying for your drugs. Most pharmaceutical companies have special programs in which they provide prescription drugs for free or reduced rates to people who can't afford them. Your doctor can tell you more.

The Downside to Statins

Like all drugs, statins have their drawbacks. While they're deemed extremely safe, given the large number of people who take them and the fact that they've been in use for more than 14 years, in rare cases they can cause problems. Among the potential side effects:

Muscle and kidney damage. In 2001 Bayer AG voluntarily recalled its statin drug, Baycol (cerivastatin), from the U.S. market because of reports of at least

Remembering to Take Your Medicine

So you're brushing your teeth before sliding into bed when it suddenly hits you: You forgot to take your cholesterol drug today. Forgetfulness is one of the most common reasons people say they don't take their medications. To avoid forgetting, use prompts like the following:

- Coordinate taking your medication with a daily activity. For instance, when you brush your teeth in the morning, you take your pill. When you eat dinner, you take your pill.
- Use alarms on clocks, watches, cell phones, and computers to remind you when to take your medication. You can even buy an electronic medicine organizer that beeps at a programmed time. You can find them in drugstores or online at www.domorehealthcare.com.
- Use pillboxes or other special medication holders to organize your medications by hour, day, and week. Then you can easily see if you've forgotten a dose.
- Keep your medication in an obvious place (for instance, on the bathroom counter) so that you see it first thing when you get up in the morning. If you need to take it with meals, keep it in plain site on the kitchen counter.
- Use a medication diary, available in drugstores or online at numerous health and medical Web sites.
- Put reminders around your house. Stick Post-it notes asking yourself if you've taken your medicine to your front door, purse, or keys.

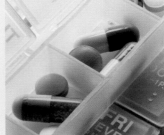

31 deaths in the United States linked to the drug. The deaths were the result of a condition called rhabdomyolysis, in which muscle cells break down, releasing proteins that become trapped in the kidneys. This interferes with the kidneys' ability to filter out toxins from the blood, leading to kidney failure and, potentially, death. Symptoms include muscle pain, weakness, tenderness, malaise, fever, dark urine, nausea, and vomiting. The pain may involve specific groups of muscles or may occur throughout the body.

While all statins have been associated with very rare reports of rhabdomyolysis, according to the FDA the risk was 16 to 80 percent higher with Baycol, particularly when used at higher doses, in elderly patients, and in combination with Lopid (gemfibrozil), another lipid-lowering drug. The rhabdomyolysis risk associated with the statins that remain on the market, especially when the drugs are used alone by people without rhabdomyolysis risk factors such as renal impairment, is extremely small.

Much less serious is the muscle weakness or pain experienced by some people taking statins. You're more susceptible if you're older than 80, have a small body frame or are frail, have a multisystem disease (such as chronic renal insufficiency), or take multiple medications. Generally about 5 percent of people taking statins will experience these side effects. They usually go away once the drug is stopped and can often be prevented by taking coenzyme Q10, which you read about in Chapter 5.

Dangerous Combinations

Taking certain drugs while you're also taking statins might increase your risk of muscle damage. These drugs include: fibrates; nicotinic acid; the antifungals Sporonox (itraconazole), Nizoral (ketoconazole), and anything in the azole class of drug; antibiotics such as erythromycin and clarithromycin; the immunosuppressant Sandimmune (cyclosporine); HIV protease inhibitors; antidepressants such as Serzone (nefazodone); the beta-blockers Calan (verapamil) and Isoptin (verapamil); and the anti-arrhythmia drug Cordarone IV (amiodarone).

Liver damage. Like most drugs, statins are broken down in the liver, thus putting additional stress on the organ. That's why your doctor will monitor your levels of liver enzymes—an indication of the health of your liver—for the first few months that you are taking the drugs. You should also limit your use of alcohol, which puts additional stress on your liver and increases the risk of liver failure if you're taking statins (or other medications). Elevated liver enzymes occur in 0.5 to 2 percent of people taking statins—generally those taking the highest doses. Full liver failure is extremely rare, and reducing the drug dose usually reverses elevated enzymes.

Depletion of coenzyme Q10. As we discussed in Chapter 5, statins also seem to decrease the body's production of the important substance coenzyme Q10. Cells need CoQ10 to help them use energy. That's why we recommend you supplement with 100 milligrams daily of CoQ10 if you take statins.

Cataracts. Statins alone don't cause cataracts. But according to a study published in the *Archives of Internal Medicine* in September 2001, taking Zocor along with the antibiotic erythromycin might increase the risk. Just a single course of antibiotic, typically taken for 10 days, appeared to double the risk of cataracts, while two or more courses tripled it. If you take statins and need antibiotics, talk with your doctor.

Nerve damage. Researchers studying 500,000 Danish residents found that people who took statins were more likely to develop a form of nerve damage called polyneuropathy than those who never took the drugs. The condition, also known as peripheral neuropathy, results in weakness, tingling, pain in the hands and feet, and difficulty walking. Taking statins for one year increased the risk of nerve damage about 15 percent, or one case for every 2,200 patients; for those taking the drug two or more years, the risk increased 26 percent.

Do Statins Cause Cancer?

For years rumors have circulated on the Internet that statins might cause cancer. The rumors trace their start to a 1996 study published in the *Journal of the American Medical Association* that suggested a link between cancer, statins, and fibrates, another class of drug that lowers cholesterol.

Researchers examining animal studies in which the two drugs were given to rats found that the rodents developed cancer more often than usual. In some cases the cancer occurred with drug doses close to those prescribed to humans. However, two later studies examining large populations of people taking statins found no connection between this class of drug and cancer.

Six Side Benefits of Statins

The more researchers study statins, the more potential uses they're finding for this class of drug, prompting some doctors to jokingly suggest that it be added to the water supply. Among its potential uses:

Lowering CRP. Numerous studies have found that statins can lower levels of C-reactive protein (CRP), a sign of inflammation that researchers now suspect may be a better predictor of heart disease than even high cholesterol. A study in the journal *Circulation* in August 2002 showed that Zocor lowered CRP levels in just two weeks.

Continued on page 190

Which Statin to Take?

As of early 2003 the FDA had approved five statin drugs for the treatment of high cholesterol. Although the drugs are similar, there are some differences in their mechanisms and effectiveness. So talk to your doctor about which statin is best for you. Here's how they break out:

Drug	Average LDL reduction* (percent)	Average HDL Increase* (percent)	Average triglycerides reduction* (percent)	Effect on cardiovascular disease and deaths	Other effects
Lescol	33	11–25	19–23	Not determined.	FDA-approved as treatment to lower apolipoprotein B. Requires the least amount of liver function testing.
Lipitor	54	5–9	19–37	Not determined.	Also reduces levels of remnant lipoprotein cholesterol levels and C-reactive protein, both signs of increased risk of heart disease.
Mevacor	35	6	21 after 12 weeks	No benefit seen in decreasing incidence of heart attack or death from heart attack.	
Pravachol	40	5	14	Reduced risk of having a first heart attack by 31 percent and reduced risk of overall death about 22 percent.	A study published in the journal *Circulation* in January 2001 suggests Pravachol may cut the risk of diabetes by 30 percent. It also reduces levels of remnant lipoprotein cholesterol and C-reactive protein.
Zocor	48	8	28–33	42 percent fewer deaths from heart disease in people who had had previous heart attacks and 30 percent reduction in overall deaths.	Also reduces levels of C-reactive protein.

*At highest dosage.

Continued from page 188

Reducing stroke risk. In several large studies of statins in patients with existing heart disease, the drugs reduced the risk of a first-time stroke between 11 and 30 percent. An analysis of several published trials suggests statins' effect on stroke risk may be due to more than just its ability to reduce cholesterol. For instance, statins improve the function of endothelial cells (the cells that make up the artery walls), probably by boosting their production of nitric oxide. This helps keep artery walls smooth and flexible and reduces the likelihood of plaque formation. Statins also reduce inflammation, make blood platelets less sticky, exert some antioxidant effects, help stabilize plaque so it doesn't burst, and help prevent blood clots.

Treating autoimmune diseases and preventing transplant rejection. In autoimmune diseases such as psoriasis and rheumatoid arthritis, an overactive immune system gets confused, thinks the body's own cells are foreign invaders, and begins attacking them. But researchers found that statins block the action of certain immune cells that play a role in these diseases. These immune cells are also involved in the rejection of transplanted organs, leading researchers to suspect that a statin-like drug could one day be used in place of other transplant-rejection medications.

> In the largest study so far, researchers found that taking statins reduced the risk of developing Alzheimer's nearly 80 percent.

By far the greatest interest in the effects of statins on the immune system lies in the treatment of multiple sclerosis (MS), an autoimmune disease. In one study in the journal *Neurology*, statins prevented the growth of immune cells that contribute to this disease. When mice with MS were treated for a week with doses of Lipitor equal to the highest human dose, the drug reversed or prevented relapses and curbed brain inflammation, a hallmark of the disease. As of this writing, clinical trials in humans with MS were to begin in 2003.

Bettering bone health. Several animal and retrospective studies (in which researchers looked back at people who had been taking statins) found that statins may help bones grow, suggesting a possible use in osteoporosis, which causes brittle bones. Today most treatments for osteoporosis simply slow bone loss. A drug that could actually get bones to grow would be a major breakthrough.

The jury is still out on whether, and by how much, statins can increase bone density. Even if they can, don't look for your doctor to prescribe them for osteoporosis anytime soon. Instead, they may pave the way for the development of drugs that have a similar molecular structure but are designed specifically for bone health.

Fighting dementia and Alzheimer's disease. As we discussed in Chapter 3, there is increasing evidence that cholesterol may play a role in the development of certain dementias, including Alzheimer's disease. This begs the question, of course, about whether cholesterol-lowering drugs could reduce the risk of Alzheimer's disease and other dementias. The answer is "maybe." In the largest study so far, researchers examined risk factors for Alzheimer's and medication history in 912 people who either definitely or probably had Alzheimer's, and 1,669 of their family members. They found that taking statins reduced the risk of developing Alzheimer's nearly 80 percent. Statins appear to work by blocking the actions of a protein called A-beta, which makes blood vessels constrict, restricting the flow of blood to the brain.

Diabetes. When researchers evaluated data from one of the largest clinical trials on statins, they found that Pravachol reduced the risk of developing diabetes by 30 percent. They theorize the effect may be due to Pravachol's ability to lower triglyceride levels. (Other statins may lower triglycerides as well.) High triglycerides lead to high circulating levels of free fatty acids, which in turn impair the ability of insulin to interact with its receptor. Lowering triglycerides is a way of preserving insulin sensitivity and preventing insulin resistance.

Cholesterol Absorption Inhibitors

Two organs primarily control cholesterol levels in your blood: the liver, which produces cholesterol and bile acids (used to digest fats), and the intestine, which absorbs cholesterol both from food and from the bile. While statins primarily lower cholesterol by preventing its production in the liver, a new class of drug called cholesterol absorption inhibitors lowers cholesterol by preventing it from being absorbed in the intestine. The first approved drug in this class, Zetia (ezetimibe), hit American markets in 2002.

By itself, Zetia reduced cholesterol about 18 percent in studies. When the drug was paired with statin drugs, cholesterol levels dropped 25 percent more than with statins alone. That's important, since on average only 60 percent of people who take statins get their cholesterol levels as low as they should. In one study just 19 percent of people taking statins alone reached their cholesterol goal; adding Zetia increased that figure to 72 percent. "Taking 10 milligrams of Zetia with a statin is equivalent to tripling the dose of statins," says Antonio Gotto, Jr., M.D., dean at Weill Cornell Medical College in New York City. Zetia also has fewer side effects than statins. For instance, it doesn't appear to cause any muscle problems. The treatment doesn't come cheaply, however; the wholesale cost for a 30-day supply is $57.90. That's on top of the cost of the statin. Merck & Co., the maker of the statin Zocor, is testing a pill that combines the two.

Side effects: The most common side effects include back, stomach, and joint pain.

Warnings: Not recommended for use in conjunction with fibrates.

Recommended dose: Zetia is administered as a once-daily tablet in a single 10-milligram strength and is taken with or without food.

Niacin

Niacin (nicotinic acid) is one of the oldest cholesterol-lowering drugs. A member of the B vitamin family, it's found in fruits, vegetables, meats, and grains, as well as in most multivitamins. At doses up to 35 milligrams per day, niacin is considered a supplement, but if you're taking it at doses high enough to lower your cholesterol— more than 100 times the recommended daily intake of 16 milligrams for men and 14 milligrams for women—you need to be taking it under the supervision of your doctor (even though it's sold over the counter).

Niacin works by reducing the production and release of LDL from the liver, lowering LDL 15 to 20 percent. It also reduces the release of free fatty acids stored in fat cells, which eventually become triglycerides. Thus, it's an excellent drug for lowering triglycerides, resulting in decreases of 20 to 50 percent. It also raises HDL between 15 and 35 percent. In fact, the branded timed-release form, Niaspan, is one of only two drugs approved to increase HDL. (In case you're wondering, the other is the fibrate gemfibrozil, brand name Lopid.)

Antioxidants and Statins: A Flawed Partnership?

In 2001 the media filled with headlines warning that taking antioxidant vitamins E and C could reduce statins' effectiveness. They were referring to a study published that year in *Atherosclerosis, Thrombosis, and Vascular Biology*. In that study 153 heart patients with especially low HDL levels were broken into four groups. The first group received a statin and niacin; the second got a combination of the antioxidants beta-carotene, vitamin C, vitamin E, and selenium; the third received placebos; and the fourth got both the drugs and the antioxidants.

After a year the group taking the drugs and the niacin had a 34 percent drop in LDL and a 25 percent rise in HDL. Those receiving antioxidants and the drugs had the same LDL drop but only an 18 percent increase in HDL. And their plaque increased 7 percent, compared with a 4 percent decrease in the drug-only group. (In case you're wondering, the vitamin-only group and the placebo group showed almost no change.)

So should you avoid taking antioxidant vitamins and minerals while also taking a statin or other cholesterol drug? While there's no definitive answer based on the research, here's what we recommend: If you take a statin, also take coenzyme Q10, which is an antioxidant, since statins deplete this important substance. Eat plenty of fruits and vegetables, and drink green tea—all sources of antioxidants. And take a daily multivitamin (a *Live It Down Plan* staple), most of which contain moderate amounts of vitamins E and C. There appears to be no clear benefit to taking additional supplements of E or C for people on statins.

Sound too good to be true? Well, there is a drawback to niacin that turns some people off: It can cause flushing and redness—an intense blush. This occurs because niacin relaxes blood vessels, enabling more blood flow. The blushing usually disappears within an hour or so after taking the drug. And taking aspirin beforehand can reduce this effect, as can gradually building up to the dose you need.

There are two types of nicotinic acid: immediate release and timed release. The timed-release version reduces the flushing, but be doubly sure you don't take this form without your doctor's supervision. If you take too much, the drug could cause liver damage and raise blood glucose levels dangerously high. It can also raise blood glucose and hemoglobin AIC levels in people with diabetes. That's why most experts recommend starting with the immediate-release form. Also, make sure you're taking nicotinic acid; another form of niacin called nicotinamide doesn't lower cholesterol levels.

Two Pills in One

If you're taking niacin and Mevacor, now you can get them both in one pill. The drug is called Advisor, and it combines the timed-release niacin drug Niaspan with 20 milligrams of the statin Mevacor. Its risks and benefits mimic those of taking both drugs separately. But convenience has its price. When the *Washington Post* compared the cost of Advisor to buying separate bottles of Niaspan and generic lovastatin, buying the drugs separately cost less. Still, for some people the convenience of a single pill might be worth the extra expense.

Side Effects: In addition to flushing, other possible side effects of niacin include:

- **Liver enzyme abnormalities.** About 5 percent of people who take more than 3 grams of nicotinic acid per day may learn they have elevated liver enzymes, an indication that their liver is under stress. If the elevation continues and your enzymes are more than three times normal levels, your doctor may want you to stop taking the drug.

- **Blood glucose control.** In about 10 percent of people—particularly those with diabetes, insulin resistance, or metabolic syndrome—nicotinic acid may make it more difficult to control blood sugar levels.

- **Gout.** About 5 to 10 percent of those people taking nicotinic acid find their production of uric acid increases. This can result in gout, a condition involving painful and inflamed joints.

- **Gastrointestinal symptoms.** Infrequently a variety of gastrointestinal symptoms, including nausea, indigestion, gas, vomiting, diarrhea, and ulcers, may also occur.

- **Muscle toxicity.** This is rare but may occur if you're combining nicotinic acid with other drugs, such as statins or fibrates (described on the next page).

Warnings: Don't take niacin if you have diabetes, liver disease, an active peptic ulcer, arterial bleeding, or unexplained liver enzyme elevations. And be careful if you're also taking blood pressure medication. Niacin can increase the effect of some blood pressure drugs, so your doctor should closely monitor your blood pressure when you first start taking niacin.

Recommended dose: 1 to 3 grams daily, taken under a doctor's supervision.

Fibrates for High Triglycerides

Fibric acid derivatives, or fibrates, affect the actions of key enzymes in the liver, enabling the liver to absorb more fatty acids, thus reducing production of triglycerides. These drugs also work well at increasing production of HDL. Although they can also lower LDL levels, they're not considered first-line treatments for high LDL or total cholesterol. Overall, they tend to lower LDL levels between 10 and 15 percent, increase HDL levels between 5 and 20 percent, and lower triglycerides between 20 and 50 percent. Fibrates are often prescribed in conjunction with other cholesterol-lowering drugs, but they shouldn't be taken with statins. They may be particularly helpful for people with insulin resistance syndrome, in which HDL tends to be low, LDL normal, and triglycerides high. Brands include Atromid-S (clofibrate), Lopid (gemfibrozil), and Tricor (fenofibrate).

Side effects: Fibrates have few side effects and most people can take them with no problem. The most common problems are gastrointestinal complaints, such as nausea and gas. The drug may also increase your likelihood of developing gallstones.

Warnings: Combining fibrates with statins could result in muscle damage. Fibrates are also not recommended if you have liver, kidney, or gallbladder disease.

Recommended dose: Fibrates are usually given in two daily doses totaling 1,200 milligrams, taken 30 minutes before morning and evening meals.

Bile Acid Sequestrants

This class of drug, in use for more than 40 years with no major problems, acts like super glue, binding with bile acids in the intestines so that the acids are removed with the stool. Bile acids (which help your body digest fatty foods) are made from cholesterol in the liver. Ordinarily, as they pass through the intestines they are reabsorbed into the bloodstream and carried back to the liver. This "recycles" the cholesterol component as well. But bile acid sequestrants interrupt this pathway, causing the bile acids to exit the body. This causes a loss of cholesterol as well. In response, the liver removes more LDL from the bloodstream. And—voilà—your blood cholesterol levels drop.

The most common drugs include cholestyramine, sold under the brand names Questran, Prevalite, and LoCholest, and colestipol (Colestid). These drugs generally lower LDL about 15 to 30 percent with relatively low doses while increasing HDL slightly (up to 5 percent). They may be prescribed with a statin if you already have heart disease. Together the two drugs can lower LDL more than 40 percent.

Side effects: These drugs may cause bloating, heartburn, constipation, and abdominal pain, and may increase triglycerides, particularly if levels are already high.

Warnings: Bile acid sequestrants may delay or reduce your ability to absorb oral medications and vitamins, so you shouldn't take them along with other medications or supplements.

Recommended dose: Bile acid sequestrants generally come as tablets or as a powdered resin that you mix with liquids or foods. A typical dose is about 10 grams per day.

Combination Drug Therapy

If medication combined with the *Live It Down Plan* doesn't enable you to reach your LDL goal within three months, your doctor may consider starting you on a second drug to boost results. Combination therapy can help reverse or slow the advance of atherosclerosis and further decrease your risk of a heart attack or death. Also, since both drugs may be prescribed in lower doses than if you were taking either alone, your risk of side effects may decrease.

Aspirin

First the proviso: Aspirin won't lower your cholesterol. But its effects on blood clotting and inflammation are so significant that anyone with known heart disease, diabetes, or two or more risk factors for heart disease (and no problems taking aspirin) should talk to their doctor about taking a daily baby aspirin. Aspirin acts like WD-40 on blood platelets, making them less likely to stick to plaque in blood vessels. It also reduces the inflammation that is a hallmark of heart disease and a part of the process that leads to the buildup of plaque.

Numerous studies have found that aspirin reduced the risk of another heart attack, stroke, or premature death in people with heart disease, and it also reduced the risk of heart attacks in healthy people. One analysis of four large studies conducted on people with no history of heart disease found a daily aspirin reduced the risk of a nonfatal heart attack 32 percent.

Side effects: Aspirin's very strength is also its greatest weakness. Because it acts on the overall system that affects bleeding, aspirin increases the risk of gastrointestinal bleeding, either from an ulcer or gastritis (inflammation of the stomach lining), and the risk of a rare but dangerous form of stroke called hemorrhagic stroke, caused not

Numerous studies found that aspirin reduced the risk of another heart attack, stroke, or premature death in people with heart disease, and it also reduced the risk of heart attacks in healthy people.

by a blood clot but by bleeding in the brain. To learn whether the benefits of aspirin therapy outweigh the risk for you personally, take the simple test at www.med-decisions.com. You will need to know your blood pressure and cholesterol readings.

Warnings: If you're taking blood-thinning medication such as Coumadin (warfarin), talk to your doctor before taking aspirin regularly. The combined effect can pose a serious hazard. And be aware that aspirin can boost the blood-thinning effects of certain supplements, such as vitamin E, ginkgo biloba, St. John's wort, and others. (Fish oil, which you'll be taking on the *Live It Down Plan*, also thins the blood, but the heart benefits of taking both fish oil and aspirin probably outweigh the risks.) Be sure to let your doctor know about any supplements you take when you discuss the pros and cons of aspirin therapy with him. Finally, don't take aspirin if you've ever had any problems with the drug, including stomach pain or allergies.

Recommended dose: One baby aspirin (81 milligrams) daily.

Looking into the Future

The American pharmaceutical industry spent more than $30 billion in 2001 researching and developing new drugs. Not surprisingly, companies tend to focus much of their research in areas that promise the biggest sales potential, such as diabetes, heart disease, and cancer. And with an estimated 36 million Americans walking around with cholesterol levels high enough to qualify them for medication, along with the success of the statin drugs, it's not surprising drug companies are anxious to bring new cholesterol medications to market. Here, then, is a snapshot of what's in the works:

CETP inhibitors. During the 1990s researchers discovered a protein called cholesterol ester transfer protein (CETP), responsible for the transfer of fats between lipoproteins. People with high blood levels of CETP generally have low levels of HDL. The finding sent pharmaceutical scientists scrambling to find a drug that would reduce or inhibit the production of CETP. Although several such drugs are in the works, the one closest to market is Pfizer Inc.'s CP-529,414. Although the drug is too experimental to have a real name, its benefits are already being bandied about in medical meetings. In trials the drug raised HDL levels a whopping 55 percent—about

10 times more than typically seen with statins. It also lowered LDL up to 20 percent. Overall, when used in combination with Pfizer's statin, Lipitor, company officials estimate it could lower LDL 70 to 80 percent, while raising HDL 55 percent. It is likely years away from FDA approval, however.

Cholesterol vaccine. Avant Immunotherapeutics Inc. is working to develop a cholesterol vaccine that controls the CETP protein, thus increasing HDL levels and helping prevent heart disease. As envisioned, the vaccine would need to be given only once every six months. Additionally, because the peptide used in the drug is simple and cheap to manufacture, Avant expects the cost of the vaccine would be considerably less than that of statins.

ACAT inhibitors. This class of drug works to inhibit an enzyme, acyl coenzyme A: cholesterol acyltransferase (ACAT), that helps foam cells—a major component of and contributor to plaque—develop. In studies these drugs appear to clear up existing plaque even as they prevent the formation of additional plaque. Pfizer's avasimibe was in late-stage clinical trials in early 2003, while Eli Lilly and Co.'s eflucimibe had just begun studies in humans. These drugs aren't expected to hit the market before mid- to late in the decade.

New statins. Two new statins under development could be approved as early as 2003 or 2004 in the United States:

- **Crestor (rosuvastatin).** This statin, which will be marketed by AstraZeneca Pharmaceuticals, was closest to approval as of this writing. It's called a "super statin" because of its impressive results in lowering LDL and total cholesterol levels. In one study Crestor reduced LDL 40 to 58 percent, beating out Lipitor, Zocor, and Pravachol. The most common side effects are nausea, diarrhea, dry mouth, and abdominal pain, although symptoms rarely resulted in patients quitting the drug. Crestor also increased HDL levels up to 14 percent, and it reduced apo(b)/A-1 levels, a CHD risk predictor.

- **Pitavastatin.** Developed by the Japanese drugmaker Sankyo Co., this drug lowered LDL levels nearly 38 percent after 12 weeks compared to Pravachol, which lowered LDL levels only 18 percent. The study found that 75 percent of patients treated with the drug reached their LDL goal, compared to just 36 percent of those taking Pravachol. Pitavastatin also reduced triglyceride levels but had no effect on HDL levels. Pharmaceutical company Novartis AG may market the drug in the United States if and when it receives FDA approval.

Ileal bile acid transport (IBAT) inhibitors. This class of drug prompts the liver to convert cholesterol into bile acids, thus reducing cholesterol levels in the liver. When this happens, the liver sends out for more cholesterol, taking it from the bloodstream and reducing blood cholesterol levels. The primary side effect is diarrhea. These drugs are several years away from FDA approval.

Dual peroxisome proliferator-activated receptor (PPAR) agonists. These drugs reduce triglycerides, raise HDL, and improve insulin resistance, making them particularly well suited for people with diabetes or metabolic syndrome. The drugs are years away from the market, however.

Putting It All Together

If you wind up needing medication, think about how fortunate we are today to have these generally safe and highly effective drugs available to us. Not too long ago all cardiologists could do for their patients was hold their hands, watching them succumb to a disease they couldn't control. Today we have the means at our disposal to shut off the rampage of atherogenesis, the formation of plaque.

That said, lifestyle changes are still the mainstay of the *Live It Down Plan*. While all drugs have potential side effects, healthy lifestyle changes are never toxic. Also, whereas drugs target a single disease or risk factor (like high cholesterol), habits like getting more exercise, lowering your stress levels, and eating a heart-healthy diet provide a vast array of health benefits no pharmaceutical product could ever match.

In the next chapter we'll walk you through the *Live It Down Plan* week by week for 12 weeks. You should follow the Plan regardless of what drug you're taking. By getting good medical care tailored to your specific needs (possibly including pre-scription medication) and following the *Live It Down Plan*, you should be able to live it up for many years to come!

The 12-Week Live It Down Plan

Congratulations! If you've made it this far, you have all of the information you need about cholesterol and how to lower it (or improve your ratios) through diet, exercise, stress reduction, and supplements. And you know how these lifestyle changes will also help protect you from other serious cardiac risk factors, including high blood pressure and inflammation. Now comes the fun part: We're going to put all of the advice we've given you in the first eight chapters into an easy-to-follow week-by-week plan. To help you put the eating advice into action, we've included more than two dozen delicious Plan-ready recipes.

Where to start? With Week 1, of course! But before you do, read about what you'll need to have at the ready in order to hit the ground running (for instance, you'll need to buy your pedometer and stock some kitchen staples, such as a good bottle of olive oil). And starting on the next page we'll show you an overview of the entire Plan as a reminder of the overall strategy.

The beauty of the 12-Week Plan is that you don't have to try to overhaul your lifestyle all at once (studies show that doesn't work). By making just a few relatively small changes one week at a time, those changes are much more likely to stick. And that's important. While most people will lower their cholesterol within 12 weeks, the point is to stay on the *Live It Down Plan* for life.

 # Eating

Protein

You'll get most of your protein from lean meat and poultry, eggs, soy, beans, and fish, with the greatest emphasis on the latter three. The Plan calls for getting about 20 percent of your calories from protein. On a 2,000-calorie diet that's about 100 grams of protein daily.

Here's what a day's worth of protein might look like:

- 1 large egg: 6 grams
- Roasted chicken breast, 3 ounces: 23 grams
- Salmon, 5 ounces: 38 grams
- Black beans, 1 cup: 14 grams
- Brown rice, 1 cup: 5 grams
- Nonfat milk, 2 cups: 16 grams

Carbohydrates

Complex carbohydrates, found in vegetables, fruit, and whole grains, should make up most of your carbohydrate intake, rather than sweets, sodas, and foods made with white flour. The Plan calls for getting 45 to 60 percent of your calories from carbohydrates. On a 2,000-calorie diet that's a range of 225 to 300 grams daily.

Here's what a day's worth of carbohydrates might look like:

- Raisin bran cereal, 1 cup: 43 grams
- Fruit juice, 8 ounces: 30 grams
- Banana, medium: 27 grams
- Broccoli, 1 cup: 5 grams
- Cooked barley, 1 cup: 44 grams
- Apple: 21 grams
- String beans, 1 cup: 10 grams
- Pear: 25 grams
- Pasta, whole wheat, 1 cup: 37 grams
- Dinner roll, whole wheat: 26 grams
- Ice cream, 1/2 cup: 20 grams

Fat

On the *Live It Down Plan* fat is fine—as long as it's unsaturated. The Plan calls for getting 20 to 30 percent of your calories from fat. On a 2,000 calorie diet that's 44 to 67 grams.

Here's what a day's worth of fat might look like:

- 1 egg: 5 grams
- Skinless chicken breast, 3 ounces: 3 grams
- Hummus, 2 tablespoons: 3 grams
- Salmon, 5 ounces: 14 grams
- Olive oil, 2 tablespoons: 28 grams

Fiber

Fiber is king on the *Live It Down Plan*. Aim to get at least 25 grams of fiber a day—relatively easy to do if you're eating your oatmeal, getting the nine servings of fruits and vegetables we recommend, and sticking to whole grain carbohydrates.

Here's what a day's worth of fiber might look like:

- High-fiber cereal or oatmeal, 1 cup: 5 grams
- Strawberries, 1 cup: 4 grams
- 1 mango: 3 grams
- Broccoli, 1 cup: 4 grams
- Steamed spinach, 1/2 cup: 2 grams
- Brown rice, 1 cup: 3 grams
- Lima beans, 1/2 cup: 7 grams
- 6 large dates: 2 grams

Fruits and Vegetables

On the Plan we want you to aim to get nine servings of fruits and vegetables a day. That's not as hard as it may sound.

Here's what a day's worth of fruits and vegetables might look like:

- 1 medium fruit (orange, pear)
- Broccoli, 1 cup (equals two servings)
- 100 percent fruit/vegetable juice, 6 ounces
- 1/2 cup beans or peas
- Smoothie with 1 cup of cut-up fruit (equals two servings)
- 1 cup raw, leafy vegetables
- 1/4 cup dried fruit (raisins, apricots)

Putting it all together | Sample menu					
Breakfast	**Midmorning snack**	**Lunch**	**Afternoon snack**	**Dinner**	**Dessert**
• 8 ounces nonfat milk • 1 cup oatmeal or high-fiber cereal • 1 banana	• 1 piece fruit	• 8 ounces fruit/vegetable juice • Broccoli and Pearl Barley Salad (page 245) or Lentil-Tomato Stew with Browned Onions (page 232) • Whole grain roll	• 1 handful almonds, walnuts, or soy nuts	• Fish en Papillote (page 236) • Bulgur Wheat Pilaf (page 241)	• Apple Raspberry Brown Betty (page 248)

 # Exercise

- Get at least 30 minutes of moderate physical activity four to five days a week (60 minutes if you need to lose weight). Walk your way up to 50,000 steps a week.
- Aim for 60 minutes of strength training each week using the 10-Minute Tune-Up (page 149) or the 30-Minute Total Body Toner (page 153).
- Do simple stretches every day to maintain flexibility (page 158).

 # Lifestyle

- Practice deep breathing four times a week for two to four minutes. And use the technique anytime you're faced with a stressful situation to mitigate your body's reactions.
- "Spin" the way you view the world so you're looking at it with a positive, rather than negative, outlook more often than not.
- Embrace those things that bring you pleasure and satisfaction. Find a hobby that you can lose yourself in. Nurture old social contacts or make new ones—maybe by joining an exercise class or walking club.

 Supplements

Everyone on the Plan will be taking a daily multivitamin, 2 grams of fish oil, and most likely a baby aspirin (81 milligrams) every day; check with your doctor before taking aspirin regularly. Some people will also benefit from other supplements. Using the chart below, write down which supplements you'll take on the Plan. (Talk to your doctor first.)

My Supplements:

☑ Multivitamin
☑ 2 grams of fish oil
☐ Aspirin
Other: _____

Supplement	Who should take it	Daily dosage
Multivitamin/ mineral	Everyone.	One pill, which should include 200 to 500 milligrams of vitamin C and 100 to 200 IU vitamin E.
Fish-oil supplements	Everyone.	2 grams of combined EPA and DHA twice daily. If you have heart disease, ask your doctor about taking higher doses.
Additional B vitamins	People with high homocysteine levels (above 9 micromoles per liter).	Talk to your doctor.
Guggul	People with high cholesterol who want an alternative to a prescription drug, especially people whose cholesterol isn't high enough to require medication.	75 milligrams of guggulsterones daily.
Red yeast rice extract	Anyone with cholesterol levels high enough to require medication but who doesn't want to take a prescription drug should consider this.	Follow manufacturer directions.
Chromium	People with metabolic syndrome or insulin resistance. Diabetics should consider it (check with your doctor first). Use chromium picolinate as your source.	200 to 400 micrograms daily for people with insulin resistance; 400 to 1,000 micrograms for people with diabetes.
Coenzyme Q10	Anyone with a high LDL level and anyone taking a statin drug should take CoQ10 if they feel they can afford it.	100 milligrams daily.
Psyllium	People who don't feel they can consistently eat foods rich in soluble fiber.	5 to 10 grams daily.
Arginine	Anyone with multiple risk factors for heart disease or who already has heart disease, and whose diet is less than ideal (it won't be if you follow the Plan faithfully).	2 to 3 grams daily in divided doses.
Hawthorne	Anyone with high cholesterol who wants to do everything they can to further lower their risk should consider this.	100 to 300 milligrams standardized extract two to three times daily.

Getting Started

Prior to Week 1 of the 12-Week Plan, you'll need to get yourself—and your kitchen—prepared. Below we've outlined the steps you should take to ensure you're ready to begin "living it down."

1. Set your sights.

Make sure you've taken the quiz starting on page 65 and that you know your LDL goal. You should also determine with your doctor whether you need to start on medication even as you start on the *Live It Down Plan.*

My LDL target: _____

2. Purchase a pedometer.

Your pedometer will not only help you keep track of how much you walk, it will also motivate you to fit more physical activity into your daily life by taking the stairs instead of the elevator, walking to nearby errands, and getting up during commercials. And you know it's always counting! Refer back to our chart on page 143 to help you choose the right model. Once you have your pedometer, be sure to follow the instructions for entering your stride length.

3. Clean out your kitchen.

You'll be stocking your refrigerator and cabinets with some of the staples you need on the Plan. But first, to make room—and remove temptation—get rid of items you won't be using anymore. Here are a few examples of what to toss:

- Soda.
- Butter (or throw it in the freezer for emergencies).
- Margarine made with hydrogenated oil.
- Frozen ground beef.
- Any frozen fried or breaded foods—fish sticks, fried chicken, etc.
- Full-fat frozen desserts.
- Chips, packaged cookies, and cakes.
- "Cream of" soups.
- Hard taco shells.
- Refried beans (the fat-free kind is okay).

4. Have the tools you need.

Heart-healthy cooking is infinitely easier when you have the right tools on hand. We suggest the following:

- Nonstick frying pan.
- Indoor grill—great for getting out the fat when it's too nasty or cold to cook outside.
- Vegetable steamer.
- Crock-Pot—thanks to slow, moist heat, this cooking requires little fat.
- Bread machine for making your own whole grain breads.
- Wok—stir-frying is an oxymoron; there's very little fat involved.
- Blender for fruit smoothies.
- Plastic or metal strainer to skim fat from stews and soups.
- A fruit bowl—studies show that people who keep fruit in plain sight are more likely to eat it.

5. Go Shopping.

Forget your former throw-whatever-looks-good-into-the-cart approach. Follow the *Live It Down* shopping list and tips, starting on the next page.

The *Live It Down* Shopping List

Staples

For the cupboard

- Canned beans, such as black, white, pinto, garbanzo, and kidney.*
- Dried fruits, such as figs, raisins, prunes, apricots, and dates.
- Whole wheat flour for baking.
- Apple sauce for baking.*
- A good bottle of virgin or extra virgin olive oil.
- Canola oil.
- Canned salmon and water-packed tuna.*
- Canned clams.*
- Canned sardines.*
- Canned fruit packed in its own juices or in light syrup.*
- Quick-cooking or old-fashioned oatmeal, but not the instant kind.
- Whole grain mix for pancakes and waffles.
- Cans of chopped tomatoes flavored with herbs, onions, or garlic for tossing with pasta.*
- Peanut butter (the natural kind, made without hydrogenated oil or added sugar).*
- Jarred artichoke hearts, sun dried tomatoes, and flavorful spreads, all of which can add pizzazz to pasta, rice, couscous, or other grains.*

Refrigerate after opening

For the fridge

- Low-fat mayonnaise.
- Hard, flavorful cheeses like Romano or Parmesan.
- A sterol-based spread such as Benecol or Take Control, or a margarine free of trans fats (such as Smart Balance).

For the freezer

- Frozen veggie or soy burgers.
- Frozen turkey meatballs.
- Frozen vegetables in bags.
- Frozen berries.
- Fillets of frozen fish, not breaded (slip unthawed pieces into simmering poaching liquid for a fast meal).

Perishables

Fruits and vegetables

- At least one fruit or vegetable of every color: red, green, orange, and yellow.
- Avocados.
- Garlic.
- Eggplant and mushrooms (for meatless meals).
- Bags of prewashed lettuce.
- Bags of baby carrots.
- Precut vegetables.
- Something new for you, like mango, star fruit, jicama, or bok choy.

Breads and grains

- Bread with the word "whole" in the first ingredient.
- Cereal with at least 5 grams of fiber per serving.
- Brown rice (regular or Minute Rice).
- Other grains, such as bulgur, barley, and quinoa.
- Whole wheat pasta.
- For a splurge, buy fresh-baked rounds of sourdough, rosemary, or olive bread for dipping in olive oil.

Meat and poultry

- Extra lean loin and round cuts.
- Chicken breasts.
- Ground turkey.
- Free-range meats, if you can find them (they're generally lower in fat).
- Game meats.

Seafood
- Fresh fish, especially salmon, tuna, and mackerel.
- Fresh shrimp, oysters, clams, crabs, or mussels.

Dairy
- Low-fat cheese.
- Strong-flavored cheeses like blue and feta.
- Nonfat or low-fat yogurt.
- Nonfat milk (low-fat is okay if you're not ready to drop all the way to nonfat just yet).
- Eggs enriched with omega-3 fatty acids.

Other
- Firm tofu.
- Soy crumbles (found in the frozen food section).
- Nuts, especially walnuts and almonds.
- Flaxseed, available in health food stores and some grocery stores.
- Wheat germ.

Condiments
- Capers.
- Hot sauces.
- Spicy mustard.
- Prechopped garlic and ginger.
- Low-fat vinegar-based salad dressings and marinades.
- Plum sauce, black bean sauce, and other Asian sauces for vegetable stir-fries.

Beverages
- Vegetable juice or 100 percent fruit juice.
- Green or black tea.
- Wine.

Tips for Successful *Live It Down* Shopping:

Read labels. Look for products that are high in fiber. If a product is high in sugar or fat or contains "partially hydrogenated" oils, put it back.

Take your time. In the beginning all of this label-reading and searching for healthy foods is going to take longer than the grocery trips you're used to. Plan accordingly.

Plan ahead. Whenever possible, plan meals ahead of time (you'll be less tempted by take-out or fast-food) and shop with a list. Use the recipes starting on page 230 for inspiration.

Shop alone. You may be less inclined to buy high-fat impulse items if you don't have company.

Make it easy for yourself. If time to cook is a factor, buy "semiprepared" foods. Some examples: boneless, skinless chicken breasts already marinated; marinated pork loin; broccoli and cauliflower florets; and salad or coleslaw in a bag.

Don't shop when you're hungry. If you're hungry, have a bite to eat before you shop. You'll be less tempted to fill your cart with high-fat convenience foods and empty calories.

Eating

GOAL | Attack saturated fat

1. Forego ground beef. If you want to make tacos or burgers, use ground turkey instead.
2. Choose only lean cuts of meat and poultry, such as chicken breast, pork loin, extra lean top round, or any of the others on page 106.
3. Start the switch to nonfat milk. If you currently drink whole milk, move to 2 percent. If you drink 2 percent, move to 1 percent. If you drink 1 percent, you're ready for nonfat.
4. Bag the butter. Dip your bread in olive oil instead, or use a sterol-based spread such as Benecol. And use olive oil or canola oil for cooking.
5. Skip the slice of cheese on your sandwich. When you do eat cheese, use just a little bit of a hard, flavorful variety like Romano.

Tip | *Use roasted garlic to add moistness and flavor in place of butter. Cut the tops off two heads of garlic, drizzle with olive oil, wrap in aluminum foil, and roast at 350°F for an hour or until soft. Cool. Squeeze out the garlic, mash, and use on bread or in mashed potatoes.*

Recipe Ideas

- **Hot and Spicy Tuna Rolls,** page 234.
- **Chicken and Pinto Bean Tacos,** page 238.
- **Mexican Pork with Salsa,** page 239.

Supplements

GOAL | Follow the supplement plan you outlined on page 202

Exercise

GOAL | 20,000 steps

1. Start wearing your pedometer all of the time. It will remind you to look for ways to fit more walking into your day.
2. On five days this week go for a 20-minute walk. Walk at whatever speed is comfortable, just get out there!

Tip | *Keep your pedometer in the bathroom, maybe even near your toothbrush, so you'll see it first thing in the morning and remember to put it on.*

Lifestyle

GOAL | Eliminate one source of stress

1. Identify one source of stress that's easily erased—and do whatever it takes to eliminate it. That could be as simple as clearing the clutter off your desk, buying files to keep your bills and other paperwork in, or placing a stick-on plastic hook on the back of your door or a kitchen cabinet for your keys so you'll always know where they are.

Tip | *Not sure what's stressing you? Keeping a journal can help. Note when you become anxious or angry, and why. Becoming more aware of what gets you stressed gives you a leg up on changing the situation, or at least your reaction to it.*

Keeping Track

THIS WEEK

Did you . . .

☐ Pass up ground beef?

☐ Eat lean cuts of meat and poultry? Write them down:

1. _____

2. _____

3. _____

☐ Use olive or canola oil for cooking?

☐ Use a sterol-based spread instead of butter?

☐ Make the switch to nonfat (or low-fat) milk?

☐ Go easy on the cheese?

☐ Eliminate one source of stress? Write it down:

_____

Area I want to do better in next week:

_____

_____

_____

EVERY WEEK

Did you . . .

☐ Take your fish-oil supplement and multi-vitamin every day?

☐ Take a baby aspirin every day if you're doctor has advised you to?

☐ Remember to laugh?

My Step-Tracker

Day	How many steps I took:
Monday	
Tuesday	
Wednesday	
Thursday	
Friday	
Saturday	
Sunday	
TOTAL	

Thought for the week |

Give yourself plenty of credit for starting the *Live It Down Plan.* Remember that you're not only cutting your risk of a heart attack, but also prolonging your life and improving its quality.

Eating

GOAL | Eat fish at least three times this week

1. Have fish for lunch. Nothing fancy is needed—think canned tuna or salmon. Try a salmon-cucumber sandwich with low-fat cream cheese.

2. Have a fish dinner at least once this week. Try a recipe below, or throw salmon or tuna steaks on the grill.

3. Check off a fish serving by using canned clams, salmon, anchovies, or sardines. Try clam sauce over pasta, an anchovy-olive spread (tapenade) as an appetizer, or salmon croquettes.

4. Treat yourself. The appeal of crab legs or lobster should not be ignored. Make one of these your treat for the week.

5. If you order pizza (go light on the cheese), top it with anchovies. Or try our tuna-topped pizza (recipe below).

Tip | *The flesh of fresh fish should spring back if you press it, its surface should glisten, and it shouldn't smell fishy. Frozen fish is generally a good bet, since it's often flash-frozen on docks or on the fishing boats themselves.*

Recipe Ideas

- **Seared Tuna and Bean Salad,** page 234.
- **Tuna and Tomato Pizza,** page 235.
- **Anchovy and Sesame-Topped Tuna,** page 236.
- **Salmon with Mango Salsa,** page 237.

Supplements

GOAL | Follow the supplement plan you outlined on page 202

Exercise

GOAL | 25,000 steps

1. On four days go for a 30-minute walk, keeping a comfortable pace. Practice good posture, with your arms bent at a 90-degree angle, your hands no higher than shoulder height in the forward motion and by the side of your body in the backward motion, your body held upright, and your shoulders pulled slightly back and down.

2. Deliberately park further from the mall entrance next time you go shopping, and eschew the elevator or escalator if you're going up three flights or fewer.

Tip | *When possible walk on a track or grass instead of a hard sidewalk or road to soften the impact on your joints.*

Lifestyle

GOAL | Learn a better way to breathe

1. Practice the slow, deep breathing exercise beginning on page 170, breathing so that your stomach expands, not your chest. Do this for one minute the first day, two or three minutes the next day, and four minutes the next. Aim for less than six breaths per minute.

Tip | *Your inhale and exhale should be approximately the same duration.*

Keeping Track

THIS WEEK

Did you . . .

☐ Have fish at least three times? Write down the meals:

1. _____

2. _____

3. _____

4. _____

5. _____

☐ Walk to an errand instead of driving?

☐ Use the stairs instead of the elevator?

☐ Park far from the mall entrance?

Area I want to do better in next week:

_____

_____

_____

EVERY WEEK

Did you . . .

☐ Avoid ground beef?

☐ Drink nonfat milk instead of whole?

☐ Use olive or canola oil or a sterol-based spread instead of butter?

☐ Wear your pedometer?

☐ Take your fish oil, aspirin, and multivitamin?

My Step-Tracker

Day	How many steps I took:
Monday	
Tuesday	
Wednesday	
Thursday	
Friday	
Saturday	
Sunday	
TOTAL	

Thought for the week |

Lowering your cholesterol doesn't require heroic measures, just small changes to some everyday habits. You can do it!

Eating

GOAL | Opt for oats

1. Start your day with oatmeal, a proven cholesterol-reducer, at least three mornings. Use the old-fashioned or quick-cooking variety, not instant.
2. Use oatmeal as a binder for your turkey meatballs instead of bread crumbs.
3. Replace up to one-third of the white flour in bread, muffin, and cookie recipes with oatmeal for extra fiber, texture, and flavor.
4. Try our delicious Pumpkin Oat Bread (recipe below) for breakfast or an afternoon snack.

Recipe Ideas

- **Fruity Muesli,** page 230.
- **Pumpkin Oat Bread,** page 247.
- **Apple Raspberry Brown Betty,** page 248.

Supplements

GOAL | Follow the supplement plan you outlined on page 202

Exercise

GOALS | 30,000 steps
Morning stretches (pages 158–159)

1. On five days go for a 30-minute walk. Check your heart rate after you finish your walk to see if you're in your target zone. (See page 142.) If you're not, try to pick up the pace a bit.
2. Keep looking for ways to add more movement to your daily life by walking to errands instead of driving, taking the stairs, getting up to change the channel, pacing while waiting at the airport— you get the idea.

Tip | *Before your walk, march in place for a few minutes to warm up your muscles, then do the stretches starting on page 144.*

Lifestyle

GOAL | Worry concretely

1. Write down your worries in a journal, and be very specific. For instance, "I'm worried that my husband will lose his job because there are rumors his plant might have layoffs," rather than, "I'm worried about our finances."
2. Ask yourself, "How likely is this to happen?" and, "What can I do to be more prepared or put my mind at ease?"

Extra credit

- Consider volunteering. Helping others lets you put your own problems into perspective and also provides social interaction.

Keeping Track

THIS WEEK

Did you . . .

- ☐ Have oatmeal for breakfast at least three times? Write down the days:

1. _____

2. _____

3. _____

- ☐ Do your morning stretches?
- ☐ Add oats to meatballs or baked goods?
- ☐ Enjoy our Pumpkin Oat Bread as a snack or dessert?

Area I want to do better in next week:

_____

_____

_____

EVERY WEEK

Did you . . .

- ☐ Eat fish three times?
- ☐ Use olive oil instead of butter?
- ☐ Wear your pedometer?
- ☐ Practice good walking posture?
- ☐ Take your multivitamin and fish-oil supplements every day?

My Step-Tracker

Day	How many steps I took:
Monday	
Tuesday	
Wednesday	
Thursday	
Friday	
Saturday	
Sunday	
TOTAL	

Thought for the week |

With the *Live It Down Plan*, you're not just cutting your cholesterol, you're slashing your overall risk of a heart attack or stroke by as much as 80 percent.

Eating

GOAL| Nine daily servings of fruits and vegetables

1. Add fruit to your morning cereal.
2. Fix salads for lunch three times this week and pile them high with at least three kinds of vegetables or fruit.
3. On days when you don't have a salad, have a piece of fruit with your lunch.
4. At dinnertime, before you put anything else on your plate, start with a salad or a heap of green beans or other vegetables. After you've eaten your vegetables, start on the rest of the meal.
5. Keep sliced vegetables in the fridge in ice water for convenient snacks.
6. Throw frozen vegetables (no need to defrost) into soups or stews.
7. Make a stir-fry and use twice the vegetables and half the meat.
8. Have a fruit-based dessert.

Tip | *A serving is a piece of fruit; $^1/_2$ cup cut-up fruit; $^1/_2$ cup cooked, raw, or frozen fruit or vegetable; 1 cup raw greens; $^3/_4$ cup 100 percent fruit juice; $^1/_4$ cup dried fruit.*

Recipe Ideas
- **Blueberry Cranberry Crunch,** page 230.
- **Thai Stir-Fried Steak with Mango,** page 240.
- **Couscous Casablanca,** page 242.
- **Apple Raspberry Brown Betty,** page 248.

Supplements

GOAL| Follow the supplement plan you outlined on page 202

Exercise

GOALS | 35,000 steps
 Morning stretches (pages 158–159)
 10-Minute Tune-Up on four days (page 149)

1. Walk for 40 minutes three days this week, and 30 minutes another two days.
2. Try to get at least 2,000 steps a day just through everyday lifestyle activities like vacuuming the house or gardening.

Tip | *Hide the remote and use commercials as signals to get up and walk up and down the stairs or circle your house until the program comes back on.*

Lifestyle

GOAL| Practice the art of spinning

1. View a challenge or setback in a more positive light this week—as a cue to change your approach, an opportunity to learn, or a bit of lousy luck that just may have an upside to it.

Tip | *Remember, it's not a stressful event that raises your blood pressure and heart disease risk, it's your reaction to that event.*

Keeping Track

THIS WEEK

My fruit and vegetable tally:

Monday	Tuesday	Wednesday	Thursday	Friday	Saturday	Sunday

Did you . . .

☐ See the positive side of a negative event?

☐ Do the 10-Minute Tune-Up four times? Mark which days:

☐ Monday ☐ Tuesday ☐ Wednesday ☐ Thursday ☐ Friday ☐ Saturday ☐ Sunday

Area I want to do better in next week:

_____

EVERY WEEK

Did you . . .

☐ Eat oatmeal on at least three mornings?

☐ Eat fish at least three times?

☐ Use a sterol-based spread?

☐ Take your fish-oil supplement and multi-vitamin every day?

☐ Practice your deep breathing?

☐ Call a friend whom you haven't spoken to in a while?

My Step-Tracker

Day	How many steps I took:
Monday	
Tuesday	
Wednesday	
Thursday	
Friday	
Saturday	
Sunday	
TOTAL	

Eating

GOAL| **Get your fill of soluble fiber**

1. Continue eating oatmeal at least three times a week.
2. Snack on apples.
3. Have beans at least three times. Some ideas: sprinkle garbanzo, black, or white beans on your salads; have lentil soup for lunch; add a can of rinsed white beans to pasta dishes; make chili (turkey or vegetarian) for dinner.
4. Make a high-fiber smoothie with 1 cup of strawberries, a carton of nonfat yogurt, and 2 tablespoons of flaxseed.
5. Eat at least three of these high-fiber foods: barley, dried peas, Brussels sprouts, lima beans, carrots, dried figs, apricots, prunes, dates, raisins, or nuts.

Tip| *Drink a full glass of water every two hours. You need the extra fluid to help your body adjust to the extra fiber.*

Recipe Ideas

- **Lentil-Tomato Stew with Browned Onions,** page 232.
- **Spinach, Sweet Potato, and Shiitake Salad,** page 232.
- **Bulgur Wheat and Prawn Salad,** page 233.
- **Seared Tuna and Bean Salad,** page 234.
- **Broccoli and Pearl Barley Salad,** page 245.

Supplements

GOAL| **Follow the supplement plan you outlined on page 202**

Exercise

GOALS| **40,000 steps**
  Morning stretches (pages 158–159)
  10-Minute Tune-Up on four days (page 149)

1. On four days this week take a 40-minute walk. On two other days walk for 20 minutes.
2. Vary your walking route so you don't get bored. Drive to a neighborhood you've always admired, or if the weather is bad, walk in the mall.
3. Keep looking for excuses to move more every day.

Tip| *Set the alarm on your computer to go off every 30 minutes. This is your signal to get up and take a five-minute break for a few stretches or a short walk.*

Lifestyle

GOAL| **Check your expectations**

1. Take one situation that always causes you stress—your daughter doesn't call as often as you'd like—and ask yourself if your expectations are realistic. Perhaps with two children she really doesn't have the time to talk twice a week. Or maybe e-mail would be more convenient for her at times.

Keeping Track

THIS WEEK

Log all of your high-fiber meals or snacks this week:

Monday	Tuesday	Wednesday	Thursday	Friday	Saturday	Sunday

Did you . . .

☐ Revamp an expectation? Write it down:

_____

Area I want to do better in next week:

_____

EVERY WEEK

Did you . . .

☐ Eat nine servings of fruits and vegetables on most days?

☐ Wear your pedometer?

☐ Have fish at least three times?

☐ Get enough sleep?

☐ Do the 10-Minute Tune-Up? Mark which days:

☐ Monday   ☐ Friday
☐ Tuesday   ☐ Saturday
☐ Wednesday   ☐ Sunday
☐ Thursday

My Step-Tracker

Day	How many steps I took:
Monday	
Tuesday	
Wednesday	
Thursday	
Friday	
Saturday	
Sunday	
TOTAL	

Eating

GOAL| Add more antioxidants

1. Brew a cup of tea each morning. If you don't like hot tea, have iced tea at lunch (go light on the sugar).

2. Enjoy a glass of red wine with dinner.

3. Concentrate on high-antioxidant fruits and vegetables (see page 112). Have an orange in the morning. Add frozen kale to soups at the last minute. Blend cooked prunes with water into a puree that can replace oils and fats in baking. Add dried prunes to stews for a delicious sweetness.

3. Snack on berries if they're in season, or use frozen berries in smoothies.

4. For dessert savor a piece of dark chocolate, chock full of heart-healthy antioxidants.

Recipe Ideas

- **Spinach, Sweet Potato, and Shiitake Salad,** page 232.
- **Broccoli and Pearl Barley Salad,** page 245.
- **Chocolate Cake with Raspberries,** page 248.

Supplements

GOAL| Follow the supplement plan you outlined on page 202

Exercise

GOALS| 45,000 steps
Morning stretches (pages 158–159)
10-Minute Tune-Up on four days (page 149)

1. This week walk for 40 minutes four times, and 30 minutes twice.

2. Make a date with a friend for at least half your walks. It will relieve any tedium and make the time go much faster.

Tip | *If you have a dog, vow to walk it more often. If you don't, offer to walk the neighbor's dog, or volunteer to walk dogs at the local animal shelter.*

Lifestyle

GOAL| Take control of your time

1. If you're the type who's always too busy, list all of your activities, chores, and commitments. Then divide them into three categories: those you must do, those you love to do, and those you do because you think you should.

2. Eliminate one item on the "because-you-think-you-should" list. Maybe you can let someone else chair the PTA this year, or hire someone to do your taxes instead of doing them yourself.

3. Whether or not you're too busy, schedule one fun activity this week. A trip to the zoo with the grandchildren, a visit to a botanical garden, a movie with friends—whatever you enjoy.

Tip | *Write a large "Just Say No" sign on a piece of paper and tape it near the phone as a reminder not to take on too much.*

Keeping Track

THIS WEEK

List the high-antioxidant fruits and vegetables you ate:

Monday	Tuesday	Wednesday	Thursday	Friday	Saturday	Sunday

Did you . . .

☐ Drink tea once a day?

☐ Enjoy a glass of wine with dinner?

☐ Eliminate a commitment?

☐ Do the 10-Minute Tune-Up? Mark which days:

☐ Monday   ☐ Friday
☐ Tuesday   ☐ Saturday
☐ Wednesday   ☐ Sunday
☐ Thursday

☐ Do something fun?

Area I want to do better in next week:

_____

_____

EVERY WEEK

Did you . . .

☐ Eat beans three times?

☐ Have oatmeal three mornings?

☐ Use olive oil or a sterol-based spread?

☐ Take your fish oil, multivitamins, and aspirin?

My Step-Tracker

Day	How many steps I took:
Monday	
Tuesday	
Wednesday	
Thursday	
Friday	
Saturday	
Sunday	
TOTAL	

Eating

GOAL | Go with the grain

1. Make sure you're eating a whole grain cereal with at least 5 grams of fiber per serving for breakfast. Raisin bran is a good choice.

2. Buy bread with the word "whole" in the first ingredient, as in "whole wheat" or "whole grain." Just because a bread is brown doesn't make it whole grain.

3. Try out a whole wheat pasta.

4. Substitute brown rice for white once this week.

5. Sprinkle wheat germ or flaxseed (both rich in omega-3 fatty acids) over salads, yogurt, and cereal, and into pancake batter.

6. Try one new grain you've never had, such as quinoa or amaranth. Most are as simple to fix as rice, yet are packed with fiber and other nutrients.

Recipe Ideas

- **Breakfast Muffins,** page 231.
- **Bulgur Wheat and Prawn Salad,** page 233.
- **Five-Star Cookies,** page 247.

Supplements

GOAL | Follow the supplement plan you outlined on page 202

Exercise

GOALS | 50,000 steps
Morning stretches (pages 158–159)
10-Minute Tune-Up on four days (page 149)

1. Walk for 45 minutes three times this week, and 30 minutes twice.

2. Continue finding ways to increase your physical activity around the house. That might be by gardening, raking, using a push-mower to cut the grass, or cleaning your entire house—including the baseboards.

Tip | *If you walk at dusk or night, wear a reflective vest and reflective tape on your shoes for safety.*

Lifestyle

GOAL | Forgive someone

1. Identify one person in your life toward whom you hold anger. Write that person a letter forgiving them. You can mail the letter or not; what's most important is writing it. Save a copy and look at it whenever you feel your anger toward this person returning.

Tip | *Are there things you'd like others to forgive you for? Write them down, then approach those people, either in person or in writing, and ask for their forgiveness.*

Keeping Track

THIS WEEK

Did you . . .

- ☐ Use wheat germ or flaxseed?
- ☐ Try a grain you'd never had before?
- ☐ Buy and use whole grain bread?
- ☐ Try a whole grain pasta?
- ☐ Eat brown rice?
- ☐ Write a letter forgiving a person in your life for some old hurt?
- ☐ Do the 10-Minute Tune-Up? Mark which days:

  ☐ Monday   ☐ Friday
  ☐ Tuesday   ☐ Saturday
  ☐ Wednesday   ☐ Sunday
  ☐ Thursday

Area I want to do better in next week:

_____

_____

_____

EVERY WEEK

Did you . . .

- ☐ Eat fish three times?
- ☐ Do your morning stretches?
- ☐ Practice good walking posture?
- ☐ Eat nine servings of fruits and vegetables?
- ☐ Have red wine or tea?
- ☐ Schedule something fun?

My Step-Tracker

Day	How many steps I took:
Monday	
Tuesday	
Wednesday	
Thursday	
Friday	
Saturday	
Sunday	
	TOTAL

Thought for the week |

Once people truly forgive those who have hurt them, they often speak of feeling as if a weight has been lifted from them.

Eating

GOAL| Pick the right protein

1. Continue choosing the leanest cuts of meat.

2. Have soy at least once this week. Add firm tofu to a stir-fry. Stir soy crumbles (found in the frozen food section) into spaghetti sauce or vegetable stew to provide some meat-like texture. Or opt for a soy burger, available in the freezer aisle at the grocery store.

3. If you haven't tried game meat, do so once this week. Venison and buffalo are both extremely low in saturated fat.

4. Instead of a roast beef sandwich, have egg salad (made with light mayo, of course). Eggs are an ideal source of protein. Look for eggs high in omega-3 fatty acids, sold at many stores.

Tip | *Don't buy tofu sold loose in open containers, as it may be contaminated with bacteria. Instead, buy packaged tofu in the refrigerated section of your grocery store.*

Recipe Ideas

- **Country Captain Chicken,** page 238.
- **Venison and Chestnut Casserole,** page 240.
- **Teriyaki-Style Noodles with Tofu,** page 243.

Supplements

GOAL| Follow the supplement plan you outlined on page 202

Exercise

GOALS| 50,000 steps
Morning stretches (pages 158–159)
30-Minute Total Body Toner on two days (page 153)

1. Walk for 45 minutes on three days, and 30 minutes on two others.

2. Vary your pace. After every 10 minutes of walking at a comfortable pace, increase your stride for five minutes, then slow down again.

Tip | *Get a freezer or refrigerator for the garage or basement and keep some staples there. It forces you to walk back and forth several times a day.*

Lifestyle

GOAL| Redirect your reactions

1. When something stressful happens, spend a minute on deep breathing. Then ask yourself:
   - Is the way I'm reacting to this situation increasing my tension?
   - Is my reaction logical and reasonable?
   - Is there another way to view the situation?

2. When a situation gets the better of you, pretend you're viewing it from afar, as if it's happening to someone else. This will help you be more objective and react more dispassionately.

Keeping Track

THIS WEEK

Did you . . .

- ☐ Try game meat for dinner?
- ☐ Prepare a tofu dish?
- ☐ Avoid ground beef?
- ☐ Redirect your reaction to a stressful event?
- ☐ Do the 30-Minute Total Body Toner twice? Mark which days:

☐ Monday	☐ Friday
☐ Tuesday	☐ Saturday
☐ Wednesday	☐ Sunday
☐ Thursday	

Area I want to do better in next week:

_____

_____

_____

EVERY WEEK

Did you . . .

- ☐ Take your fish-oil supplement and multi-vitamin every day?
- ☐ Sprinkle wheat germ or flaxseed over yogurt and cereal or into pancake mix?
- ☐ Have an exotic, high-fiber grain?
- ☐ Eat fish three times?
- ☐ Have oatmeal on several mornings?
- ☐ Do your morning stretches?

My Step-Tracker

Day	How many steps I took:
Monday	
Tuesday	
Wednesday	
Thursday	
Friday	
Saturday	
Sunday	
TOTAL	

Thought for the week |

You aren't following the *Live It Down Plan* just for yourself; you're also doing it for the people who love you.

Eating

GOAL | Fall in love with olive oil

1. Visit the gourmet section of your grocery store and choose three or four high-end olive oils for a tasting. (Follow the instructions on page 92.)

2. Drizzle olive oil on your toast or bagel, or dip hunks of bread into it instead of spreading on butter or margarine.

3. Substitute olive oil for margarine in recipes. Just use one-quarter less than what the recipe requires.

4. Sauté nuts in a little extra virgin olive oil, then store in the refrigerator. Use chopped over salads for extra protein, crunch, and cholesterol-lowering zing.

5. Baste turkey and chicken with extra virgin olive oil for extra flavor.

6. Try the roasted olive recipe on page 91.

7. Use extra virgin olive oil to replace smoked meats and sausages typically used to flavor bean and pea soups.

8. For a tasty dessert sauté bananas, apples, pears, or other fruits in light olive oil. Sprinkle with cinnamon and sugar and serve.

Recipe Ideas

- **Lentil-Tomato Stew with Browned Onions,** page 232.
- **Seared Tuna and Bean Salad,** page 234.
- **Salmon with Mango Salsa,** page 237.

Supplements

GOAL | Follow the supplement plan you outlined on page 202

Exercise

GOALS | 50,000 steps
Morning stretches (pages 158–159)
30-Minute Total Body Toner on two days (page 153)

1. Walk for 45 minutes on three days, and 30 minutes on two others.

Tip | *Adopt a stretch of road that you pledge to keep clean, then walk it several times a week to pick up trash.*

Lifestyle

GOAL | Rediscover (or discover) a hobby

1. Think about things you used to enjoy doing—or have always wanted to try—and decide to take up a hobby if you don't already have one. It could be needlepoint, woodworking, hiking, bird watching—something that you can throw yourself into and that makes time pass quickly.

Tip | *Can't think of a hobby? Write down all of the things you enjoyed as a child, then find one you can transfer to your adult life. For instance, if you loved to draw, sign up for a drawing class at the local community college or recreation center.*

Keeping Track

THIS WEEK

Did you . . .

- ☐ Buy some fancy olive oils and host a tasting?
- ☐ Dip your bread into olive oil and substitute olive oil for other fats in recipes?
- ☐ Find or rediscover a hobby?

Area I want to do better in next week:

_____

_____

_____

EVERY WEEK

Did you . . .

- ☐ Eat soy at least once this week?
- ☐ Practice your deep breathing?
- ☐ Get nine servings of fruits and vegetables on most days?
- ☐ Have oatmeal or a high-fiber cereal in the morning, along with a cup of tea?
- ☐ Drink plenty of water to help your body handle the extra fiber you're eating?

- ☐ Do the 30-Minute Total Body Toner twice? Mark which days:

  ☐ Monday   ☐ Friday
  ☐ Tuesday   ☐ Saturday
  ☐ Wednesday   ☐ Sunday
  ☐ Thursday

My Step-Tracker

Day	How many steps I took:
Monday	
Tuesday	
Wednesday	
Thursday	
Friday	
Saturday	
Sunday	
TOTAL	

Thought for the week |

Your mind and body truly are connected, and they both affect your health. The *Live It Down Plan* attends to both, providing a holistic approach to total health and well-being.

Eating

GOAL | Practice portion control

1. When you eat out this week, ask to have half of your main dish boxed up before it's even brought to the table.

2. Eyeball your meals. A portion of meat is about the size of a deck of cards or a computer mouse; a portion of pasta or rice is about the size of a baseball.

3. Eat more slowly to give yourself time to feel full. Then put down your fork when you're no longer hungry—not when the plate is empty.

4. Measure your morning cereal. A portion is 1 cup, yet most Americans take at least twice that.

5. Dole out your snacks. Instead of digging into an open bag of pretzels, place a few pretzels on a napkin, then put the bag away.

6. Buy the smallest size. Studies find that when you buy larger sizes, you eat more. So get a small popcorn, Italian ice, or whatever you're eating.

Recipe Ideas

- **Tuna and Tomato Pizza,** page 235.
- **Couscous Casablanca,** page 242.
- **Veggie Burger,** page 244.

Supplements

GOAL | Follow the supplement plan you outlined on page 202

Exercise

GOALS | 50,000 steps
Morning stretches (pages 158–159)
30-Minute Total Body Toner on two days (page 153)

1. Walk for 45 minutes on three days, and 30 minutes on two others.

2. Vary your pace. After 15 minutes at your normal pace, walk faster for 15 minutes before slowing down again.

3. Give a pedometer to a friend or spouse and hold a competition to see who can reach their steps goal first.

Tip | *Trade in your new shoes when you've walked 350 to 550 miles in them. If you're logging about 15 miles a week (2 to 3 miles a day, five days a week), that means replacing them about every six months.*

Lifestyle

GOAL | Make yourself happy

1. Do at least one thing from the list of "20 Simple Ways to Get Happy" (page 177) each day.

Tip | *Feeling truly overwhelmed and stressed? Take a nap. Even if you don't fall asleep, an hour in a quiet, dark room will do wonders for your mood and mind, not to mention your blood pressure.*

Keeping Track

THIS WEEK

Did you . . .

- ☐ Bring home half your entrée every time you ate out?
- ☐ Measure your morning cereal?
- ☐ Eat more slowly?
- ☐ Keep snacking under control?

Areas I want to do better in next week:

_____

_____

_____

EVERY WEEK

Did you . . .

- ☐ Fill up on vegetables first?
- ☐ Read labels at the grocery store?
- ☐ Practice good walking posture?
- ☐ Spend some time with a friend?
- ☐ Get a good night's sleep?
- ☐ Do the 30-Minute Total Body Toner twice? Mark which days:

  - ☐ Monday   ☐ Friday
  - ☐ Tuesday   ☐ Saturday
  - ☐ Wednesday   ☐ Sunday
  - ☐ Thursday

My Step-Tracker

Day	How many steps I took:
Monday	
Tuesday	
Wednesday	
Thursday	
Friday	
Saturday	
Sunday	
TOTAL	

Thought for the week |

Your body was designed for motion. As you become more fit, take pleasure in your vigor, in the simple physical prowess of your muscles.

Eating

GOAL| Switch your snacks

1. Keep the fridge stocked with cut-up vegetables and fruits so it doesn't take any effort to reach for a healthy snack.

2. For an extra treat dip apples, celery, or carrots in peanut butter (buy the natural kind with no trans fats). Just limit the portion, or you could find yourself eating an entire week's worth of fat calories in one sitting.

3. Instead of potato chips, have a handful of nuts. Walnuts and almonds are good choices. Toast them to bring out their full flavor.

4. For a delightful change of pace, try roasted soy nuts, available in many grocery and health food stores.

5. Bake your own tortilla chips: Simply spray flour tortillas with cooking spray, salt lightly, cut into wedges with kitchen shears, and bake at 325°F until crisp. Enjoy them with salsa or guacamole (full of heart-healthy fats).

6. Bake some heart-healthy sweets, such as oatmeal cookies (use oil in place of butter) or either of the recipes below.

Recipe Ideas

- **Five-Star Cookies,** page 247.
- **Date and Walnut Cake,** page 249.

Supplements

GOAL| Follow the supplement plan you outlined on page 202

Exercise

GOALS| 50,000 steps
Morning stretches (pages 158–159)
30-Minute Total Body Toner on two days (page 153)

1. Walk for 45 minutes on three days, and 30 minutes on two others, or choose another moderate-level activity, such as ballroom dancing.

Tip| *Anytime you get tired of walking, try working out to one of the exercise videos mentioned on page 160 and 161 instead.*

Lifestyle

GOAL| Live in the moment

1. Too often we're on "autopilot," doing a million things at once and not giving anything our full attention. This week focus on concentrating fully on whatever task you're engaged in. Instead of doing the dishes while you talk on the phone, curl up in a comfortable chair and get into the conversation. Instead of worrying about your checkup tomorrow while you have dinner with your family, focus on the here and now—the food, the company, the conversation.

Keeping Track

THIS WEEK

Track all of the snacks—healthy and otherwise —you had this week. Write down how you did:

_____

_____

_____

_____

_____

Did you . . .

☐ Avoid potato chips and candy bars?

☐ Bake a heart-healthy treat?

☐ Substitute another moderate physical activity for walking?

☐ Practice living "in the moment"?

Area I want to do better in next week:

_____

EVERY WEEK

Did you . . .

☐ Take your fish-oil supplement and multi-vitamin every day?

☐ Keep portion sizes reasonable?

☐ Have at least one soy or bean dish?

☐ Hug someone?

☐ Do the 30-Minute Total Body Toner twice? Mark which days:

☐ Monday   ☐ Friday
☐ Tuesday   ☐ Saturday
☐ Wednesday   ☐ Sunday
☐ Thursday

My Step-Tracker

Day	How many steps I took:
Monday	
Tuesday	
Wednesday	
Thursday	
Friday	
Saturday	
Sunday	
TOTAL	

Thought for the week |

Remember, you're human; you may occasionally have a bad day and "fall off" the Plan. Forgive yourself, then get back on track!

Eating

GOAL | **Eat out the *Live It Down* Way**

1. Hit Subway for lunch, ordering a veggie or turkey sub. Or go to any of the restaurants on pages 120–121 and order something that gets less than 25 percent of its calories from fat.

2. Ask for extra rice—brown, if possible—with your Chinese takeout. Mix it into the dish, then put half of the dish in the fridge for another day.

3. Have the waiter put half of your meal in a doggie bag before it's even served.

4. Practice your assertiveness. If a dish comes with a cream sauce, ask for a tomato sauce instead. If it comes with french fries, ask to substitute a salad or a side of steamed vegetables. Find out if the dish comes with butter on top, and ask to have it omitted.

5. Ask for dressings on the side.

6. Request olive oil instead of butter for your bread.

7. Ask the waiter to take away the tortilla chips.

Tip | *Any menu description that uses the words "creamy," "breaded," "crisp," or "stuffed" is likely a dish loaded with fat.*

Recipe Ideas
- **No recipes this week since you're eating out. But you should have plenty of leftovers from your doggie bags.**

Supplements

GOAL | **Follow the supplement plan you outlined on page 202**

Exercise

GOALS | **50,000 steps**
Morning stretches (pages 158–159)
30-Minute Total Body Toner on two days (page 153)

1. Walk for 45 minutes on three days, and 30 minutes on two others.

Tip | *Anytime you wish you can substitute a different activity for walking, such as playing volleyball, ballroom dancing, swimming, or bicycling.*

Lifestyle

GOAL | **Nurture a friendship**

1. Studies find that friendships are wonderful antidotes to stress. Spend some time this week with a friend. Make a date for lunch, take a walk together, or see an afternoon movie, followed by a cup of tea or glass of wine.

Tip | *Feel like you're lacking friends? Call someone you'd count only as a casual acquaintance and invite them to breakfast.*

Keeping Track

THIS WEEK

Did you . . .

- ☐ Go to Subway for lunch and order a veggie or turkey sub?
- ☐ Practice your assertiveness while ordering?
- ☐ Avoid ordering fried entrées or anything smothered in butter or cheese?
- ☐ Request a salad instead of fries?
- ☐ Ask for doggie bags?

Area I want to do better in going forward:

_____

_____

_____

EVERY WEEK

Did you . . .

- ☐ Take your fish oil, multivitamin, and aspirin?
- ☐ Eat lean cuts of meat?
- ☐ Have fish at least three times?
- ☐ Have oatmeal at least three mornings?
- ☐ Snack on fruit?
- ☐ Replace butter with olive oil?
- ☐ Practice your deep breathing?
- ☐ Have some fun?
- ☐ Get a good night's sleep?
- ☐ Do the 30-Minute Total Body Toner twice? Mark which days:

  - ☐ Monday
  - ☐ Tuesday
  - ☐ Wednesday
  - ☐ Thursday
  - ☐ Friday
  - ☐ Saturday
  - ☐ Sunday

My Step-Tracker

Day	How many steps I took:
Monday	
Tuesday	
Wednesday	
Thursday	
Friday	
Saturday	
Sunday	
TOTAL	

Thought for the week |

Congratulations! You've completed 12 weeks of the *Live It Down Plan*. But don't stop now. The changes you've made are for life—your life!

Good Beginnings |
Breakfast

Fruity Muesli

See photo | page 98 | **Serves 4**

For a nutty, high-fiber start to your day, try this cereal, inspired by a recipe developed more than a century ago in Zurich, Switzerland.

1/2 **cup rolled oats**
1/2 **cup raisins**
 1 **cup nonfat milk**
 1 **apple, grated**
 2 **teaspoons lemon juice**
 2 **tablespoons hazelnuts, roughly chopped**
 1 **tablespoon pumpkin seeds**
 1 **tablespoon sesame seeds**
 4 **ounces strawberries, chopped**
 4 **tablespoons plain low-fat yogurt**
 4 **teaspoons honey**

Preparation time | 10 minutes, plus overnight soaking

1. Place the oats and raisins in a large bowl and add the milk. Stir well, cover, and place in the refrigerator. Soak overnight.

2. The next day, just before serving, grate the apple, discarding the core. Toss the apple with the lemon juice to prevent browning.

3. Stir the hazelnuts, pumpkin seeds, and sesame seeds into the oat mixture, then stir in the grated apple and chopped strawberries.

4. Divide the muesli among 4 cereal bowls, and top each with the yogurt and honey.

Each serving provides | Calories 239, fat 6 g, saturated fat 1 g, cholesterol 3 mg, sodium 56 mg, carbohydrates 41 g, fiber 4 g, protein 8 g.

Blueberry Cranberry Crunch

See photo | page 111 | **Makes 6 cups**

This cereal starts with a box of low-fat raisin granola and adds berries, nuts, and seeds for extra heart friendliness.

 4 **cups low-fat packaged raisin granola**
1/2 **cup dried cranberries**
1/3 **cup dried blueberries**
1/4 **cup slivered blanched almonds**
 2 **tablespoons light brown sugar**
 2 **tablespoons sunflower seeds**
 1 **tablespoon sesame seeds**
 2 **tablespoons fresh orange juice**
 2 **tablespoons maple syrup**
 2 **tablespoons canola oil**

Preparation time | 10 minutes
Cooking time | 25 minutes

1. Preheat the oven to 325°F and set out a shallow baking pan with sides, about 10 by 15 by 1 inches. In a large bowl combine the granola, dried cranberries and blueberries, almonds, sugar, and the sunflower and sesame seeds.

2. In a measuring cup whisk together the orange juice, maple syrup, and oil. Drizzle this mixture over the dry ingredients. Toss well.

3. Spread in a single layer in the pan. Bake until slightly crisp and lightly browned, about 25 minutes. Stir every 10 minutes to ensure even browning.

4. Remove from the oven and let cool. Serve with low-fat vanilla yogurt or nonfat milk. This can be stored in an airtight container at room temperature for up to 2 weeks.

More ideas |
• Replace cranberries and blueberries with 1/4 cup chopped dried apricots and 1/4 cup golden raisins.

Each serving (1/2 cup) provides | Calories 218, fat 6 g, saturated fat 1 g, cholesterol 0 mg, sodium 75 mg, carbohydrates 39 g, fiber 3 g, protein 3 g.

Breakfast Muffins

See photo | page 97 | **Makes 12 muffins**

We call these breakfast muffins, but the truth is that you can enjoy them any time of day.

¹/₂ **cup whole wheat flour**
³/₄ **cup all purpose flour**
 2 **teaspoons baking soda**
Pinch of salt
¹/₄ **teaspoon ground cinnamon**
¹/₄ **cup brown sugar**
 2 **tablespoons wheat germ**
³/₄ **cup raisins**
 1 **container (8 ounces) plain low-fat yogurt**
 4 **tablespoons canola oil**
 1 **egg**
Grated zest of ¹/₂ **orange**
 3 **tablespoons orange juice**

Preparation time | 15 minutes
Cooking time | 15–20 minutes

1. Preheat the oven to 400°F. Line 12 muffin cups with paper liners, or coat with nonstick cooking spray. Set aside.

2. Sift the flours, baking soda, salt, and cinnamon into a large bowl. Stir in the brown sugar, wheat germ, and raisins, and make a well in the center of the dry ingredients.

3. Lightly whisk together the yogurt, oil, egg, orange zest, and juice. Pour into the well and stir only enough to moisten.

4. Spoon into the muffin cups. Bake until the muffins are golden brown and the centers are firm when gently touched, about 15–20 minutes. Leave muffins to cool in the tray for 2–3 minutes, then turn out onto a wire rack. The muffins are best eaten fresh, preferably still slightly warm from the oven, but can be cooled completely and then kept in an airtight container for as many as 2 days.

More ideas |
• Substitute chopped prunes or dried dates for the raisins.
• For carrot and spice muffins, add a dash of nutmeg, stir 2 small grated carrots into the flour mixture with the wheat germ, and reduce the amount of raisins to ¹/₄ cup.

Each muffin provides | Calories 154, fat 6 g, saturated fat 1 g, cholesterol 19 mg, sodium 232 mg, carbohydrates 24 g, fiber 1 g, protein 4 g.

Lip-Smacking and Light |
Lunch

Open-Faced Sardine, Watercress, and Carrot Sandwich

Serves 4

A quick and easy way to get 1 of your 3 weekly servings of fish.

 1 **carrot, grated**
 2 **cups watercress, roughly chopped**
 2 **tablespoons chopped fresh chives**
 5 **ounces reduced-fat cream cheese**
 8 **thick slices rye bread**
 2 **cans (7 ounces each) sardines packed in olive oil, drained**
 1 **small red onion, thinly sliced**

Garnish: several whole fresh chives

Preparation time | 10 minutes

1. Mix the grated carrot, watercress, and chives into the cream cheese. Season to taste with pepper.

2. Spread the cheese mixture evenly over a side of each slice of rye bread. Halve the sardines lengthwise, then arrange them skin-side up on top of the cheese.

3. Arrange the red onion slices over the sardines and top with a few long pieces of chive. Sprinkle with pepper and serve.

Each serving provides | Calories 453, fat 20 g, saturated fat 7 g, cholesterol 147 mg, sodium 1,021 mg, carbohydrates 37 g, fiber 5 g, protein 31 g.

Spinach, Sweet Potato, and Shiitake Salad

See photo | page 90 | **Serves 4**

Loaded with fiber, this is a wonderful winter salad. To save time, instead of baking the sliced sweet potatoes in the oven, microwave whole, unpeeled potatoes and then peel and slice them after cooking.

- 1 **pound sweet potatoes, peeled, halved lengthwise, and cut crosswise into $^{1}/_{3}$-inch slices**
- $^{1}/_{3}$ **cup walnuts, shelled**
- 2 **cloves garlic, minced**
- 12 **ounces fresh shiitake mushrooms, stems discarded and caps thickly sliced**
- $^{1}/_{4}$ **teaspoon salt**
- 12 **cups spinach leaves**
- 4 **teaspoons olive oil**
- $^{1}/_{2}$ **cup red wine vinegar**
- 1 **tablespoon Dijon mustard**

Preparation time | 10 minutes
Cooking time | 25–30 minutes

1. Preheat the oven to 400°F. Place the sweet potatoes on a baking sheet coated with non-stick cooking spray, and bake until tender, about 15–20 minutes. Remove the potatoes from the oven and cool. Toast the walnuts in a separate pan in the oven until crisp, about 5–7 minutes. Coarsely chop the nuts when they are cool enough to handle.

2. Heat a large nonstick skillet coated with cooking spray over medium heat. Add the garlic and cook until fragrant, about 30 seconds.

3. Add half the mushrooms, sprinkle them with the salt, and cook until they begin to soften, about 4 minutes. Add the remaining mushrooms and cook until all the mushrooms are tender, about 5 minutes.

4. Place the spinach in a large bowl. Add the sweet potatoes and walnuts. Remove the mushrooms from the skillet with a slotted spoon and add to the bowl with the spinach.

5. Add the oil, vinegar, and mustard to the skillet, and whisk over high heat until warm. Pour the dressing over the salad and toss to combine.

Each serving provides | Calories 256, fat 11 g, saturated fat 1 g, cholesterol 0 mg, sodium 320 mg, carbohydrates 37 g, fiber 7 g, protein 7 g.

Lentil-Tomato Stew with Browned Onions

Serves 6

This hearty, fiber-rich dish can also serve as a main meal.

- 1 **cup dried shiitake mushrooms**
- 1 **cup boiling water**
- 1 **tablespoon olive oil**
- 3 **carrots, quartered lengthwise and thinly sliced crosswise**
- 8 **cloves garlic, thinly sliced**
- $^{3}/_{4}$ **cup lentils, rinsed and picked over**
- 1 **cup canned crushed tomatoes**
- $^{3}/_{4}$ **teaspoon salt**
- $^{3}/_{4}$ **teaspoon ground cumin**

³/₄ teaspoon ground ginger
¹/₂ teaspoon rubbed sage
 3 cups water
 1 large onion, halved and thinly sliced
 2 teaspoons sugar
 1 cup frozen peas

Preparation time | 15 minutes
Cooking time | 1 hour

1. In a small bowl combine the shiitake mushrooms and boiling water. Let stand until the mushrooms are softened, about 20 minutes. Remove the mushrooms with a slotted spoon and reserve the liquid. Trim any stems from the mushrooms and thinly slice the caps. Strain the reserved liquid through a fine-meshed sieve or coffee filter. Set aside.

2. In a large saucepan heat 2 teaspoons of the oil over medium heat. Add the carrots and garlic, and cook until softened, about 5 minutes.

3. Stir in the lentils, tomatoes, salt, cumin, ginger, sage, mushrooms, and reserved liquid. Add 3 cups of water and bring to a boil. Reduce to a simmer; cover and cook until the lentils are tender, about 35 minutes.

4. Meanwhile, in a large skillet heat the remaining 1 teaspoon of oil over medium heat. Add the onion and sugar; cook, stirring frequently until the onion is lightly browned, about 5 minutes.

5. Add the peas to the stew and cook for 2 minutes to heat through. Serve the stew topped with the browned onions.

More ideas |
• 2 cups of fresh, sliced mushrooms can be used in place of the dried mushrooms. Eliminate the hot water and the soaking step.
• Any vegetables can be added to this stew. Celery, red potatoes, sweet potatoes, and parsnips make wonderful additions. Chop finely and add with the carrots.

Each serving provides | Calories 237, fat 3 g, saturated fat 0 g, cholesterol 0 mg, sodium 496 mg, carbohydrates 43 g, fiber 13g, protein 13 g.

Bulgur Wheat and Prawn Salad

See photo | page 82 | **Serves 4**

Bulgur is coarsely ground wheat that has been parboiled, so it's quick and easy to prepare. This nutty-textured, colorful salad is a great main dish for a summer lunch or picnic.

 1 cup bulgur wheat
 3 cups water
 1 small red onion, very thinly sliced
 1 carrot, coarsely grated
 1 tomato, diced
 1 can (8 ounces) baby corn, sliced into rounds
¹/₂ cucumber, diced
 7 ounces peeled cooked prawns or shrimp

Lime and chili dressing:
 3 tablespoons extra virgin olive oil
 2 tablespoons fresh lime juice
 1 garlic clove, crushed
¹/₄ teaspoon crushed dried chilies
Salt and pepper to taste

Preparation and cooking time | 20–25 minutes

1. Put the bulgur wheat in a saucepan with 3 cups of water. Bring to a boil, then simmer until the bulgur is tender and all of the water has been absorbed, about 10 minutes. Spread in a flat dish and allow to cool slightly.

2. Combine the onion, carrot, tomato, corn, cucumber, and prawns in a large salad bowl. Add the bulgur and stir together.

3. For the dressing, place the oil, lime juice, garlic, and chilies in a small bowl; add salt and pepper to taste. Whisk with a fork. Stir the dressing into the salad, tossing to coat all the ingredients evenly. Cover the salad and keep it in the refrigerator if not serving immediately.

More ideas |
• For a bulgur wheat and feta salad, replace the prawns with 3 ounces of diced feta cheese. Another alternative to the prawns is diced tofu.

Each serving provides | Calories 299, fat 11 g, saturated fat 1 g, cholesterol 96 mg, sodium 133 mg, carbohydrates 36 g, fiber 9 g, protein 16 g.

Seared Tuna and Bean Salad

Serves 4

Perhaps the ideal cholesterol-lowering meal!

- 1 **piece (14 ounces) tuna steak, about 2 inches thick**
- 2 **tablespoons extra virgin olive oil**
- 1 **tablespoon lemon juice (or to taste)**
- 1 **garlic clove, crushed**
- 1 **tablespoon Dijon mustard**
- 1 **can (15 ounces) cannellini beans, drained and rinsed**
- 1 **small red onion, thinly sliced**
- 2 **red peppers, seeded and thinly sliced**
- 1/2 **cucumber, halved lengthwise and thinly sliced**
- 6 **cups watercress**

Salt and pepper
Lemon wedges to garnish

Preparation and cooking time | 30 minutes

1. Heat a ridged grill pan (preferably cast iron) coated with cooking spray over medium-high heat. Season the tuna steak on both sides with coarsely ground black pepper.

2. Cook the fish for 4 minutes on each side—the outside should be browned and the center light pink. Take care not to overcook. Remove from the pan and set aside.

3. Mix together the oil, lemon juice, garlic, and mustard in a salad bowl. Season with salt and pepper to taste, and add more lemon juice if needed. Add the cannellini beans, onion, and peppers. Cut the cucumber lengthwise into quarters, then cut the quarters into 1/2-inch slices. Add to the bowl together with the watercress. Toss gently to mix.

4. Cut the tuna into slices about 1/2-inch thick. Arrange on top of the salad. Serve with lemon wedges.

Each serving provides | Calories 335, fat 12 g, saturated fat 1 g, cholesterol 37 mg, sodium 225 mg, carbohydrates 26 g, fiber 7 g, protein 32 g.

Hot and Spicy Tuna Rolls

Serves 4

Here the soft interiors of crusty bread rolls are hollowed out to provide a crisp casing for a gently spiced mix of tuna, corn, and kidney beans, and then warmed in the oven. Serve with a salad of mixed greens and tomatoes.

- 4 **small, round whole wheat bread rolls, about 3 inches across**
- 2 **tablespoons low-fat sour cream**
- 2 **tablespoons reduced-fat mayonnaise**
- 1 **teaspoon hot chili sauce**
- 2 **teaspoons fresh lime juice**
- 1 **can (6 ounces) tuna in spring water, drained**
- 1 **can (8 ounces) corn, drained**
- 1 **can (15 ounces) red kidney beans, drained and rinsed**
- 1/2 **green pepper, seeded and diced**
- 2 **tablespoons chopped fresh cilantro**

Salt and pepper

Preparation time | 15 minutes
Cooking time | 10 minutes

1. Preheat the oven to 350°F. Slice the tops off the bread rolls and set aside. Scoop out most of the soft interior, leaving a "shell" about 1/2-inch thick.

2. Make the scooped-out bread into crumbs, either by crumbling with your fingers or using a food processor. Spread 1/2 cup of the bread

crumbs on a baking tray and toast in the oven until dry and crisp, about 10 minutes. Remove from the oven and set aside. Leave the oven on.

3. In a medium bowl mix together the sour cream, mayonnaise, chili sauce, and lime juice. Add the tuna, corn, kidney beans, green pepper, cilantro, and dried bread crumbs. Season with salt and pepper to taste. Stir well, taking care not to break up the chunks of tuna too much.

4. Spoon the tuna mixture into the hollowed-out rolls and replace the lids. Set on the baking tray and cover loosely with foil. Bake for 5 minutes, then remove the foil and bake for an additional 5 minutes to crisp the bread crust. The filling should be warm but not bubbling. Serve immediately.

Each serving provides | Calories 279, fat 3 g, saturated fat 1 g, cholesterol 13 mg, sodium 579 mg, carbohydrates 43 g, fiber 7g, protein 20 g.

Tuna and Tomato Pizza

See photo | page 89 | **Serves 4**

Who says pizza can't be heart-healthy? If you don't want to use a store-bought pizza crust, use any type of crusty Italian bread or whole wheat English muffins.

- 2 **teaspoons olive oil**
- 1 **onion, finely chopped**
- 1 **can (14 1/2 ounces) chopped tomatoes**
- 1/2 **teaspoon dried oregano**
- **Pinch of sugar**
- 2 **ready-made pizza crusts,
  about 8 1/4 ounces each**
- 2 **tablespoons tomato puree**
- 1 **can (7 ounces) tuna in spring water,
  drained and flaked**
- 4 **teaspoons capers**
- 8 **black olives, pitted and sliced**
- **Salt and pepper**
- **Fresh basil leaves to garnish**

Preparation time | 15 minutes
Cooking time | 10 minutes

1. Preheat the oven to 425°F. Heat 1 teaspoon of the oil in a small saucepan, add the onion, and cook over medium heat until softened, about 4 minutes. Add the tomatoes, their juice, oregano, and sugar. Season with salt and pepper to taste, and simmer for 10 minutes, stirring occasionally.

2. Put the pizza crusts on 2 baking sheets. Spread 1 tablespoon of tomato puree over each crust. Spoon the tomato sauce over the pizzas, then add the tuna. Sprinkle with the capers and sliced olives, and drizzle the remaining olive oil over the top.

3. Bake the pizzas until the crusts are crisp and golden, about 10 minutes. Sprinkle with torn basil leaves and serve immediately.

More ideas |
• Substitute canned salmon or sardines for tuna.

Each serving provides | Calories 449, fat 4 g, saturated fat 0 g, cholesterol 13 mg, sodium 740 mg, carbohydrates 80 g, fiber 7 g, protein 22 g.

What's the Catch? |
Main Dish Fish

Anchovy and Sesame-Topped Tuna

Serves 4

Tuna is one of the top sources of omega-3 fatty acids. Pair this dish with a crisp salad or lightly steamed broccoli for a complete meal.

- 1 **large onion, thinly sliced**
- 1 **large red pepper, seeded and thinly sliced**
- 1 **large yellow pepper, seeded and thinly sliced**
- 2 **garlic cloves, finely chopped**
- 1 **can (14 1/2 ounces) chopped tomatoes**
- 1 **tablespoon tomato puree**
- 1 **bay leaf**
- 1/2 **teaspoon hot chili sauce**
- 2 **tuna steaks (about 1 pound total), 3/4-inch thick**

Anchovy and sesame topping:
- 1/4 **cup fresh whole wheat bread crumbs**
- 1 **garlic clove**
- 4 **anchovy fillets, drained**
- 1/4 **cup trimmed fresh parsley**
- 2 **tablespoons sesame seeds**
- 2 **teaspoons olive oil**
- **Salt and pepper**

Preparation time | 20 minutes
Cooking time | 10 minutes

1. Preheat the oven to 400°F. Heat a large non-stick skillet coated with cooking spray over medium heat and add the onion, peppers, and garlic. Cover and cook, stirring frequently until the onion has softened, about 3–4 minutes. Stir in the tomatoes and their juice, the tomato puree, bay leaf, and chili sauce. Cover again and cook, stirring frequently until the peppers are just tender, about 7 minutes.

2. Meanwhile, make the topping. Combine all of the ingredients in a blender or food processor and process until finely chopped. Or chop the bread crumbs, garlic, anchovies, and parsley, put in a bowl, and mix in the sesame seeds and oil with a fork until well combined.

3. Spread the pepper mixture in the bottom of an ovenproof dish large enough to hold the fish in 1 layer. Lightly sprinkle the tuna steaks with salt and pepper, and cut each in half. Place the 4 pieces in the dish and cover evenly with the topping mixture. Bake until the fish is just cooked, about 10 minutes; it should be a little pink in the center. If you prefer tuna more well done, cook 1–2 minutes longer.

Each serving provides | Calories 298, fat 11 g, saturated fat 1 g, cholesterol 47 mg, sodium 425 mg, carbohydrates 19 g, fiber 5 g, protein 31 g.

Fish en Papillote

See photo | page 107 | **Serves 4**

Baking in foil packets is a simple and trouble-free way to prepare fish. It's healthy, too, as no water-soluble nutrients are lost.

- 10 **ounces mixed Asian greens, such as bok choy and Chinese cabbage, chopped**
- 4 **skinless salmon or hake steaks (about 5 ounces each)**
- **Grated zest and juice of 1/2 small orange**
- 3 **tablespoons shredded fresh basil**
- 2 **garlic cloves, finely chopped**
- 1/2 **cup dry white wine**
- 1 **tablespoon olive oil**
- 1/2 **medium-sized bulb of fennel, thinly sliced**
- 1 **carrot, cut into thin strips**

Bulgur and herb pilaf:
 1 **cup bulgur**
 3 **cups water**
 1 **tablespoon olive oil**
Juice of 1/2 **lemon**
 1 **garlic clove, finely chopped**
 2 **tablespoons shredded fresh basil**
 2 **tablespoons chopped fresh cilantro**
 3 **spring onions, sliced**
Salt and pepper

Preparation time | 20 minutes
Cooking time | 10–15 minutes

1. Preheat the oven to 475°F. Cut out 4 12-inch squares of foil or baking parchment. Arrange a quarter of the chopped Asian greens in the middle of each foil or paper square. Top with a fish steak, and sprinkle with the orange zest and juice, basil, garlic, white wine, olive oil, fennel, carrot, and salt and pepper to taste. Fold over the foil or paper to form a packet, leaving a little air inside so the ingredients can steam, and twist the edges to seal. Put the packets on a baking sheet and set aside.

2. Combine the bulgur with 3 cups of water in a large saucepan and bring to a boil. Reduce the heat to medium-low, cover, and cook until the bulgur is just tender, about 12–15 minutes. Drain the bulgur if necessary.

3. While the bulgur is cooking, put the fish packets into the oven and bake for 10 minutes. Open 1 of the parcels to check that the fish is cooked and will flake easily.

4. Use a fork to fluff the cooked bulgur and mix in the olive oil, lemon juice, garlic, basil, cilantro, and spring onions. Season with salt and pepper to taste. Serve each person a fish packet to open at the table, with the bulgur pilaf in a bowl.

Each serving provides | Calories 469, fat 20 g, saturated fat 3 g, cholesterol 88 mg, sodium 127 mg, carbohydrates 36 g, fiber 10 g, protein 37 g.

Salmon with Mango Salsa

See photo | page 85 | **Serves 4**

This salsa is also delicious with other oily fish, such as tuna, swordfish, and mackerel.

 4 **salmon fillets (5 ounces each)**
 4 **teaspoons mixed peppercorns
    (black, white, green, and pink)**
1 1/2 **pounds baby new potatoes, scrubbed
    and halved if large**
 5 **cups watercress**

Mango salsa
 1 **ripe mango**
 3 **spring onions, finely chopped**
 3 **tablespoons chopped fresh cilantro**
 2 **tablespoons fresh lime juice**
 2 **teaspoons olive oil**
Tabasco sauce to taste

Preparation time | 20 minutes
Cooking time | 20 minutes

1. Check the salmon for any tiny bones and remove them. Roughly crush the peppercorns with a mortar and pestle. Press them into the flesh side of the salmon. Set aside.

2. Cut the potatoes into a saucepan, cover with water, and bring to a boil. Reduce the heat and simmer until tender, about 10–12 minutes.

3. Meanwhile, make the salsa. Peel and seed the mango, dice the flesh, and put into a large bowl. Mix in the spring onions, coriander, lime juice, olive oil, and a dash of Tabasco.

4. Heat a ridged grill pan coated with nonstick cooking spray over medium-high heat. Place the salmon fillets in the pan, skin-side down. Cook for 4 minutes. Turn the fish over and cook until the fish is done, about another 4 minutes. Drain the potatoes.

5. Arrange the watercress and new potatoes on 4 serving plates. Place the salmon on top and serve with the mango salsa.

Each serving provides | Calories 450, fat 15 g, saturated fat 2 g, cholesterol 96 mg, sodium 102 mg, carbohydrates 45 g, fiber 5 g, protein 35 g.

Double-Duty Dishes |
Meat and Poultry

Chicken and Pinto Bean Tacos

See photo | page 81 | **Serves 8**

Soft tortillas—instead of fried—make the difference in these tacos, which are an excellent way to get a serving of beans and avocado, rich in heart-healthy monounsaturated fats.

3/4 **pound skinless boneless chicken breasts, cut into strips**
3 **garlic cloves, chopped**
Juice of 1 lime
1 **tablespoon taco seasoning mix**
1 **tablespoon olive oil**
2 **red, green, or yellow peppers, seeded and thinly sliced**
1 **can (15 ounces) pinto beans, drained and rinsed**
8 **soft corn tortillas**
1 **avocado**
4 **cups romaine lettuce leaves, torn or shredded**
3 **spring onions, thinly sliced**
3 **tablespoons fresh cilantro**
1 **tomato, diced or sliced**
Tabasco or other hot sauce to taste
4 **tablespoons low-fat sour cream**
Salt and pepper

Preparation time | 20 minutes
Cooking time | 8 minutes

1. Preheat the oven to 350°F. Place the chicken, garlic, lime juice, and taco seasoning mix in a bowl, and season to taste with salt and pepper. Mix well.

2. Heat the oil in a large nonstick skillet or wok over medium-high heat. Add the chicken mixture and cook for 1 minute without stirring. Add the peppers and stir-fry over a high heat until the chicken is lightly browned, about 3–5 minutes. Add the beans and heat them through, stirring occasionally.

3. Meanwhile, place the tortillas on a baking sheet and warm in the oven for 2–3 minutes, or place them between paper towels and microwave on medium for 1 minute. Peel and dice the avocado.

4. Spoon the chicken and pepper mixture into the tortillas. Add the avocado, lettuce, spring onions, tomato, cilantro, and Tabasco or other hot sauce to taste. Serve at once, topped with the sour cream.

Each serving provides | Calories 243, fat 8 g, saturated fat 2 g, cholesterol 28 mg, sodium 206 mg, carbohydrates 28 g, fiber 7 g, protein 16 g.

Country Captain Chicken

See photo | page 105 | **Serves 4**

Country Captain is now considered a classic American dish, but it is likely named for a British army captain who first brought curry seasonings from India to his home port.

2 **teaspoons olive oil**
4 **boneless, skinless chicken breast halves (5 ounces each)**
1 **small onion, thinly sliced**
3 **cloves garlic, minced**
1 **tablespoon curry powder**
1 1/3 **cups canned crushed tomatoes**
1/4 **cup dried apricots, thinly sliced**
1/2 **teaspoon salt**
1/2 **teaspoon dried thyme**
1/4 **teaspoon pepper**
1/4 **cup sliced almonds**

Preparation time | 10 minutes
Cooking time | 35 minutes

1. Heat oil in large nonstick Dutch oven over medium heat. Add chicken and sauté until golden brown, about 3 minutes a side. Transfer chicken to plate with tongs or slotted spoon.

2. Add onion and garlic to pan and cook until onion is tender, about 5 minutes.

3. Stir in curry powder and cook for 1 minute. Add tomatoes, apricots, salt, thyme, and pepper, and bring to a boil.

4. Return chicken (and any accumulated juices) to Dutch oven. Reduce to a simmer, cover, and cook until chicken is cooked through, about 20 minutes. (Recipe can be made ahead to this point and refrigerated. Reheat in 325°F oven.) Serve sprinkled with almonds.

Each serving provides | Calories 258, fat 8 g, saturated fat 1 g, cholesterol 82 mg, sodium 431 mg, carbohydrates 12 g, fiber 3g, protein 35g.

Mexican Pork with Salsa

See photo | page 119 | **Serves 4**

Lean pork marinated in a Mexican spice and citrus mixture and sautéed until succulent makes an excellent filling for soft flour tortillas. The finishing touch is a crown of fresh avocado salsa.

14 ounces pork tenderloin, trimmed of fat
2 onions, thickly sliced
2 red or yellow peppers, seeded and cut into chunks
4 flour tortillas (10-inch)

Citrus marinade:
3 garlic cloves, minced
Juice of 1 lime
Juice of 1 grapefruit or 1 small blood orange
1 teaspoon olive oil
2 teaspoons mild chili powder
1 teaspoon paprika
1/2 teaspoon ground cumin
1/4 teaspoon dried oregano or mixed herbs such as herbes de Provence
Pinch of ground cinnamon
3 spring onions, chopped

Avocado and radish salsa:
1 avocado
3 radishes, diced
1 garlic clove, minced
1 ripe tomato, diced
Juice of 1/2 lime, or to taste
1 spring onion, chopped
1 tablespoon chopped fresh cilantro
Salt and pepper

Preparation time | 30 minutes
Marinating time | 30 minutes
Cooking time | 15 minutes

1. Mix all of the ingredients for the marinade in a shallow dish. Add the pork tenderloin and turn to coat. Cover and marinate for at least 30 minutes, or overnight.

2. To prepare the salsa, halve and peel the avocado and remove its pit, then mash the flesh in a bowl. Add the remaining salsa ingredients and mix well, then season to taste. Cover and chill until serving time.

3. Preheat the oven to 350°F. Heat a large non-stick skillet over a medium-high heat until hot. Remove the meat from the marinade and pat it dry with a paper towel. Coat the pan with cooking spray, add the pork, and cook on all sides until brown.

4. Push the pork to the side and add the onions and peppers to the pan. Cook until the vegetables are tender and lightly charred and the pork is cooked through, about 12–15 minutes.

5. Meanwhile, wrap the tortillas (stacked) in foil and warm in the oven for 5–10 minutes, or stack them between paper towels and heat on medium in the microwave for 1 minute.

6. Remove the skillet from the heat. Lift out the pork and cut it into thin strips, then return it to the pan and mix it well with the onions and peppers.

7. To serve, pile the pork, onions, and peppers into the tortillas, roll into cone shapes, and top with salsa.

Each serving provides | Calories 494, fat 17 g, saturated fat 4 g, cholesterol 56 mg, sodium 393 mg, carbohydrates 58 g, fiber 8 g, protein 30 g.

Venison and Chestnut Casserole

See photo | page 74 | **Serves 4**

Full of flavor but low in saturated fat, venison makes a wonderful alternative to beef in a casserole.

1 1/2 tablespoons olive oil
  1 pound boneless venison shoulder, cut into 1 1/2 -inch cubes
  2 medium onions, sliced
  2 garlic cloves, crushed
  2 cooked fresh beets, each cut into 6 wedges
Grated zest and juice of 1/2 large orange
 1/2 cup port wine
1 1/4 cup low-fat reduced-sodium beef broth
3 1/2 ounces vacuum-packed peeled whole chestnuts
  3 carrots, halved lengthwise, cut into 1-inch pieces
  1 piece ginger (2 inches), grated
  4 shallots, unpeeled but roots sliced off
  1 tablespoon flour
  2 tablespoons nonfat milk
Salt and pepper

Preparation time | 20 minutes
Cooking time | about 1 hour and 45 minutes

1. Preheat the oven to 350°F. Heat half of the olive oil in a large Dutch oven. Add the venison in 1 layer and let it brown on each side for about 5 minutes, turning once. Do this in 2 batches if necessary. Using a slotted spoon, remove the meat from the pan and set it aside on a plate.

2. Add the sliced onions to the Dutch oven and stir well. Cook over a low heat, stirring occasionally, until the onions are softened and just beginning to brown, about 10 minutes.

3. Add the garlic, beets, orange zest, and juice. Stir well, then return the venison and its juices to the pan, and add the port and beef stock. Bring to a simmer. Cover the pan and transfer to the oven. Cook until the venison is tender, about 1 hour and 20 minutes, adding the chestnuts in the last 15 minutes of cooking.

4. Meanwhile, place the carrots, ginger, and shallots in a roasting pan, add the remaining oil, and stir until the vegetables are evenly coated. Place in the oven above the Dutch oven and roast for 1 hour, turning the vegetables over halfway through the cooking time.

5. Blend the flour with the milk to make a paste. Move the Dutch oven from the oven to the top of the stove. Place over medium-high heat and add the paste a little at a time, whisking constantly and simmering until the gravy thickens. Season to taste. Serve the venison casserole hot, with the roasted vegetables.

Some more ideas |
• Alcohol gives color and richness as well as flavor to the casserole, but it can be left out—just add more broth.

Each serving provides | Calories 341, fat 8 g, saturated fat 2 g, cholesterol 96 mg, sodium 241 mg, carbohydrates 34 g, fiber 5 g, protein 30 g.

Thai Stir-Fried Steak with Mango

Serves 4

Here's a dish that is surprisingly low in fat and bursting with a variety of spices and fresh flavors.

Dressing:
 1/4 cup rice vinegar or cider vinegar
  2 tablespoons honey
  2 tablespoons mild chili powder
  2 tablespoons paprika
  1 tablespoon grated fresh ginger
 3/4 cup water
  3 tablespoons fresh lime or lemon juice

Salad:
  2 large ripe mangoes
  4 ripe plums (about 1 pound)
  3 cups watercress leaves
1 1/2 cups shredded red cabbage
  1 cup cucumber, cut into matchsticks
  1 red pepper, cut into strips
  4 green onions, sliced
 1/2 cup chopped fresh cilantro
 1/2 cup chopped fresh mint
  2 tablespoons coarsely chopped roasted unsalted peanuts

Stir-fried beef steak:
- **1 pound lean sirloin steak**
- **2 teaspoons reduced-sodium soy sauce**
- **3 large garlic cloves, minced**
- **1 teaspoon sugar**
- **1 tablespoon canola oil**

Preparation time | 45 minutes
Cooking time | 10 minutes

1. Make the dressing first. In a small saucepan whisk together the vinegar, honey, chili powder, paprika, and ginger. Slowly whisk in the water and bring to a boil over high heat. Reduce the heat to medium and simmer uncovered for 5 minutes. Remove from the heat and whisk in the lime or lemon juice. Set aside.

2. Peel the mangoes (but not the plums), cut the fruits in half, remove the pits, and cut into ¹/₂-inch thick slices. Place in a large, shallow bowl (you should have about 5 cups). Add the watercress, cabbage, cucumber, red pepper, green onions, cilantro, and mint. Toss gently to mix. Set aside.

3. Diagonally cut the steak into ¹/₄-inch thick strips. In a large bowl coat the steak with 3 tablespoons of the dressing, the soy sauce, garlic, and sugar. Heat a wok or nonstick skillet over high heat, add the oil, and then the steak. Stir-fry until the steak strips are cooked to taste.

4. Spoon the steak over the salad. Drizzle with the rest of the dressing and sprinkle with the peanuts.

Each serving provides | Calories 413, fat 13 g, saturated fat 3 g, cholesterol 64 mg, sodium 215 mg, carbohydrates 54 g, fiber 8 g, protein 28 g.

Hale and Hearty |
Meatless Mains

Bulgur Wheat Pilaf

Serves 4

The combination of grains and beans is common to all cuisines with a tradition of vegetarian meals. In this delicious 1-pot main dish, ground coriander, cinnamon, and dried apricots add a Middle Eastern flavor.

- **2 eggs**
- **1 teaspoon canola oil**
- **1 large onion, finely chopped**
- **2 large garlic cloves, minced**
- **1¹/₂ teaspoons ground coriander**
- **1 teaspoon ground cinnamon**
- **1 teaspoon turmeric**
- **Pinch of crushed dried chilies (optional)**
- **1 can (15 ounces) pinto beans or chickpeas, drained and rinsed**
- **¹/₂ cup dried apricots**
- **1¹/₄ cup bulgur wheat**
- **1 cup green beans, halved**
- **Salt and pepper**
- **Fresh cilantro leaves to garnish**

Preparation and cooking time | 30 minutes

1. Place the eggs in a saucepan of cold water, bring to a boil, and boil gently for 10 minutes. Drain the eggs and cool under cold running water. Set aside.

2. While the eggs are cooking, heat the oil in a large saucepan over medium-high heat. Add the onion and garlic, and sauté for 3 minutes, stirring occasionally. Stir in the ground coriander, cinnamon, turmeric, and chilies (if using). Stir for 1 minute.

3. Add the pinto beans or chickpeas and apricots, and stir to coat them with the spices. Stir in the bulgur and green beans, then pour in enough water to cover by about 1/2 inch. Bring to a boil, then reduce the heat to low. Cover and simmer for 20 minutes, or until all of the liquid has been absorbed.

4. While the bulgur is cooking, shell and slice the eggs. Fluff the bulgur with a fork and season lightly with salt and pepper. Serve hot, garnished with the egg slices and sprinkled with cilantro leaves.

Each serving provides | Calories 373, fat 5 g, saturated fat 1 g, cholesterol 107 mg, sodium 145 mg, carbohydrates 71 g, fiber 18 g, protein 16 g.

Couscous Casablanca

See photo | page 103 **| Serves 8**

Couscous is a staple in much of North Africa, where it is often served topped with tender, colorful vegetables. In Tunisia it is usually spiced with a traditional hot chili sauce called harissa.

- **10 1/2 ounces couscous**
- **1 cup raisins**
- **1 teaspoon ground cumin**
- **2 tablespoons chopped fresh cilantro**
- **1 tablespoon lemon juice**
- **Chili sauce to taste**
- **Pinch of ground cinnamon**
- **1/2 teaspoon orange zest**

Vegetable stew:
- **1 tablespoon olive oil**
- **2 large onions, chopped**
- **4 garlic cloves, chopped**
- **4 teaspoons ground cumin**
- **1 teaspoon chili powder**
- **1/2 teaspoon each ground cinnamon, turmeric, cloves, coriander, and ginger**
- **1 can (14 1/2 ounces) chopped tomatoes**
- **5 cups vegetable broth**
- **1 cup pumpkin, cut into 1/2-inch pieces**
- **1 small sweet potato, cut into 1/2-inch pieces**
- **2 celery stalks, sliced**
- **1 carrot, sliced**
- **1 turnip, cut into 1/2-inch pieces**
- **1 cup green beans, cut into short pieces**
- **1 zucchini, cut into 1/2-inch pieces**
- **1 can (15 ounces) chickpeas, drained**
- **Salt and pepper**

Preparation time | 40 minutes, plus 15 minutes standing
Cooking time | 40–45 minutes

1. Start with the vegetable stew. Heat the oil in a large saucepan or stockpot over medium-high heat. Add the onions and half of the garlic, and cook until slightly softened, about 4 minutes. Stir in the cumin, chili powder, cinnamon, turmeric, cloves, coriander, and ginger. Cook for a few seconds.

2. Add the tomatoes with their juice, the vegetable broth, pumpkin, sweet potato, celery, carrot, turnip, and green beans. Bring to a boil, then reduce the heat and simmer until the vegetables are just tender, about 15–20 minutes.

3. Stir in the zucchini, chickpeas, and remaining garlic. Cook until all of the vegetables are tender, about 15 minutes. Season lightly with salt and pepper if needed.

4. Meanwhile, place the couscous and raisins in a large bowl. Add 1 cup of boiling water and mix well. Soak for 5 minutes.

5. When the vegetables have finished cooking, ladle 2 cups of the hot liquid from the stew over the couscous. Cover and soak for 10 minutes. Cover the pan of vegetables and remove from the heat.

6. To make the harissa sauce, ladle a cup of hot cooking liquid from the vegetables into a bowl, and stir in the ground cumin, chopped cilantro, and lemon juice. Add chili sauce to taste.

7. To serve, reheat the vegetable stew if necessary. Fluff the couscous with a fork, then mound it on a platter or in a large bowl, and sprinkle with the cinnamon and the orange zest. Ladle some of the vegetable stew over the couscous and serve the rest separately.

Serve the spicy harissa sauce on the side.

Each serving provides | Calories 342, fat 3 g, saturated fat 0 g, cholesterol 0 mg, sodium 799 mg, carbohydrates 71 g, fiber 9 g, protein 11 g.

Teriyaki-Style Noodles with Tofu

See photo | page 109 | **Serves 2**

This rich, Japanese-style broth, flavored with vibrant fresh herbs, ginger, and garlic, peps up firm tofu and long strands of earthy buckwheat noodles.

- 5 ounces soba (Japanese buckwheat noodles)
- 2 cups mixed vegetables (asparagus tips, broccoli, carrots, cauliflower, or green beans)
- 1/3 cup reduced-sodium soy sauce
- 1 1/4 cups vegetable broth
- 4 tablespoons rice wine (sake or mirin) or dry sherry
- 10 ounces firm light tofu, diced
- 2 spring onions, chopped
- 1 fresh red chili, seeded and chopped
- 1 tablespoon chopped fresh mint
- 1 tablespoon chopped fresh cilantro
- 1 large garlic clove, crushed
- 1/2 teaspoon grated fresh ginger

Preparation time | 15 minutes
Cooking time | 10 minutes

1. Bring a large saucepan of water to a boil and cook the soba noodles according to package instructions, or until al dente, about 6 minutes.

2. Meanwhile, cut all of the mixed vegetables into bite-sized pieces. Add to the simmering pasta for the final 3–4 minutes of cooking.

3. Drain the pasta and vegetables in a large colander. Place all remaining ingredients in the empty saucepan and return it to the heat. Heat until simmering, then reduce to low. Return the pasta and vegetables to the pan, and cook very briefly until they are reheated.

4. Serve in deep soup bowls, with a spoon to drink the broth and a fork or chopsticks for picking up the solid ingredients.

Some more ideas |
• Replace the tofu with 8 ounces peeled, cooked shrimp or diced, cooked chicken or turkey (without the skin).

Each serving provides | Calories 317, fat 2 g, saturated fat 0 g, cholesterol 0 mg, sodium 1,842 mg, carbohydrates 56 g, fiber 6 g, protein 21 g.

Roasted Vegetable and Pasta Bake

Serves 4

Here's a hearty vegetarian dish that the whole family will enjoy.

- 1 small butternut squash (about 1 pound), peeled, seeded, and cut into 2-inch cubes
- 2 red onions, cut into large chunks
- 2 garlic cloves, minced
- 1 tablespoon olive oil
- 2 leeks, thickly sliced
- 6 ounces asparagus spears, cut across in half
- 10 ounces rigatoni or penne
- 2 cups nonfat milk
- 3 tablespoons flour
- 1/3 cup sharp reduced-fat cheddar cheese, grated
- 2 teaspoons coarse mustard
Salt and pepper

Preparation time | 20 minutes
Cooking time | about 1 hour

1. Preheat the oven to 425°F. Place the squash and red onions in a large roasting pan and sprinkle with the garlic. Drizzle with the oil and season with salt and pepper to taste. Toss to coat the vegetables with the oil, then place the pan in the oven and roast for 15 minutes.

2. Remove the pan from the oven and add the leeks and asparagus. Toss gently, then return to the oven. Roast until all the vegetables are tender and starting to brown, about 20 minutes.

3. Meanwhile, cook the pasta in a large saucepan of boiling water according to the package instructions, or until al dente, about 10–12 minutes.

4. While the pasta is cooking, make the sauce. Measure 4 tablespoons of the milk into a medium bowl, add the flour, and stir to make a smooth paste. Heat the remaining milk in a saucepan until almost boiling. Stir the hot milk into the flour mixture, then return to the sauce-pan and heat gently, stirring, until the mixture boils and thickens. Simmer for 2 minutes.

5. Remove the sauce from the heat and add about $2/3$ of the cheese and the mustard. Season with salt and pepper to taste.

6. Remove the pan of roasted vegetables from the oven. Drain the pasta, add it to the vegetables, and gently stir to combine. Stir in the sauce. Sprinkle the remaining cheese evenly over the top. Return to the oven and bake until golden and bubbling, about 10–15 minutes. Serve hot.

Each serving provides | Calories 476, fat 7 g, saturated fat 2 g, cholesterol 9 mg, sodium 223 mg, carbohydrates 82 g, fiber 6 g, protein 22 g.

Veggie Burger

See photo | page 88 | **Serves 4**

A few simple ingredients make a truly tasty meatless burger. The secret ingredient? Peanut butter!

1 **large onion, finely chopped**
1 **garlic clove, finely chopped**
1 $1/2$ **cups grated carrot**
1 $1/2$ **cups grated zucchini**
1 $1/2$ **teaspoons ground cumin**
1 $1/2$ **teaspoons ground coriander**
2 **tablespoons peanut butter**
2 **tablespoons chopped fresh cilantro**
$1/2$ **cup fresh whole wheat bread crumbs**
1 **egg, beaten**
Salt and pepper
2 **teaspoons olive oil**

To serve:
2 **tomatoes, seeded and chopped**
2 **tablespoons ketchup or relish**
4 **sesame-seed burger buns**
2 **tablespoons reduced-fat mayonnaise**
4 **iceberg lettuce leaves, shredded**
1 **shallot, thinly sliced**

Preparation time | 40 minutes
Cooking time | 10 minutes

1. Heat a large nonstick skillet coated with cooking spray over medium heat. Add the onion and garlic, and cook until the onion is soft and beginning to brown, about 5 minutes. Stir frequently. Add the carrots and zucchini, and sauté until the vegetables have softened, about 10 minutes. Stir frequently.

2. Stir in the ground cumin and coriander, peanut butter, and fresh cilantro; mix well. Season with salt and pepper. Remove the pan from the heat and set aside to cool slightly.

3. Mix in the bread crumbs and egg until thoroughly combined. The mixture should bind together well. Shape the mixture into 4 thick burgers about 4 inches in diameter.

4. Wipe the skillet with a paper towel and then heat the oil over medium heat. Add the burgers and cook until firm and golden, about 5 minutes on each side.

5. Stir the tomatoes and ketchup together. Split the hamburger buns horizontally and toast the cut sides. Spread 1 teaspoon mayonnaise (if using) on each bun, then add some lettuce and a burger to each. Spread with the tomato mixture and top with the shallot slices. Replace the tops of the buns and serve.

More ideas |

• These burgers freeze well once cooked. Allow them to cool, then wrap individually in plastic wrap and place in a freezer bag. To serve, unwrap and reheat in a 400°F oven for about 20 minutes, turning occasionally.

Each serving provides | Calories 328, fat 13 g, saturated fat 2 g, cholesterol 56 mg, sodium 499 mg, carbohydrates 44 g, fiber 6 g, protein 11g.

Full of the Good |
Sides

Broccoli and Pearl Barley Salad

See photo | page 100 | **Serves 4**

Barley has proven cholesterol-lowering powers and makes an interesting change from rice.

5 ¹/₂ **ounces pearl barley**
 2 **cups water**
 7 **ounces broccoli, cut into small florets**
 3 **zucchinis, thickly sliced**
 2 **cups sugar snap peas, halved**
¹/₂ **cup dried apricots, thinly sliced**
¹/₄ **cup pumpkin seeds**
Salt and pepper

Spicy tomato dressing:
1 ¹/₂ **tablespoons olive oil**
 1 **tablespoon tomato puree**
 2 **tablespoons fresh lime juice**
 2 **teaspoons ground cumin**
Dash of Tabasco sauce
 1 **garlic clove, crushed**
 2 **tablespoons chopped fresh cilantro or parsley (optional)**

Preparation time | 20 minutes
Cooking time | 35 minutes

1. Rinse the barley in a strainer under cool water. Drain and place in a saucepan. Cover with 2 cups of cold water. Bring to a boil, then reduce the heat to low and cover. Simmer very gently until most of the water has been absorbed and the grains are tender but still firm, about 30 minutes. Drain the barley well.

2. While the barley is cooking, bring a second pot of water to a boil. Add the broccoli florets, zucchini, and peas, and bring back to a boil. Reduce the heat and simmer the vegetables until they are just tender but still crisp, about 3–4 minutes, then drain well and rinse briefly with cold water.

3. Whisk all dressing ingredients together in a large bowl. Stir in the apricots. Add the barley and vegetables as soon as they are cooked, and mix well to coat with the dressing. Cover and allow to cool until just warm.

4. Add the pumpkin seeds just before serving, and salt and pepper to taste.

Some more ideas |

• Other grains to try in this salad include quinoa or buckwheat, both available from natural food stores. Prepare these grains according to the package instructions.

Each serving provides | Calories 357, fat 13 g, saturated fat 2 g, cholesterol 0 mg, sodium 36 mg, carbohydrates 54 g, fiber 11 g, protein 14 g.

Sesame Greens and Bean Sprouts

Serves 4

This succulent stir-fry is full of flavor and crunch. It is ideal as part of an Asian menu, or equally delicious with grilled fish, poultry, or meat.

    2 tablespoons sesame seeds
    1 teaspoon canola oil
    1 onion, chopped
    2 garlic cloves, chopped
    1 small savoy cabbage (10 1/2 ounces),
      finely shredded
 1/2 head of bok choy, finely shredded
 1 1/2 cups bean sprouts
    4 tablespoons oyster sauce
Dash of black pepper

Preparation time | 10 minutes
Cooking time | 4–6 minutes

1. Heat a large nonstick skillet over medium-high heat. Toast the sesame seeds in the pan until lightly brown and fragrant. Pour the seeds into a small bowl to cool. Set aside.

2. Heat the oil in the skillet over medium-high heat. Add the onion and sauté until tender, about 3-4 minutes. Add the garlic, cabbage, and bok choy; stir-fry until cabbage is wilted but still slightly crisp, about 5 minutes. Add the bean sprouts, oyster sauce, and sesame seeds, and cook for 2 minutes. Season with a dash of black pepper and serve warm.

More ideas |
• Substitute 2 tablespoons of crushed cashew nuts or almonds for the sesame seeds.

Each serving provides | Calories 101, fat 4 g, saturated fat 1 g, cholesterol 0 mg, sodium 499 mg, carbohydrates 15 g, fiber 5 g, protein 5g.

Wild and Brown Rice with Toasted Pecans

Serves 6 to 8

Don't like plain brown rice? You'll like this versatile side dish. Serve it with roasted meat, poultry, or seafood. If you have any leftovers, toss them with a light dressing for a super rice salad.

 2/3 **cup wild rice**
 1 1/3 **cup brown rice**
 1/2 **cup coarsely chopped pecans**
   1 **tablespoon unsalted butter or margarine**
 1/2 **teaspoon salt**
 1/2 **teaspoon black pepper**
 1/4 **cup snipped fresh chives or minced**
     parsley

Preparation time | 10 minutes
Cooking time | 50 minutes

1. Preheat the oven to 300°F. Bring a large saucepan of unsalted water to a boil over moderate heat. Add the wild rice and boil uncovered for 15 minutes. Add the brown rice and boil 20 minutes more. Drain.

2. Meanwhile, scatter the pecans on a baking sheet and toast in the oven, stirring occasionally to prevent burning, about 10 to 15 minutes or until lightly toasted. Set aside.

3. Transfer the rice to a steamer or colander. Set over boiling water in a large saucepan, cover, and steam for 15 to 20 minutes or until tender. Transfer the rice to a warm serving bowl and stir in the butter, pecans, salt, pepper, and chives.

Each serving provides | Calories 294, fat 9 g, saturated fat 2 g, cholesterol 6 mg, sodium 182 mg, carbohydrates 47 g, fiber 3 g, protein 7 g.

Something Sweet |
Bonus-Added Baked Goods

Five-Star Cookies

Makes 16 cookies

These nutty, moist cookies are satisfying with-out being too sweet. Barley flakes, which are slightly crisper than oatmeal, are available from most health food stores.

2 tablespoons hazelnuts, finely chopped
2 tablespoons sunflower seeds,
  finely chopped
1/4 cup dried apricots, finely chopped
1/4 cup stoned dried dates, finely chopped
1 tablespoon light brown sugar
1/2 cup barley flakes
1/2 cup whole wheat flour
1/2 teaspoon baking soda
2 tablespoons canola oil
4 tablespoons apple juice

Preparation time | 10–15 minutes
Cooking time | 10 minutes

1. Preheat the oven to 350°F. Mix the chopped hazelnuts, sunflower seeds, apricots, and dates together in a bowl. Add the sugar, barley flakes, flour, and baking soda, and stir to combine.

2. Mix together the canola oil and apple juice, and pour over the dry mixture. Stir until the dry ingredients are just moistened.

3. Drop the batter by rounded teaspoonfuls onto a baking sheet coated with cooking spray. Using the back of a fork dipped in flour, gently flatten each ball and neaten the edges with your fingers.

4. Bake until golden brown, about 10 minutes. Transfer to a wire rack and cool. These can be kept in an airtight container for up to 4 days.

Some more ideas |
● Use unsalted cashew nuts instead of hazelnuts.
● Substitute oatmeal for the barley flakes.

Each cookie provides | Calories 61, fat 3 g, saturated fat 0 g, cholesterol 0 mg, sodium 41 mg, carbohydrates 9 g, fiber 1 g, protein 1 g.

Pumpkin Oat Bread

Makes 12 3/4-inch slices

Oats, walnuts, and pumpkin—an excellent source of the antioxidant beta-carotene—are all packed into this moist, flavorful loaf, per-fect for snacking or for dessert.

1 1/4 cups all purpose flour
  2 teaspoons baking powder
1/2 teaspoon baking soda
1/2 teaspoon salt
1/2 teaspoon ground cinnamon
1/4 teaspoon ground mace
1/8 teaspoon ground cloves
3/4 cup oat bran
  1 cup canned pumpkin puree
  1 large egg
  1 large egg white
1/4 cup vegetable oil
3/4 cup firmly packed brown sugar
1/4 cup orange juice
  2 teaspoons grated orange rind
1/2 cup chopped walnuts (2 ounces)

Preparation time | 15 minutes
Cooking time | 1 hour

1. Preheat the oven to 325°F. Lightly grease a 9-by-5-by-3-inch loaf pan. In a large bowl stir together the flour, baking powder, baking soda, salt, cinnamon, mace, and cloves. Stir in the oat bran.

2. In a medium bowl combine the pumpkin, egg, egg white, oil, sugar, orange juice, and orange rind. Add this mixture to the dry ingredients and stir until just combined. Fold in the walnuts.

3. Pour the batter into the loaf pan and bake for 1 hour, or until a toothpick inserted in the center comes out clean. Let the bread cool in the pan for 5 minutes, then turn it out onto a rack to cool. Makes 12 $^3/_4$-inch slices.

Each serving provides | Calories 197, fat 8 g, saturated fat 1 g, cholesterol 18 mg, sodium 194 mg, carbohydrates 30 g, fiber 2 g, protein 4 g.

Apple Raspberry Brown Betty

Serves 6

This dessert is simple to make and a guaranteed crowd-pleaser. The type of fruit used for the filling can be adjusted depending on what's in season. Top with low-fat vanilla frozen yogurt to finish off this treat.

$^1/_4$ **cup unsweetened apple juice**
$^1/_4$ **cup apple or currant jelly**
 1 tablespoon cornstarch
 5 apples (1 $^1/_4$ pounds), unpeeled, cored, and thinly sliced
$^1/_3$ **cup currants or raisins**
 1 cup frozen raspberries (no sugar added), thawed

For the topping:
$^1/_4$ **cup rolled oats**
 3 tablespoons fresh bread crumbs
 2 tablespoons brown sugar
 1 tablespoon butter or margarine, melted
$^1/_2$ **teaspoon ground cinnamon**

Preparation time | 20 minutes
Cooking time | 25–30 minutes

1. Lightly grease an 8-inch-square baking dish. In a large saucepan combine apple juice, apple jelly, and cornstarch. Stir until blended.

2. Stir in apples and cook over medium-high

heat until mixture comes to a boil. Cook for 1 minute, stirring constantly. Remove from heat and allow to cool. Gently fold currants or raisins into mixture and then spoon into the baking dish. Layer the raspberries on top.

3. Preheat oven to 400°F. In a small bowl combine the topping ingredients and mix well. Sprinkle over the fruit and bake until topping is nicely browned, about 25–30 minutes.

Each serving provides | Calories 193, fat 3 g, saturated fat 1 g, cholesterol 5 mg, sodium 37 mg, carbohydrates 43 g, fiber 4 g, protein 1 g.

Chocolate Cake with Raspberries

See photo | page 113 | **Serves 9**

Count on chocolate and raspberries—both powerful antioxidants—as delicious weapons against plaque formation. This cake only has 2 grams of fat per serving.

 1$^1/_2$ cups all purpose flour
$^1/_2$ **cup unsweetened cocoa powder**
 1 teaspoon baking powder
$^1/_2$ **teaspoon baking soda**
$^1/_2$ **teaspoon salt**
 1$^1/_4$ cups sugar
$^1/_2$ **cup unsweetened applesauce**
 1 egg or 2 egg whites
 1 cup nonfat milk or water
 2 teaspoons vanilla extract
$^1/_4$ **cup seedless raspberry jam**
Confectioners' sugar
 1 pint fresh raspberries

Preparation time | 15 minutes
Cooking time | 45 minutes

1. Preheat the oven to 350°F. Lightly spray an 8-by-8-by-2-inch baking pan with nonstick cooking spray. Dust with cocoa powder.

2. In a medium bowl whisk together the flour, cocoa powder, baking powder, baking soda, and salt.

3. In a large bowl, using an electric mixer on low speed, beat together the sugar, applesauce, and egg until smooth. Beat in the milk and vanilla until blended. Add the flour mixture and beat until blended.

4. Turn the batter into the pan. Bake 40–45 minutes, or until a pick inserted in the center comes out clean. Cool in the pan on a wire rack for 10 minutes. Turn out onto the rack or a serving plate to cool completely.

5. To serve, melt the jam in a saucepan over low heat. Brush over the top of the cooled cake. Top with raspberries and dust with confectioners' sugar.

Each serving provides | Calories 256, fat 2 g, saturated fat 1 g, cholesterol 24 mg, sodium 268 mg, carbohydrates 58 g, fiber 4 g, protein 5 g.

Date and Walnut Cake

See photo | page 95 | **Serves 10**

The dates give this low-fat cake a delicious moistness. It's delightfully easy to make, and keeps well, too.

  1 cup pitted dried dates, chopped
  2 tablespoons butter or margarine
  1 teaspoon baking soda
  1 cup boiling water
 3/4 cup light brown sugar
  2 eggs
  2 cups flour
  2 teaspoons baking powder
1 1/2 teaspoons pumpkin pie spice
Pinch of salt
 1/2 cup walnuts, chopped

Preparation time | 20 minutes, plus soaking
Cooking time | 1 hour

1. Place the dates in a bowl with the butter or margarine and baking soda. Pour the boiling water over the dates and stir until the butter has melted. Set aside to cool.

2. Preheat the oven to 350°F. Coat an 8-inch round cake pan with cooking spray and line the bottom with baking parchment. Coat the parchment with cooking spray.

3. Place the sugar and eggs in a large bowl and stir well with a whisk. Add the cooled date mixture, then sift in the flour, baking powder,

spice mix, and salt. Fold in the walnuts.

4. Turn the batter into the pan. Bake until the cake is nicely browned and a toothpick inserted in the center comes out clean, about 1 hour.

5. Turn out onto a wire rack and leave to cool. The cake can be wrapped in foil or stored in an airtight container for up to 5 days.

Some more ideas |
● Replace some or all of the dates with chopped prunes or dried figs.
● Use half white and half whole wheat flour to add extra fiber.

Each serving provides | Calories 276, fat 7 g, saturated fat 2 g, cholesterol 49 mg, sodium 243 mg, carbohydrates 50 g, fiber 2 g, protein 5 g.

Index